RALLY YEARBOOK
World Rally Championship
2002

CHRONOSPORTS
EDITEUR

SHARING THE PASSION FOR WINNING.

1st, 2nd, 3rd, 4th, 5th, and 6th on the 2002 Rally GB for Pirelli-shod cars, with Petter Solberg in his Subaru taking the top honours.
Pirelli is also 2002 British Rally Champion with Jonny Milner and Toyota.

POWER IS NOTHING WITHOUT CONTROL.

RALLY YEARBOOK
World Rally Championship
2002

Photography
McKlein

Words
Philippe Joubin
Jean-Philippe Vennin "Rallyes Magazine"

**Artistic director
and page layout**
Cyril Davillerd

Coordination
Sidonie Perrin

Results
Sabrina Favre, Tino Cortese, Désirée Ianovici

ISBN 2-84707-017-6
© November 2002, Chronosports S.A.
Jordils Park, Chemin des Jordils 40, CH-1025 St-Sulpice, Suisse.
Tél. : (+41 21) 694 24 44. Fax : (+41 21) 694 24 46.
e-mail: info@chronosports.com   internet: www.chronosports.com

Printed in France by Imprimerie Sézanne,
11 rue du 35ᵉ Régiment d'Aviation, F-69500 Bron.
Bound by SIRC, Zone Industrielle, F-10350 Marigny-le-Châtel.

As Tommi Mäkinen well knows after doing it four years on the trot, one of the privileges each year's winner of the World Rally Championship enjoys is writing the Foreword for the World Rally Yearbook.

I had a year's respite, as last year was a lot less satisfying than the one before – and this one. My second title may not have been quite as hard-earned as the first one, but there were five more wins, one of them in my home country for the third year running: what more could a man ask? In my younger days I used to hope I would win one or two rallies, but I never even thought about the Championship. Most people would love to win one title, so I think I should be very happy with two! But then again there are more important things in life, such as my home and my family.

My dearest wish today is to enjoy driving some fantastic cars, in a team where the bonds we have forged over the last four years go far beyond the sporting realm. But the season just finished is the real subject of this book, so I had better say a word or two about it. I think what told in our favour was that my navigator Timo Rautiäinen and I made very few mistakes. That's what you had to do to come out on top in a Championship that had gone to a higher level than ever. And I don't think I could have won in any other car.

Now I must let you get acquainted with the book you have in your hands. But don't take too long to read it! As you well know, the new rallying season comes round again very soon. By mid-January we will be on the Monte Carlo trail. Then it's Sweden, a rally and a country I am very fond of. And then... Testing has started already. My 206 is waiting, so I have to go. See you next year, same time, same place?

Marcus Grönholm

Sunrise.
Sunset.
Inmarsat.

MOBILE BUSINESS COMMUNICATIONS THE WORLD RELIES ON.

There are few things in life you can be sure of. Inmarsat is one of them. We are a leading mobile satellite network that is relied upon by businesses all over the world, from multi-national companies to broadcast journalists. Our high speed operations and worldwide coverage make us the perfect exclusive global partner for the FIA World Rally Championship. Today Inmarsat continues to innovate with our range of highly reliable, high speed services including e-mail, Internet and remote LAN access and voice. With over 21 years experience, you can trust Inmarsat to get it right.

www.inmarsat.com
an **inmarsat ventures** company

EXCLUSIVE GLOBAL PARTNER OF THE FIA WORLD RALLY CHAMPIONSHIP.

Contents

WARNING MOTORSPORT CAN BE DANGEROUS

Despite the organisers taking all reasonable precautions, unavoidable accidents can happen.
In respect of these you are present at your own risk.

Family resemblance

Peugeot's third crown in three years, Marcus Grönholm's second: there was a touch of déjà vu about the season, but there was no lack of interest, thanks in particular to a whole new generation coming through. The 'Lionesses' may have some rivals in 2003 – in the shape of their French cousins from Citroën.

Formula One is the thing that springs to mind: Ferrari here, Schumacher there, total domination. In fact dominant forces seemed to be the order of the day in motorised world championships in 2002, and rallying proved no exception to that rule.

Crowned right at the death in 2000 (constructors' and drivers') and 2001 (constructors' only), the Peugeot team skipped through the Championship this time, taking two more titles for a total of five from a possible six.

Peugeot took eight wins, and as many one-two finishes, a tally that puts you in mind of Ferrari's, but there the resemblance ends. The F1 season was ruined by team orders which Ferrari employed to excess, while the French marque never resorted to that kind of policy.

No team orders: the unspoken agreement had been struck between Peugeot Sport boss Corrado Provera and his drivers before hostilities began. Was the proud, cigar-smoking Italian so sure of his ground? The decision really hinged on his team's having the last two World Champions and the driver recognized as the best there is on tarmac, as well as on an admirable notion of what sport is all about. You don't tell blokes of the calibre of Marcus Grönholm, Richard Burns and Gilles Panizzi – no forelock-tuggers among that lot – how to go about their business.

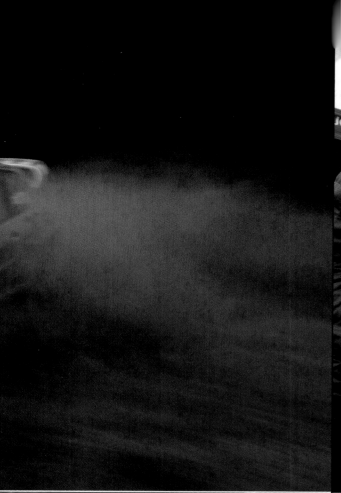

Magic Grönholm

Reigning World Champion with Subaru, Richard Burns was disappointing given that he was in the best car around. He didn't take a single win and only twice in 14 rallies did he prove faster fair and square than Grönholm: on tarmac in Catalonia and in New Zealand, where he staked all in his title bid but saw his race end in a dramatic series of barrel-rolls. And then in his home rally in Britain, an event he has won three times, Burns fell over his own feet – twice – when the only pressure was that of trying to save a little face. Yes, Grönholm went off too, in the Welsh forests, but before bowing out he had always been quicker than his main rival.

In truth, while Peugeot were clearly a cut above, it seems just as obvious that Grönholm in particular was head and shoulders above the rest. The final standings are there to prove it: Marcus finished up with twice as many points as his three teammates, who were all much of a muchness, and three other drivers pushed their way in between Marcus and them.

As we saw, Peugeot took eight one-two finishes, but the only Peugeot man who never missed one of those podiums went by the name of Grönholm. Burns was too inconsistent as well as not often having Lady Luck on his side. Rovanperä, the 'other' Finn, brought home his share of points, notably with his four second places. As for Gilles Panizzi, that's a different matter: the Frenchman is never going to earn many points for his team on gravel, but in theory and even with an injured shoulder, as on the Sanremo, he is unbeatable on tarmac, the surface where he learned his trade.

A new era

In just a few short years Peugeot have made a seismic change to the world rally scene, setting new benchmarks and raising the bar ever higher. This year they seemed to have the other teams more firmly by the throat than ever. Ford, who put up such stubborn resistance throughout the two previous seasons, were a pale shadow of their former selves. Colin McRae won two rallies, Carlos Sainz finished in the top three overall – yet again – just ahead of his Scottish teammate, but the Focus never seemed a real threat to the Lioness. The Subaru kept the impetus from 2001 going, but not with the leader we were expecting. Four-time World Champion with Mitsubishi Tommi Mäkinen, brought in to make up for Burns' departure, bowed to young colleague Petter Solberg, with the exception of the Monte, which he won in the stewards' room. Both those teams, equipped with Pirelli tyres, suffered from the advantage now enjoyed on all surfaces by the other rally supplier, Michelin.

As for the other teams, they sank without trace – Citroën excepted, as yet again they did not contest an entire season. Everything, of course, is relative: if we may be forgiven another comparison with Formula One, at least in WRC Mitsubishi, Hyundai (both did it) or Skoda still have the chance to set a

fastest time on a special stage when all the conditions are right. But those three were all just picking up the crumbs. We expected no miracles from Skoda, at least not yet, but their progress was disappointingly slow, and it was sad to watch Mitsubishi – badly missing Mäkinen and all at sea in their efforts to sort out the Lancer WRC – go downhill so alarmingly.

The trouble is there is nothing to suggest that the gap will close in 2003. The WRC may well be going through a wonderful spell, with seven constructors entered in 14 events next year, but there are real problems. And while the regulations allow constructors to enter three works cars on each rally (the best two finishers will score Championship points, unless there is a rule change that everyone – with one exception – wants to see), Peugeot are the only ones who will be able to do so throughout the coming season – the same Peugeot who invested whatever it took in technical and human resources to achieve their aims, the same Peugeot who are about to enjoy the backing of a certain tobacco firm with red and white livery. At the same time the other major carmakers involved, Ford, have to contend with budget restrictions which have seen them release their star drivers so that they can afford to develop the new Focus WRC, expected in 2005. And the other teams will all be battling to secure their financial footing.

d Citroën head-to-head?

st opposition in 2003 may well come from Citroën. The PSA
–name brand will at last be right in at the deep end, with a
already an old car after having taken so long to tip-toe its way
Championship scene. This season the 'Reds' were a little
t while awaiting the arrival of McRae and maybe Sainz they
fray by taking a podium finish on the Safari through Radstrom
that superb success of Sébastien Loeb's in Germany. And
'won' the Monte Carlo Rally until a penalty dropped him back

The new wave

Sébastian Loeb winning in Germany, Petter Solberg destroying Mäkinen and taking a copybook win in Britain, Markko Märtin out of reach in Greece until a silly puncture and gradually getting the better of his experienced teammates until he finished on the podium in wales and Ford team leader for 2003: the other great lesson to emerge from the 2002 season was the confirmation that a new generation of drivers had arrived. While rallying puts a higher premium on experience than any other sport, its move towards limited reconnaissance runs, repeated runs through the same timed sectors and the ever-increasing pace of events have shifted the goalposts. The young guys will be pushing even harder in 2003, but the likes of the returning Didier Auriol, Carlos Sainz (hopefully) and François Delecour won't be pushed around. Still, it's the respresentatives of the generation in between – Grönholm, Burns, McRae – who will again be favourites.

World Rally Championship

2002, Business as usual, Sparco products
win the World Rally Championship,
as they have done
for most of the last 20 years.

Champions!

1985, 1986, 2000, 2001, 2002
Peugeot Sport & Sparco, have
achieved World Rally Championship
victory every year that they have
worked together, proving
to be an unbeatable
partnership.

Sparco would also like to thank all the teams
that choose our products,
rewarding our dedication & passion for motorsport.

Sparco domination continues...

#1 in World Motorsport

Tel. +39 011 42.119.38 / +39 011 42.119.34 / +39 011 42.119.11 - Fax +39 011 42.119.00 - e-mail: info@sparco.it

Marcus

Mark II

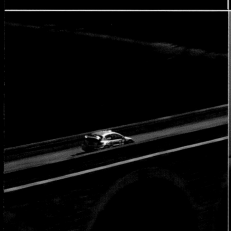

As was the case with Ari Vatanen, Marcus Grönholm's careeer now seems inextricably linked with Peugeot. Starting the season as favourite, the Finn became World Champion for the second time. How long will the run continue?

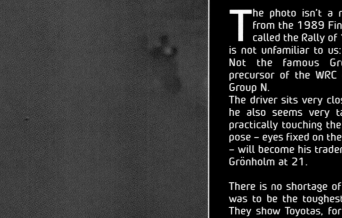

The photo isn't a recent one: it dates from the 1989 Finland Rally, then still called the Rally of 1000 Lakes. The car is not unfamiliar to us: it's a Lancia Delta. Not the famous Group A 'Integrale', precursor of the WRC cars. Just a simple Group N.

The driver sits very close to the wheel and he also seems very tall – his helmet is practically touching the roof of the car. The pose – eyes fixed on the prey, jaw jutting out – will become his trademark: This is Marcus Grönholm at 21.

There is no shortage of pictures from what was to be the toughest part of his career. They show Toyotas, for the most part: the Celica, then the Corolla WRC in 1997. But not just any old car: a works model, which Marcus planted in the lead of the Finland Rally after the first leg before losing an eventual third place because of a harmless little problem. Put it down to youthful error – the team's, that is. Then came '98: another Corolla, though not a works one. Not entirely, that is, for it was entered by Toyota Finland and carried several stickers from the driver's personal sponsors. That time Marcus went off, something that happened all too often in those days, making him feel like giving it all up and heading back to the family farm at Espoo in the country's south. It didn't matter that Marcus set an impressive series of scratch times that made him the best performer on his home event: he seemed destined, at 30, to stay a penniless prospect taking too long to confirm his potential.

But this time there was something different. Along those Finnish roads a man was watching as the big Finn went through, for the same big Finn had taken his fate in his own hands a few weeks earlier and called to suggest that this man make the trip. The man was Jean-Pierre Nicolas, head of Peugeot Sport's Rally Division. After years of trying, he had been given the green light by his superiors: Peugeot were coming back

to the World Championship, with a 206 WRC whose mission was to repeat the successes of the 205 T16 back in the Eighties.

But they needed drivers. With only a six-rally schedule for '99 it was pointless trying to attract one of the big names. They nearly got Didier Auriol, but no: the 'French Dream Team' of Delecour-Panizzi-Auriol would remain just that – a dream. Back in Paris, Jean-Pierre Nicolas was sure of it: the lanky Finn, so quick, so likeable and just a little bit cheeky with it, would do nicely.

Fast forward to Britain 2002. In the middle of the second leg, concentration flagging and forced back on manual gear changes, Marcus Grönholm lost his 206 in a series of barrel rolls, and with it the chance of a record six wins in a single season, held by Auriol since 1992. But what did he care? In three years Marcus had won it all: two world titles, 11 victories and the respect of all and sundry, his rivals first and foremost. Grönholm has also found a second home in the Peugeot Sport family, where he was quickly taken in and made a fuss of. Marcus, the good-natured chap, the man with a wink and a smile, the man who would never say no... There were some tensions, though, notably when his boss Corrado Provera, who claimed he swore by his boy Grönholm, promptly saddled him with arch-enemy Richard Burns. But it didn't take long: some tough negotiating, a couple of rallies and Marcus was top dog at Peugeot – and everywhere else – again. He is tied to the Lion till the end of 2004, but Corrado and Jean-Pierre are standing by with contract and pen in hand to try and persuade him to stay on for a further two years.

Listening to him, you'd say he won't do it. For Marcus hasn't changed. Fame and fortune haven't rubbed off on Grönholm the man. He knows that pretty soon he will have more time to spend on the farm with his family by his side. He just has a few little trips to make – trips that will take him all around the world. ∎

Colin McRae • Ford Focus RS WRC 02 • Kenya
Sébastien Loeb • Citroën Xsara WRC • Germany

Victories...

WRC
WORLD RALL

THE STARS

MARCUS GRÖNHOLM
PEUGEOT

IDENTITY CARD
- Nationality: Finnish
- Date of birth: February 5, 1968
- Place of birth: Espoo (Finland)
- Resident: Inkoo (Finland)
- Marital status: Married
- Children: 3 (Jessica, Johanna and Niclas)
- Co-driver: Timo Rautiainen (SF)

- Web: www.mgr.fi

CAREER
- First Rally: 1989
- Number of Rallies: 71
- Number of victories: 11

1996 - 10th in Championship
1997 - 12th in Championship
1998 - 16th in Championship
1999 - 15th in Championship
2000 - World Champion
2001 - 4th in Championship
2002 - World Champion

World Champion in 2000, Marcus Grönholm couldn't hang on to the title the year after. That was partly down to his 206 WRC: it was an undeveloped version that was used in the early part of the season, it had been caught up in terms of performance and it was on the edge where reliability was concerned. But it was also partly down to the driver, who made a few forgivable mistakes, some of them due to overdriving in the effort to match the pace set by Burns (then with Subaru), McRae (at Ford) or Mäkinen (Mitsubishi). He put in a much more convincing second half-season. Despite a degree of tension between him and Peugeot over the imminent arrival of Richard Burns, he made a whirlwind finish to his year, winning in Finland and twice more on the last two events in Australia and Great Britain. With fourth place in the Championship, it was enough to make him the favourite for 2003.
Marcus duly kept that appointment. From the Swedish Rally on, his confidence was unshakable, his grip on the Championship absolute. Yes, the 206 was the gun car again, but Grönholm simply ran away from new teammate Burns and all his other rivals. The only one to beat him consistently was Panizzi, and that of course was only on tarmac. One disappointing little thing: it was a pity Grönholm didn't stay focused long enough to win fair and square in Great Britain and steal it from under the noses of McRae and Burns.

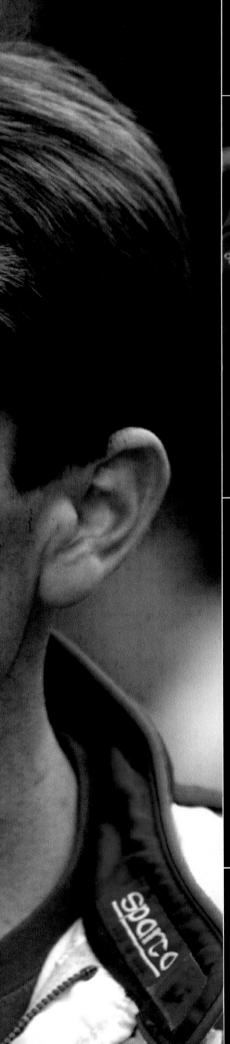

PETTER SOLBERG
SUBARU

Solberg – superb. From the season's start right through to the end, with the possible exception of Monte Carlo – and even then – the young Norwegian had the measure of his teammate Tommi Mäkinen and proved himself the most consistent rival to the Peugeots. Delayed by a few little mistakes and mechanical problems, his first win finally arrived, and when it did it was on the most treacherous rally of them all, Great Britain, where Grönholm, Burns and McRae were all caught out. But Solberg wasn't. Better still, that success took him on to the second step of the podium for the season overall, which puts Peugeot's dominance into perspective and shows how much it owes to Grönholm.

Discovered by Malcolm Wilson in 1999 and 'nicked' from Ford by Subaru at the end of the following year, Solberg quickly became the leading figure among the new generation of rally drivers. We knew he was quick – very quick – but also prone to going off the road repeatedly. But it was also clear that as soon as he learned how to channel his energy the rest would feel it – and they did. Solberg is a pleasant, warm individual (not always the case with your Nordics), a man who always has a smile on his face: a man with the charisma to be a future leader of the discipline. Meanwhile, those Peugeot drivers had better watch out for him in 2003.

IDENTITY CARD
- Nationality: Norwegian
- Date of birth: November 18, 1974
- Place of birth: Spydeberg (Norway)
- Marital status: Single
- Children: 1
- Co-driver: Phil Mills (GB)

- Web: www.pettersolberg.com

CAREER
- First Rally: 1996
- Number of Rallies: 46
- Number of victories: 1

1999 - 18th in Championship
2000 - 10th in Championship
2001 - 9th in Championship
2002 - 2nd in Championship

SEBASTIEN LOEB
CITROËN

It's not all that long since we were all worrying about Sébastien Loeb. He had a huge talent, no doubt about that: but 'Seb' had come late to rallying, and his career didn't seem to be going fast enough to bridge the gap in terms of experience to lads like Solberg or Märtin, both his juniors but both thrown into the deep end of World Rally Cars much sooner. So much time wasted, we thought, on 'tarmac' and 'gravel' in the French Championships, and we started to blame his rather touchy ways on Guy Fréquelin, who wouldn't give him a regular drive.

That happened in 2002, and the season put paid to any lingering doubts. Moral victor on the Monte, where a far-fetched penalty relegated him to second, it was on his own doorstep in Germany that the 2001 Junior Champion beat Petter and Markko in the race to see who would be first to win a World Championship rally.

Loeb is not only quick on tarmac, he's a quick learner on gravel too. Apart from Sweden, where he was no slouch but had a teammate enjoying home advantage, he was consistently quicker than Thomas Radstrom, made few mistakes and learned a huge amount in tricky places like Australia and Kenya. And the best is yet to come. 2003 is nearly here, and with it Monte Carlo. Colin, you should be shaking in your shoes...

IDENTITY CARD
- Nationality: French
- Date of birth: February 26, 1974
- Place of birth: Haguenau (France)
- Resident: Oberhoffen (France)
- Marital status: Single
- Co-driver: Daniel Eléna (MC)

- Web: www.fanloeb.com

CAREER
- First Rally: 1995
- Number of Rallies: 22
- Number of victories: 1

2002 - 10th in Championship

FREDDY LOIX
HYUNDAI

This was the comeback story of the year, even if his Championship scorecard didn't really reflect that fact. Freddy has really come back from the edge, those three nightmare seasons with Mitsubishi that crushed all the potential glimpsed in his time with Toyota up until 1998. On the Monte, where he crunched a bridge, it looked as if his move to Hyundai hadn't changed things, those old demons were still in place. But by Sweden (where he was getting around on crutches) he was showing us that wasn't the case. Sadly, bad luck hadn't left him. Over the whole season he was the most convincing of the drivers in a team that cut quite a dash, with Schwarz and Kankkunen also in its ranks.

IDENTITY CARD
- Nationality: Belgian
- Date of birth:
  November 10, 1970
- Place of birth: Tongres
  (Belgium)
- Resident: Millen (Belgium)
- Marital status: Single
- Hobbies: Squash,
  mountainbike
- Co-driver: Sven Smeets (B)

- Web: www.freddyloix.com

CAREER
- First Rally: 1993
- Number of Rallies: 78
- Best result: 2nd

1996 - 8th in Championship
1997 - 9th in Championship
1998 - 8th in Championship
1999 - 8th in Championship
2000 - 12th in Championship
2001 - 11th in Championship
2002 - 17th in Championship

GILLES PANIZZI
PEUGEOT

Acknowledged as the world's best on tarmac, Gilles Panizzi was supposed – at last – to be having his first full season. It didn't turn out that way: a broken shoulder (a domestic fall) forced him to forfeit Finland and Germany. Then in Australia, where his car was destroyed by Burns in pre-rally testing, Peugeot didn't bother to have a replacement sent out. Ah well... Though Gilles had his wings clipped by mechanical failure even before the start of the Monte, he was untouchable in Corsica, Catalonia and Snremo, and put in other good performances on gravel, in Kenya especially. With as many tarmac events as gravel, he could be a title contender.

IDENTITY CARD
- Nationality: French
- Date of birth: September 19, 1975
- Place of birth: Roquebrune Cap
  Martin (France)
- Resident: Monaco
- Marital status: Married, 1 daughter
- Co-driver: Hervé Panizzi (F)

- Web: www.club-panizzi.com

CAREER
- First Rally: 1990
- Number of Rallies: 44
- Number of victories: 6

1997 - 9th in Championship
1998 - 12th in Championship
1999 - 10th in Championship
2000 - 7th in Championship
2001 - 7th in Championship
2002 - 6th in Championship

COLIN McRAE
FORD

Colin McRae endured another weird sort of a season. Two wins at the start of the summer made him the outright record-holder with 25. After that: nothing. Or rather, plenty: he made mistakes (again), his heart clearly wasn't in it on several occasions (especially on tarmac), he had some bad luck (his Focus catching fire on the last special stage in Finland) and near the end of the season he finally split with Nicky Grist, his co-driver since 1996. A victim, supposedly, of Ford's cost-cutting, Colin is taking a big gamble in 2003: the touchy Scot is joining the very young, very French Citroën team. Maybe it's his chance to kick-start a career that has been going nowhere for the last few years.

IDENTITY CARD
- Nationality: British
- Date of birth:
  August 5, 1968
- Place of birth:
  Lanark (Scotland)
- Resident: Scotland, Monaco
- Marital status: Married
- Children: 1 daughter
- Hobbies: Water skiing ,
  motocross
- Co-driver: Nicky Grist (GB),
  then Derek Ringer (GB) in
  Australia and Britain.

- Web: www.colinmcrae.com

CAREER
- First Rally: 1986
- Number of Rallies: 129
- Number of victories: 25

1992 - 8th in Championship
1993 - 5th in Championship
1994 - 4th in Championship
1995 - World Champion
1996 - 2nd in Championship
1997 - 2nd in Championship
1998 - 3rd in Championship
1999 - 6th in Championship
2000 - 4th in Championship
2001 - 2nd in Championship
2002 - 4th in Championship

RICHARD BURNS
PEUGEOT

In the end, Burns gave us more to write about last winter with the legalistic and financial shenanigans that accompanied his move from Subaru to Peugeot than he did all season. "All that for that?" one is tempted to ask. World Champion by dint of wearing the others down, with just one success in 2001, Richard didn't win a single event in 2002 and didn't even finish in the top three overall. There's no shortage of excuses: the Englishman was getting to grips with a new car and a new team, a French one to boot. And the machinery didn't make life any easier for him, with a string of breakdowns. But he was still completely outclassed by Grönholm, who overtook him in the number of titles and wins, so we shall expect him to be firmly out for revenge in 2003.

IDENTITY CARD
- Nationality: British
- Date of birth: January 17, 1971
- Place of birth: Reading (England)
- Resident: Reading (England)
- Marital status: Single
- Hobbies: Motorbikes, Mountain Bike
- Co-driver: Robert Reid (GB)

- Web: www.richardburns.com

CAREER
- First Rally: 1990
- Number of Rallies: 90
- Number of victories: 10

1994 - 19th in Championship
1995 - 9th in Championship
1996 - 9th in Championship
1997 - 7th in Championship
1998 - 6th in Championship
1999 - 2nd in Championship
2000 - 2nd in Championship
2001 - World Champion
2002 - 5th in Championship

MARKKO MÄRTIN
FORD

In 2001 Märtin was Petter Solberg's teammate at Subaru, but the team didn't really play the game – they did fewer rallies than expected – and, to be fair, his performances caught the eye much less than those of the Norwegian (with the exception of Finland) and the latter's much more outgoing nature tended to detract from them. So Markko took refuge with Ford and, in the shadow of McRae and Sainz, he put in a self-effacing but successful season. There was none quicker than him in Greece, where a puncture deprived him of a first success. And then in Britain, where he finally had to give best to the same Solberg, the young Estonian led, was always up among the front-runners and showed that leadership of the Ford team in 2003 was his rightful place.

IDENTITY CARD
- Nationality: Estonian
- Date of birth: November 10, 1975
- Place of birth: Tartu (Estonia)
- Resident: Tartu
- Marital status: single
- Hobbies: basket-ball, moutain-bike
- Co-driver: Michael Park (GB)

CAREER
- First Rally: 1994
- Number of Rallies: 37
- Best result : 2nd

1998 - Not classified
1999 - 18th in Championship
2000 - 21st in Championship
2001 - 17th in Championship
2002 - 9th in Championship

TOMMI MÄKINEN
SUBARU

IDENTITY CARD
- Nationality: Finnish
- Date of birth: June 26, 1964
- Place of birth: Puupola (Sf)
- Resident: Puupola and Monaco
- Marital status: Single
- Children: 1 son (Henry)
- Hobbies: Golf, skiind, hiking
- Co-driver: Kaj Lindström (SF)

- Web: www.tommimakinen.net

CAREER
- First Rally: 1984
- Number of Rallies: 125
- Number of victories: 24

It was a rather lacklustre Tommi Makinen who left Mitsubishi, with whom he took 22 wins and four world titles, to join Subaru as replacement for Richard Burns in 2002. On the Monte we were quick to sing his praises for adapting so quickly to a new car and new tyres in those ever-changing conditions, but there wasn't much to write home about for the rest of the season. As he did in 2001, Tommi made a bit of a habit of going off, once terrifyingly in Argentina, near the end of the one rally where he was fighting Grönholm for the win. Mäkinen never really got his edge back all year, and the contrast with Solberg's sharpness was very instructive.

1990 - 20th in Championship	1995 - 5th in Championship	1999 - World Champion
1991 - 29th in Championship	1996 - World Champion	2000 - 5th in Championship
1993 - 10th in Championship	1997 - World Champion	2001 - 3rd in Championship
1994 - 10th in Championship	1998 - World Champion	2002 - 8th in Championship

CARLOS SAINZ
FORD

Carlos: what a man! This year he didn't carry his title challenge through to the end of the season as he had done so often in the past. But he did finish on the podium overall – for the eighth time! That result, of course, came about because of his consistency. Sainz even won a rally, in Argentina, though that came after the Peugeots had been disqualified. Unlike McRae, the Spaniard was prepared to take a pay cut to keep his place at Ford for 2003, but Malcolm Wilson had decided to give youth its fling and would have none of it. As the Rally Yearbook closed for press, just after the Rally of Great Britain, it looked as if his last chance of a drive lay with Citroén.

IDENTITY CARD
- Nationality: Spanish
- Date of birth: April 12, 1962
- Place of birth: Madrid (Spain)
- Resident: Madrid (Spain)
- Marital status: Married
- Children: 3 (Bianca, Carlos et Ana)
- Hobbies: Football, squash, tennis
- Co-driver: Luis Moya (E), replaced by Marc Forti (E) in Catalonia because of injury

- Web: www.carlos-sainz.com

CAREER
- First Rally: 1987
- Number of Rallies: 165
- Number of victories: 24

1988 - 11th in Championship
1989 - 8th in Championship
1990 - World Champion
1991 - 2nd in Championship
1992 - World Champion
1993 - 8th in Championship
1994 - 2nd in Championship
1995 - 2nd in Championship
1997 - 3rd in Championship
1998 - 2nd in Championship
1999 - 4th in Championship
2000 - 3rd in Championship
2001 - 5th in Championship
2001 - 5th in Championship
2002 - 3rd in Championship

FRANÇOIS DELECOUR
MITSUBISHI

While he was only the third Ford driver in 2001, that saeson did at least kick-start the 'enfant terrible' of French rallying's career after the damage done by his split with Peugeot the previous year. Joining Mitsubishi in place of Mäkinen, Delecour revised his ambitions upward – but that made the let-down all the worse. The Lancer WRC was never in the hunt, François earned just a few constructors' points and was reduced to races within races against teammates Alister McRae and Paasonen. The year ended in pain, with two high-speed offs, especially the one on Rally Australia which sadly left co-driver Daniel Grataloup with multiple fractures.

IDENTITY CARD
- Nationality: French
- Date of birth: August 30,1962
- Place of birth: Cassel (France)
- Resident: Plan de la Tour (France)
- Marital status: Single
- Children: 2 (Anne-Lise, Gabriel)
- Hobbies: Jet-ski, mountain-bike
- Co-driver: Daniel Grataloup (F) replaced because of injury by Dominique Savignoni (F), in Great Britain

- Web: www.delecour.com

CAREER
- First Rally: 1984
- Number of Rallies: 98
- Number of victories: 4

1991 - 7th in Championship
1992 - 6th in Championship
1993 - 2nd in Championship
1994 - 8th in Championship
1995 - 4th in Championship
1997 - 17th in Championship
1998 - 10th in Championship
1999 - 16th in Championship
2000 - 6th in Championship
2001 - 8th in Championship
2002 - 22nd in Championship

ARMIN SCHWARZ
HYUNDAI

Another disappointment. It looked as if Armin had got things back on track after putting everything on the line with some difficult but determined seasons at Skoda, and the move to a more ambitious Hyundai outfit might take him to the next stage. We also thought he would have Freddy Loix for breakfast. Wrong on both counts. The German fell back into his old ways – and into a few ditches, notably on the Sanremo and again on the home event he had been looking forward to so much. His efforts convinced no-one, least of all his boss David Whitehead, when he did keep it on the road and when the fragile machine gave him some peace. But the likeable Armin will fulfil the second year of his contract in 2003, and let's hope it sees him turn the corner.

IDENTITY CARD
- Nationality: Allemande
- Date of birth: July 16, 1963
- Place of birth: Oberreichenbach (Germany)
- Resident: Monaco
- Marital status: Married
- Hobbies: Jet-ski, music
- Co-driver: Manfred Hiemer (D)

- www.armin-schwarz.com

CAREER
- First Rally: 1988
- Number of Rallies: 90
- Number of victories: 1

1991 - 6th in Championship
1994 - 7th in Championship
1995 - Excluded (Toyota)
1997 - 8th in Championship
1999 - Not classified
2000 - 17th in Championship
2001 - 11th in Championship
2002 - 24th in Championship

TONI GARDEMEISTER
SKODA

IDENTITY CARD
- Nationality: Finnish
- Date of birth: March 31, 1975
- Place of birth: Kouvola (Finland)
- Resident: Monaco and Kouvola
- Marital status: single
- Co-driver: Paavo Lükander (SF)

CAREER
- First Rally: 1997
- Number of Rallies: 47
- Best result : 3rd

1999 : 10th in Championship
2000 : 12th in Championship
2001 : Not classified
2002 : 13th in Championship

Left without work by Seat's pull-out at the end of 2000, Gardemeister did just three rallies in 2001 with Mitsubishi. A few bent panels later, young Toni and genial Ralliart boss Andrew Cowan didn't exactly part on the best of terms. Not kept on by Mitsubishi when they were choosing replacements for Mäkinen and Loix, Gardemeister promptly found a new job with Skoda, and a fine season he had with them in 2002. Trouble was, nobody really saw it – a problem that seems to affect the cumbersome Octavia as much as it does World Championship rallying! In 2003 Toni will team up again with Didier Auriol, his old friend from the Seat days, and that will be a good thing on the set-up front.

JANI PAASONEN
MITSUBISHI

IDENTITY CARD
- Nationality: Finnish
- Date of birth: April 11, 1975
- Place of birth: Mäntyharju (Finland)
- Resident: Espoo (Finland)
- Marital status: Single
- Hobbies: snow motorcycling
- Co-driver: Daniel Grataloup (F)

- Web: www.janipaasonen.com

CAREER
- First Rally : 1995
- Number of Rallies: 15

2002 - 27th in Championship

Before the start of season 2002, Paasonen was best-known for the ubiquitous 2001 clip that showed a Ford Focus converted to a pick-up truck the way only a Colin McRae can do it. No problem: though he had had his fingers burned with Gardemeister, Andrew Cowan took on the other, even younger Finn for three rallies in 2002 with the official Mitsubishi works team, and they became five when a stand-in had to be found for Alister McRae late in the season. After beating his teammates in Sweden, he went one better in Finland by giving the Lancer WRC its first and so far only scratch time, though it all finished up with an off. In 2003 he will have a part-time drive with Mitsubishi or Ford.

HARRI ROVANPERÄ
PEUGEOT

Of the drivers who make up Peugeot's 'Gang of Four', now its 'Dream Team', Rovanperä is the one who spends least time in the limelight. But the Lion's 'other' Finn is as solid as a rock, notably whenever his teammates show any frailty, human or mechanical. Harri can also bite: in Australia he gobbled up Sainz and Solberg to round off Peugeot's eight and last 1-2 finish of the year. His record may still show just one win, in Sweden in 2001, but Rovanperä took second place four times this year as easy as you like. One jarring note: he doesn't seem to have made any progress on tarmac, though it has to be said he doesn't get many chances to drive on that surface: no testing, and on the events themselves he only has a 'privateer' car.

IDENTITY CARD
- Nationality: Finnish
- Date of birth: April 8, 1966
- Place of birth: Jÿvaskÿla (Finland)
- Resident: Jÿvaskÿla
- Hobbies: winter sports
- Marital status: married, a child
- Co-driver: Risto Pietiläinen (SF), replaced because of illness by Voitto Silander (SF) between Finland and Sanremo.

- Web: www.rovanpera.com

CAREER
- First Rally: 1989
- Number of Rallies: 68
- Number of victories: 1

1999 - 9th in Championship
2000 - 9th in Championship
2001 - 4th in Championship
2002 - 7th in Championship

KENNETH ERIKSSON
SKODA

Either Kenneth Eriksson just loves a challenge, or he doesn't know how to turn his back on racing. Not retained by Hyundai, for whom he worked so hard after his successful years with Mitsubishi and Subaru, he joined Skoda for only the second full season of his long career. Even his faithful co-driver Staffan Parmander had given up and gone home. The veteran spared no effort but with the exception of his favourite places, notably Argentina, there were no miracles in a heavy Octavia which he just couldn't convert to his way of driving, especially on tarmac. All that effort, just to be replaced by Didier Auriol for 2003. Maybe it's time to call it a day...

IDENTITY CARD
- Nationality: Swedish
- Date of birth: May 13, 1956
- Place of birth: Appelbo (Sweden)
- Resident: Appelbo, Monaco
- Marital status: Single
- Hobbies: fishing, hunting, plane
- Co-driver: Tina Thörner (S)

CAREER
- First Rally: 1977
- Number of Rallies: 139
- Number of victories: 6

1986 - 10th in Championship
1987 - 4th in Championship
1989 - 6th in Championship
1991 - 5th in Championship
1993 - 7th in Championship
1995 - 3rd in Championship
1996 - 4th in Championship
1997 - 5th in Championship
2000 - 11th in Championship
2001 - 20th in Championship
2002 - 18th in Championship

PHILIPPE BUGALSKI
CITROËN

Entered in just the three tarmac rallies Citroën contested, 'Bug' did a lot of behind-the-scenes development work on the Xsara WRC, gravel included. With his engine breaking even before the Monte got under way, he went off twice, in Germany and on the Sanremo. Twice, like last year... Co-driver Jean-Paul Chiaroni has had problems with his eyesight since hitting that rock in Italy, so let's hope he gets better soon. Fourth place in Corsica, in a Xsara belonging to Citroën Sport's Spanish arm Piedrafita, and a podium in Spain rescued their season.

IDENTITY CARD
- Nationality: French
- Date of birth: June 12, 1963
- Place of birth: Busset (France)
- Resident: Busset
- Marital status: married, two children
- Co-driver: Jean-Paul "Coco" Chiaroni (F)

CAREER
- First Rally: 1982
- Number of Rallies: 31
- Number of victories: 2

1998 - 16th in Championship
1999 - 7th in Championship
2000 - Not classified
2001 - 20e in Championship
2002 - 11e in Championship

ALISTER McRAE
MITSUBISHI

Poor Alister: leaving Hyundai for Mitsubishi, Colin's likeable younger brother at last found himself in a top team with legitimate hopes of moving up the order. Alas, no: the Lancer Evolution WRC, whether in its original version or Step 2, was consistently slowest of the works cars, and it seemed there was nothing to be got out of it. Alister threw himself into it nonetheless, but it was all a waste of time. To crown a season in hell, he bruised his liver in a mountain-bike fall at Sanremo and missed the last three dates on the calendar – the long hauls to New Zealand and Australia, and his home rally in Great Britain. Hard to take.

IDENTITY CARD
- Nationality: British
- Date of birth: December 20, 1970
- Place of birth: Lanark (Scotland)
- Marital status: Single
- Hobbies: Moto-cross, Mountain-bike
- Co-driver: David Senior (GB)

CAREER
- First Rally: 1988
- Number of Rallies: 66
- Best result : 4th 2001

1995 - 10th in Championship
2000 - Not classified
2002- 15th in Championship

JUHA KANKKUNEN
HYUNDAI

Hello stranger! Dismissed by Subaru at the end of 2000 to make way for Solberg and Märtin – whose combined ages were hardly greater than his own – Kankkunen took himself back to his lakeside farm. But one year without driving, other than with Hyundai in Finland, was too much, so back he came for another crack this year, signing up with the Anglo-Korean outfit for nine rallies. And it must be said that Juha was far from being made to look foolish by teammates Schwarz and Loix. In fact he put in some solid performances, in Australia for example. But his lack of interest in the development of the Lancer WRC disappointed the men in charge, as did a tendency – unusual for him – to go off the road.

IDENTITY CARD
- Nationality: Finnish
- Date of birth: April 2, 1959
- Place of birth: Laukaa (Finland)
- Resident: Laukaa (Finland)
- Marital status: Married, a son (Tino)
- Hobbies: Golf, fishing
- Co-driver: Juha Repo (SF)

CAREER
- First Rally: 1981
- Number of Rallies: 152
- Number of victories: 23

1983 - 16th in Championship	1994 - 3rd in Championship
1984 - 24th in Championship	1995 - Exlu (Toyota)
1985 - 5th in Championship	1996 - 7th in Championship
1986 - World Champion	1997 - 4th in Championship
1987 - World Champion	1998 - 4th in Championship
1989 - 3rd in Championship	1999 - 4th in Championship
1990 - 3rd in Championship	2000 - 8th in Championship
1991 - World Champion	2001 - Not classified
1992 - 2nd in Championship	2002 - 14th in Championship
1993 - World Champion	

FRANÇOIS DUVAL
FORD

This man makes Sébastien Loeb, even Petter Solberg and Markko Märtin, seem like veterans. But François Duval already has a good grounding in karts and quads in his 'youth', as it were, then in more grown-up cars in Belgian rallying. Under Malcolm Wilson's tutelage he contested a number of WRC events this year in tandem with the Junior Championship in a Puma. His greatest feat was leading the Cyprus Rally after two stages. In 2003 Duval will contest a full season alongside Märtin in a Ford team that's going to look a bit like a nursery! Joking apart, the older guys won't spend too much time laughing at these boys.

IDENTITY CARD
- Nationality: Belgian
- Date of birth: November 18, 1980
- Place of birth: Chimay (Belgium)
- Marital status: Single
- Hobbies: quads, jet-skiing
- Co-driver: Jean-Marc Fortin (B)
- Web: www.euroautoduval.com/fduval

CAREER
- First Rally: 1999
- Number of Rallies: 21
- Best result : 1st in Junior Championship

2002 - 30th in Championship

THOMAS RADSTRÖM
CITROËN

When Citroën Sport boss Guy Fréquelin failed to secure the services of a top-line driver, and amazingly brushed Didier Auriol's application aside, he brought back Thomas Radstrom despite his fall from grace at the end of 2001. The Swede being no great shakes as a communicator, he put him together with a French co-driver to ease relations with the team, particularly on the technical front. Unfortunately Thomas lapsed back into his old ways, going off in Sweden – where he was, at least, running with the quick men – then more seriously in Catalonia, where he was supposed to be learning about tarmac. Affter that came the magnificent podium finish in Kenya, a reward for the crew's hard work – but Radstrom's fate was already sealed by then.

IDENTITY CARD
- Nationality: Swedish
- Date of birth: July 22, 1966
- Place of birth: Vannas (Sweden)
- Marital status: Single
- Co-driver: Denis Giraudet (F)

CAREER
- First Rally: 1984
- Number of Rallies: 40
- Best result : 2nd

	1998 - 19th in Championship
	1999 - 10th in Championship
	2000 - 16th in Championship
	2001 - 13th in Championship
	2002 - 12th in Championship

Citroën again

As they did last year with Sébastien Loeb in the first Championship, which then went by the less graphic title of 'Super 1600', Citroën and French team PH Sport won the 'little' World Championship with a Saxo in the hands of Catalan prospect Daniel Sola. 'Dani' won on home soil at the start of the season, again in Germany and in the last event in Great Britain. Even with three wins from six rallies he had to wait till the very last round to be sure the crown was his.

Italian Andrea Dallavilla – no longer a driver with potential, gieb that he is well into his thirties – finished second, as he had in 2001, and he won on home soil too in the Sanremo. The only thing that had changed was that he had abandoned the Fiat Punto in favour of a Saxo. Another Citroën rounded off the podium, this one – the second PH Sport-prepared entry – belonging to Finland's Tuohino, winner in Greece. François Duval in his Ford Puma also won one round (Monte Carlo) of a Championship which Peugeot offically withdrew from this year. In 2003, incidentally, the age limit for competitors will be set at 28.

Sola

Tuohino

Duval

Singh on top

The experienced Malaysian Karajmit Singh (he's nearly 40) took the Championship for 'Production' cars, run over the eight rounds not featured on the Junior calendar. He garnered two wins and took full advantage when Finland's Kristian Sohlberg, also a two-time winner, struck trouble in the last round. Peruvian Ramon Ferreyros also won twice, while former transalpine celebrity Alex Fiorio and the more-or-less Subaru works driver Toshihiro Araâ claimed one rally each. The Japanese apart, they were all in Mitsubishis.

Singh

Arai

Ferreyros

Barratt

BLACK ART

Michelin's success in the World Rally Championship is unsurpassed. Their technological miracles can make the difference between success and failure, but thanks to some magic compounds and tread patterns, the French tyre heads the WRC pack

For most of us, choosing a tyre is something we do once, maybe twice, every couple of years, but if you are one of Michelin's World Rally Championship stars, you'll use up to a dozen sets of rubber on every rally. Find the right one and it could win the stage, get it wrong and the car will feel like you've put your shoes on the wrong feet. Tyres are that important.

Michelin's tremendous rallying success is built upon what it calls the Triple Alliance. It's the fusion between driver, car and tyre that makes for those magical moments behind the wheel. Find the sweet spot and stage times will look better than Bill Gates' bank balance. A close working relationship is the key, which is why you'll often see drivers deep in conversation with the folk in blue and yellow. A last-minute conversation with your tyre engineer could be the ticket to buying chunks of time from your rivals.

Rallying's special challenge is the massive variety of surfaces that it takes place on, so Michelin's wizards must create tyres for every circumstance – from the icy roads of Monte Carlo to the rough stages of Greece, the smooth asphalt of Spain to the snowy forests of Sweden. And if you really must know, the gravel of New Zealand is even different from the stuff you'll find in Argentina. It makes choosing your clothes for a Friday night out seem easy.

Occasionally, Michelin will even develop a tyre especially for a particular stage. On this year's Rally Deutschland, it introduced a new asphalt cover for the Baumholder group of stages. It clearly worked, and contributed to seven stage victories

on the military ranges and vaulted Francois Delecour's Mitsubishi Lancer Evo to second place on one test – the car's best ever result at the time. Citroen's Sebastien Loeb won the rally on, you guessed it, Michelins.

More usually, tyres are developed to perform within a wider range of conditions. This offers a flexible compromise to drivers, who might otherwise struggle in a changeable environment. Michelin's tactical designs work effectively across a broader spectrum than other rally rubber, making that all-important tyre choice easier for the driver.

Peugeot star Richard Burns explains: "There are fewer choices than other makes of tyre, so it makes life a little less stressful!"

Winning is a feeling familiar to Michelin-shod drivers – since 1982 the drivers' title has been won 16 times by the French tyres. This year, the honour fell to Marcus Gronholm, while Peugeot claimed its third manufacturers' championship on the trot.

Team principal Corrado Provera is quick to acknowledge the role tyres play.

"Our relationship with Michelin forms a huge part of our success," he says. "We work well together because we share the same sporting ethos: there is constant two-way communication between them and us. Our ways of working and desire for success are identical. One thing I admire most about Michelin is their rigorous approach to problem solving. It's the perfect partnership because we understand each other so well."

But it's not just Peugeot reaping the rewards. In addition to its win with Citroen this year, Michelin has enjoyed big success with Mitsubishi, Toyota and Ford over the years. And that's just in rallying.

As the world's leading tyre supplier to motorsport (including Formula 1, MotoGP, sportscars and World Superbikes), the company learns an enormous amount about what happens when tyres are pushed to, and beyond, their limits. Michelin's 'chefs' use between 150 and 200 ingredients for each rally tyre, and most are in the products you can buy. Complex polymers and chemicals are added to rubber and

(Top to bottom) Gronholm: a winner on Michelins; star-studded success; the tyre technician is a valuable member of any team

Kevlar, with a dash of silica, carbon and sulphur. Hmm, tasty! An army of technical wizards at the company's Ladoux Research and Development centre near Clermont-Ferrand push the boundaries of tyre performance to new limits for the WRC. And experience gained on special stages provides a deeper knowledge of tyre technology for the company's road tyres.

Motorsport boss Pierre Dupasquier says: "Rallying is a university for tyre engineers – we graduate eventually!"

That happened a long time ago. Michelin has been in world rallying for 30 years now without a break and is the most successful tyre company in WRC history. As things stand, the future looks equally promising. ∎

Michelin
by numbers

16,000 studs for Gronholm's Swedish win

Up to 4500 tyres for each event

192 WRC victories since 1973

60 kilometres – the normal life of a WRC tyre!

33 world titles – 17 manufacturers', 16 drivers'

12 trucks travel in convoy to each WRC event

9 wins in 2002

3 all-Michelin podiums in 2002

THE TEAMS

PEUGEOT
206 WRC

Engine
- Type: XU9J4
- Layout: front transverse
- Number of cylinders: 4
- Capacity: 1,998 cc
- Bore x stroke: 85 x 88 mm
- Power: 300 bhp > 5,250 rpm
- Maximum torque: 535 kgs/m > 3,500 rpm
- Cylinder head: aluminium
- Valves: 4 per cylinder
- Cylinder block: aluminium
- Camshaft: double overhead
- Engine management system: Magneti Marelli Step 9
- Turbo: Garrett Allied Signal
- Lubrification: carbon wet sump

Transmission
- Clutch: 5.5" or 6" AP carbon tri-disc
- Gearbox: longitudinal 6-speed X-Trac sequential
- Differentials: programmable

Suspension
- Front and rear: McPherson-type
- Dampers: Peugeot

Steering
- Power-assisted rack and pinion

Brakes
- Front: ventilated discs, 355 mm diametre, 6-piston calipers
- Rear: ventilated discs, 300 mm diametre, 4-piston calipers

Tyres
- Michelin

Dimensions
- Wheelbase: 2,468 mm
- Length: 4,005 mm
- Width: 1,770 mm
- Rims: OZ 8 x 18"
- Weight: 1,230 kgs
- Fuel tank capacity: 85 litres

Web
www.peugeot.com

In 2000 and 2001 Peugeot took the title by scoring more than half of their points on tarmac. The 206 WRC also went well on 'easy' gravel surfaces such as Finland and New Zealand, but not so well on the car-breaking surfaces of Greece, Cyprus or Kenya, where the French team was left to pick up the crumbs dropped by the robust Ford Focuses, or even Subaru and Mitsubishi. The new evolution of the little Lioness that came out in Spring 2002 changed all that. Since the performance was already a given, they had put the accent on reliability, and we know what happened next: the 206 became the benchmark on every type of surface. It seems to have plenty in hand over the opposition still, but they're already talking about its replacement, the 307.

Position
- 1973 - 3rd
- 1973 - 15th
- 1974 - 13th
- 1975 - 5th
- 1976 - 8th
- 1977 - 13th
- 1978 - 8th
- 1979 - 11th
- 1980 - 8th
- 1981 - 9v
- 1983 - 10th
- 1984 - 3rd
- 1985 - 1st
- 1986 - 1st
- 1988 - 10th
- 1993* - 3rd
- 1994* - 5th
- 1995* - 1st
- 1996* - 4th
- 1997* - 3rd
- 1998* - 2nd
- 1999 - 6th
- 2000 - 1st
- 2001 - 1st
- 2002 - 1st

(* = 2 liters)

FORD
FOCUS RS
WRC 02

Web
- www.fordracing.net

Engine
- Type: Ford Zetec E
- Number of cylinders: 4
- Capacity: 1,995 cc
- Bore x stroke: 84.8 x 88 mm
- Power: 300 bhp > 6,500 rpm
- Maximun torque: 550 kgs/m > 4,000 rpm
- Engine management system: M-Sport
- Turbo: Garrett
- Lubrification: wet sump

Transmission:
- Clutch: Sachs
- Gearbox: 6-speed X-Trac sequential
- Differentials: M-Sport

Suspension
- Front and rear: McPherson
- Dampers: Reiger

Steering
- Power-assited rack and pinion

Brakes
- Front and rear: ventilated discs, 4- piston calipers

Tyres
- Pirelli

Dimensions
- Wheelbase: 2,615 mm
- Length: 4,152 mm
- Width: 1,770 mm
- Weight: 1,230 kgs

Malcolm Wilson's team did not homologate a car this year, putting it off until 2003 while waiting for the all-new car, based on the second-generation production Focus, to arrive in 2005. So there were only a few developments, mainly on the engine front, and that was not enough to reel in the Peugeots or even, on occasion, the Subarus. McRae did win the events that were hardest on the machinery, Greece and the Safari, but unlike previous years Peugeot did a brilliant damage limitation job and actually won in Cyprus. With budgets revised downwards and their stars departed, the Ford team may have to endure a few transitional seasons.

SUBARU
IMPREZA WRC 2002

Engine
- Type: 4 cylindres à plat Number of cylinders: 4
- Capacity: 1,994 cc
- Bore x stroke: 92 x 75 mm
- Power: 300 bhp > 5,500 rpm
- Maximun torque: 48 kgs/m > 4,000 rpm
- Turbo: IHI

Transmission
- Gearbox: 6-speed Prodrive manual/semi-automatic
- Differentials: electro-hydraulically controlled

Suspension
- Front: McPherson strut
- Rear: McPherson strut, longitudinal and transversal rod
- Dampers: Bilstein

Steering
- Power-assisted rack and pinion

Brakes
- Front and rear: ventilated discs, 305 mm diametre, 4-piston calipers
- For tarmac: 366 mm discs, 6-piston calipers

Tyres
- Pirelli

Dimensions
- Wheelbase: 2,535 mm
- Length: 4,405 mm
- Width: 1,770 mm
- Rims: OZ 8 x 18"
- Weight: 1,230 kgs
- Fuel tank capacity: 75 litres

Web www.swrt.com

Subaru went through another strange sort of a season. After a rather monochrome 2001, Richard Burns blossomed in late season to take the title. This time round, the Imprezaas won the first rally of the year... and the last. In terms of sheer performance, especially on tarmac, and on the reliability front, they seemed at least a match for the Fords, but they ended up behind them in the Championship. Maybe Solberg needed to turn more of his excellent showings into solid points, or Mäkinen needed to have his mind more on the job, or they needed to enter three cars on a regular basis. In 2003, Subaru, like Citroën, should be leading contenders – for second place.

HYUNDAI ACCENT WRC 3

Engine
- Type: DOHC
- Number of cylinders : 4
- Capacity: 1,998 cc
- Bore x stroke: 84 x 90 mm
- Power: 300 bhp > 5,200 rpm
- Maximum torque: 520 kgs/m
- Valves: 4 per cylinder
- Turbo: Garrett
- Lubrification: wet sump

Transmission
- Clutch: tri-disc, 140 mm, carbon
- Gearbox: 6-speed X-Trac sequential
- Differentials: programmable central diff

Suspension
- Front and rear: McPherson strut
- Dampers: Ohlins

Brakes
- Front: ventilated discs, 304 mm diametre, 4-piston calipers
- For tarmac: 368 mm discs, 6-piston calipers
- Rear: ventilated discs, 304 mm diametre, 4-piston calipers

Tyres
- Michelin

Dimensions
- Wheelbase: 2,440 mm
- Length: 4,200 mm
- Width: 1,770 mm
- Rims: OZ 8 x 18'''
- Weight: 1,230 kgs

Web
- www.hyundaiwrc.com

By finishing 8th on the Rally of Great Britain, and with help from the "nominations" game – only the two best-placed official entries from each team scored points – Freddy Loix snared the single point that made all the difference, giving Hyundai fourth place, the target the boss had set them at the outset. The Anglo-Korean team went into the final rally equal on points with Skoda and Mitsubishi, neither of whom scored a point. But Hyundai's progress still needs to be turned into solid achievement, they are still iffy on reliability, and the WRC3 that came out this year didn't turn out to be a big step forward. Hanging on to that fourth place in 2003 will be no easy task.

Position		
1996* - 7th	1998* - 5th	2001 - 6th
1997* - 6th	1999* - 2nd	2002 - 4th
	2000 - 6th	

SKODA
OCTAVIA WRC Evo 2 / Evo 3

They went surprisingly well, even if fourth place did elude them. At the wheel of the ageing Octavia WRC, Kenneth Eriksson and Toni Gardemeister – the unlikeliest pairing in the Championship, and the one separated by the widest age gap – proved spectacular, sometimes at their own expense, as happened with the Swede on tarmac. Neither of them is much good at setting the car up, which didn't help matters much until they got to Australia and after Didier Auriol had put his oar in. Next season, possibly in Spring, Skoda will debut their new Fabia, a much more interesting-looking candidate. It may well be the real start for a team whose resources and ambitions have been rounded firmly upwards.

Engine
- Type: 4 cylindres
- Capacity: 1,999 cc
- Bore x stroke: 82.5 x 93.5 mm
- Power: 296 bhp > 6,000 rpm
- Maximum torque: 50.1 kgs/m > 3,250 rpm
- Valves: 5 per cylinder
- Turbo: Garrett

Transmission
- Gearbox: 6-speed sequential
- Differentials: programmable central diff

Suspension
- Front and rear: McPherson strut
- Dampers: Proflex

Steering
- Power-assisted rack and pinion

Brakes
- Front and rear: ventilated discs

Tyres
- Michelin

Dimensions
- Wheelbase: 2,512 mm
- Length: 4,511 mm
- Width: 1,770 mm
- Weight: 1,230 kgs

Web www.skoda-auto.cz

Position	
1993* - 2nd	
1994* - 1st	
1995* - 3rd	
1996* - 3rd	
1997* - 2nd	
1999 - 7th	
2000 - 6th	
2001 - 5th	
2002 - 5th	

MITSUBISHI LANCER EVO WRC 2

How can a team that took four drivers' and constructors' titles between '96 and '99 lose so much ground so quickly? Mäkinen's going didn't help matters, but the real reason lies in the fact that Mitsubishi's management hummed and hawed and were very late in starting the development of a Lancer WRC to follow the still-competitive Group A car. The new machine appeared only at the end of 2001 and was only part way to being a WRC car. This year, developments kept being pushed back, and again they never actually appeared. Changes are in the pipeline, prompted by new Mitsubishi owners Daimler-Benz, but the rally programme appears to be under no threat despite Marlboro's withdrawal.

Position
- 1973 - 3rd
- 1973 - 16th
- 1974 - 11th
- 1975 - 11th
- 1976 - 10th
- 1977 - 10th
- 1978 - 13th
- 1979 - 13th
- 1980 - 15th
- 1981 - 14th
- 1982 - 8th
- 1983 - 16th
- 1984 - 14th
- 1988 - 14th
- 1989 - 4th
- 1990 - 3rd
- 1991 - 3rd
- 1992 - 5th
- 1993 - 5th
- 1995 - 2nd
- 1996 - 2nd
- 1997 - 1st
- 1998 - 4th
- 1999 - 3rd
- 2000 - 4th
- 2001 - 4th
- 2002 - 6th

Engine
- Type: 4G 63 - DOHC
- Number of cylinders: 4
- Capacity: 1,996 cc
- Bore x stroke: 85,5 x 86,9 mm
- Power: 300 bhp > 6000 rpm
- Maximun torque: 539 kgs/m > 3,500 rpm
- Valves: 4 per cylinder
- Turbo: Mitsubishi

Transmission
- Clutch: carbon
- Gearbox: 6-speed sequential (INVECS)
- Differentials: active control of anti-locking system

Suspension
- Front: independent, with McPherson strut with coil springs
- Rear: independent, with pullrods with coil springs
- Dampers: Ohlins with adjustable system

Steering
- Power-assisted rack and pinion

Brakes
- Front: ventilated discs, 4-pot calipers
- Rear: ventilated discs, 4-pot calipers

Tyres
- Michelin

Dimensions
- Wheelbase: 2,600 mm
- Length: 4,360 mm
- Width: 1,770 mm
- Rims: OZ 8 x 18"
- Front: 1,550 mm
- Rear: 1,550mm

Web
www.mitsubishi-motors.co.jp

CITROËN XSARA WRC

Citroën were due to contest only seven rallies (eight, in the end) this year, outside the Championship proper. The target Guy Fréquelin set was at least one win. Halfway through the calendar we were still waiting to see the Xsaras as frisky as they were in 2001: they had been caught up, left behind in fact, on tarmac by the 206's and they didn't seem much better off on gravel than they were the year before. It looked as if Citroën were throwing a year's development down the drain. But then – phew! – came the podium and fifth place in Kenya, and that win in Germany. Next year will be their first full season, and there is a great deal to play for. Everyone is waiting for Citroën to slip up: this is where the hard work really starts.

Position
- 1982 - 12th
- 1983 - 14th
- 1984 - 13th
- 1985 - 18th
- 1986 - 10th
- 2001 - not classified
- 2002 - not classified

Engine
- Type: XU7JP4
- Layout: transverse, tilted at a 30° angle
- Number of cylinders: 4
- Capacity: 1,998 cc
- Bore x stroke: 85 x 88 mm
- Power: 300 bhp > 5500 rpm
- Maximun torque: 53 kg/m > 4000 rpm
- Valves: 4 per cylinder
- Camshaft: double overhead
- Engine managmnt system: Magneti Marelli
- Turbo: Garrett

Transmission
- Clutch: carbon two-disc
- Gearbox: longitudinal 6-speed X-Trac sequential

Suspension
- Front and rear: McPherson with helicoidal springs
- Dampers: Extrem Tech

Steering
- Hydraulic, power-assisted rack and pinion

Brakes
- Front: ventilated discs, 376 mm diametre, 6-piston calipers
- Rear: ventilated discs, 318 mm diametre, 4-piston calipers

Tyres
- Michelin

Dimensions
- Wheelbase: 2,555 mm
- Length: 4,167 mm
- Width: 1,770 mm
- Rims: OZ 8 x 18"
- Weight: 1,230 kgs

Web
- www.citroen.fr

Latitude. Longitude. Altitude. Inmarsat.

MOBILE BUSINESS COMMUNICATIONS THE WORLD RELIES ON.

There are few things in life you can be sure of. Inmarsat is one of them. We are a leading mobile satellite network that is relied upon by businesses all over the world, from multi-national companies to broadcast journalists. Our high speed operations and worldwide coverage make us the perfect exclusive global partner for the FIA World Rally Championship. Today Inmarsat continues to innovate with our range of highly reliable, high speed services including e-mail, Internet and remote LAN access and voice. With over 21 years experience, you can trust Inmarsat to get it right. www.inmarsat.com

an **inmarsat** ventures company

EXCLUSIVE GLOBAL PARTNER OF THE FIA WORLD RALLY CHAMPIONSHIP.

SUBARU IMPREZA WRC 2002

TOMMI MÄKINEN   NEW ZEALAND

KAJ LINDSTRÖM

WRC
WORLD RALLY
CHAMPIONSHIP

unrivalled **preparation**
unbeatable **results**

Karamjit Singh/Allen Oh - Proton PERT: **2002 FIA Group N World & Asia Pacific Champions**

WRCII
EXTREME
2002
PRO-CHALLEN

SOLBERG vs LOIX vs GARDEMEISTER vs P

WHO IS THE GREATEST PLAYER OF THEM ALL? TURN OVER

PlayStation 2

EXTREME MEASURES

WRC Extreme II, the only official WRC game for Sony's PS2, can sort the men from the boys, but how would Petter Solberg, Gilles Panizzi, Toni Gardemeister and Freddy Loix rate? We sat them down before Rally Great Britain for a virtual shoot-out. At stake, a limited edition silver PlayStation 2. So who stood tall and walked off with the prize?

SUNDAYS were made for this. Four world class rally drivers perched on a brown leather sofa, fighting over Sony's newest PlayStation epic, *WRCII Extreme.* OK, so it's a bit unusual for the sofa to be in the middle of a stage on Rally Great Britain, but it worked for us.

It's a straightforward enough job for our quartet of heroes. Gilles Panizzi, Toni Gardemeister, Freddy Loix and Petter Solberg must each choose a rally for our four-stage challenge. The driver with the fastest cumulative time wins a very special prize – a limited edition, silver PlayStation 2. They all want it.

So where are we going, fellas? All 14 WRC rounds are included in the game, made up of 115 stages and more than 800km of roads. There are no surprises from Finnish hero Gardemeister, who loves nothing better than to yump his Skoda Octavia WRC on Rally Finland. We're going to try Lankamaa, a 5.28km

test with its colossal leaps and super-fast sweeps. It's a real buttock-clencher.

Loix has picked the Safari Rally, an odd choice given his huge crash there in 1999. The Orien stage promises plenty of car-breaking material.

Solberg likes it rough as well. He's chosen Greece. His stage is a corker: tight twists, flat-out blasts and the typical rough Acropolis gravel that clatters underneath the car along every inch of the road.

The obvious choice for Panizzi is Sanremo, an event the little Frenchman virtually owns. There is one small twist. We've made it a night stage, and it is a real test of concentration.

Though there are PlayStations for all four, they want to watch (read insult) each other. This could take all night.

All manufacturer-backed cars and drivers feature in the game, so each of our heroes will play as themselves. Toni

kicks off, and makes a shaky start. Less than a kilometre into the Finnish stage, he clouts a rock, which stops his Octavia dead in its tracks. He gets going again and sets a blistering pace thereafter. He's a keen game player and it shows as he adapts to English pace notes read by Richard Burns' co-driver, Robert Reid.

At the end, a replay (with more angles to choose than a protractor) reveals Toni's early mishap not only mashed his bumper, but also led to a puncture. In spectacular detail, we see that he ended the stage on the wheel rim.

Next up is Petter, a self-confessed games nut, though these days his playing is restricted by time.

As he begins the stage, he shows a deft touch. He's a real player, and despite the odd mishap, he goes 10 seconds faster than Toni. The gauntlet is down.

There was a time when Loix had a reputation for sticking it in the hedges most days and *WRC II Extreme* seems to be bringing out the bad old days!

As he pounds through the Finnish forests, it is not long before the inevitable major shunt takes place. Over and over he goes, making a dreadful mess of his Hyundai Accent WRC. One of *WRC II Extremes'* most extraordinary features is the carnage you can create on screen.

When he gets going again, there's a major problem. His bonnet is flapping. Luckily, Sony has planned for such a crisis, and offers six views of the game. There are two overhead options, two inside the car and two exterior onboard options. Freddy switches to bumper-cam, and escapes the misbehaving bonnet.

Loix's chaotic run eventually grinds to a steaming halt. The time is not good. He's a full two minutes down on Petter.

Panizzi is next up. Pretty soon we see that he's easily better than Freddy, but not on the same level as Toni and Petter. He's 23 seconds away from the lead.

Gardemeister and Solberg resume their battle at the front in Greece. The Skoda claws back time from the Subaru to take a slender 1.3-second lead. Gilles surprisingly handles the gravel well, but is still 26 seconds off Toni's pace. Freddy is making progress, but he's still two minutes slower than the others.

On to Kenya and one of the game's most remarkable environments. It even has an elephant call among the popping and banging of each World Rally Car. The stage is true to reality, with flat-out sections punctuated by muddy quagmires that slow the cars almost to a crawl. The surface looks remarkably natural. It's the next best thing to doing it for real.

Petter and Toni resume battle, and the Skoda comes out on top again, by 11 seconds. This is getting serious for Petter, who now has a hefty deficit to overcome on the final stage. Gilles is third again, while Freddy plugs away, muttering about how he spends all his time on a mountain bike, not a sofa. Excuses, excuses.

And so to the final stage. It's Panizzi's favourite: asphalt. But, strangely enough, while he has gone pretty well on gravel, he struggles on the Sanremo stage, bouncing off the crash barriers and skidding up the earth banks. He shakes his head, saying: "I'm glad that I don't drive like this normally!" Still, he is a comfortable third from Loix.

To Petter's horror he loses again to Toni, making it game, set and match to the Finn. The Norwegian cries foul, claiming his PlayStation isn't as good as the others. On Gardemeister's pod,

he is 10 seconds quicker at Sanremo, but it's too late, the result stands.

"At the moment Skoda is fastest!" says a delighted Gardemeister.

"Until the rally starts," says Freddy, who thinks a steering wheel might have been better than a controller. "If you play with a wheel and pedals, it's very nice," he says. "You have to concentrate, to listen to the notes – and it's fantastic."

Unsurprisingly, the winner gives the game a ringing endorsement. "It's

much more difficult than the previous game – that was easier!" says Gardemeister. "But for sure this is much better. It's more realistic and it looks better."

As Petter leaves the building, he's still cursing his luck, and we hear through the grapevine that everybody he meets that evening gets to find out how he was 'robbed'. We hope that winning Rally GB for real made up for the disappointment, Petter! ■

PRO-CHALLENGE 2002 STAGE TIMES

Driver	Finland	Greece	Safari	Sanremo	Total
Toni Gardemeister	2m07.05s	3m40.59s	3m07.79s	3m52.48s	12m54.91s
Petter Solberg	1m57.17s	3m51.74s	3m18.79s	3m58.88s	12m57.11s +2.20s
Gilles Panizzi	2m20.04s	4m06.14s	3m35.55s	5m00.80s	15m02.53s +2m05.42s
Freddy Loix	3m56.43s	5m49.75s	4m27.00s	5m36.58s	19m49.76s +4m47.23s

Limited edition silver PS2 and WRCII Extreme are available at uk.playstation.com

Monte Carlo

Decided in the committee room rather than on the bitumen, the 2002 Monte Carlo Rally went to Tommi Makinen at Sebastien Loeb's expense. Though faster on the road, the Frenchman paid the ultimate price for an innocent mistake by his team. And the 206 WRC's? They were the pre-event favourites, but once again this event was to elude them.

1

No question about it, the Citroën driver was the main man on this Monte, and he more than anyone deserved to win it.

THE RACE
Subaru steals a march

The Monte Carlo Rally may well start and finish in the famous Principality but the season-opening event is strictly played out on French tarmac. Not since 1994 when Francois Delecour triumphed for Ford has there been a victory for a local driver. And the last time a French car won the Monte? 1985 and the legendary Peugeot 205 T16. There was a time when this event was a French speciality, the full bells and whistles. Since the 206 WRC came out, the Lion has been telling

us year in, year out that one of its major goals is to win this, the most prestigious event on the calendar. But so far it has eluded them. Indeed Delecour and fellow Frenchman Didier Auriol have never found it to their liking and have been regularly beaten by others who were stronger on the day.

In 2002, however, a young Frenchman in a hurry driving for a constructor still in their WRC infancy very nearly pulled off the perfect result. On Sunday January 20, Sébastien Loeb and local hero Daniel Eléna did indeed mount the top step

of the podium, with the regulation laurels, bubbly and what-have-you, but that made their subsequent fall all the harder when an unfortunate mix-up saw them relegated to second place (see below). But before we got that unlikely ending, we had a race, and a damned fine race it was too.

Carlos Sainz has flair and an outsize ego to go with it, so there was no question that anyone else might get away with claiming the first scratch time of the first rally of the new season and being its first leader. But it was all just a flash in the pan:

plagued by a power steering failure in the next stage, his Focus made way for Petter Solberg to shine. But by that stage the time sheets made for some interesting reading. Tommi Mäkinen was consistently setting the second-fastest time. A new car, which handled radically differently from his Mitsubishi, new tyres, a new team, new surroundings a far cry from what he had become accustomed to at Mitsubishi – and virtually a new co-driver in Lindstrom (he had only had him alongside at Rally GB 2001), coming in for Risto Männisenmäki, who was still not fully recovered from the

There were a few failures to begin with, but Tommi Mäkinen is now Mr Monte Carlo, the man with unrivalled flair in the Alps.

injuries he suffered in the last Tour de Corse. Yet here he was, already out in front. That's the mark of a champion. But the three-time Monte winner eventually hit a snag, and it took the shape of another potential champion: Sébastien Loeb. Familiar with the event, having already done it in a Saxo and having driven some of the stages in the French Championship event there, Citroën's new young recruit set the last two scratch times of the first day (five timed sections, one of them

cancelled) to nose ahead of the pack at the end of the opening leg. Meanwhile the Finnish star had rather overcooked it, spinning on the Sisteron-Thoard stage, the second-last of the day, and conceding a 36.7s lead at the end of the day. Colin McRae rounded out the top three.

So what had happened to the Peugeots? They had gone AWOL as they often do here. Richard Burns celebrated the wearing of his World

Championship crown by going off on the first timed stage. After coming close to a penalty, the Englishman cooled down and took things a little easier. Gilles Panizzi was red-hot favourite given the dry conditions for this Monte, but he was out of the running early on with a leak in his car's hydraulic system even before the first special stage. He picked up a 2m10s penalty, because of the interminable time it took to do the work on his car – gearbox and diff replacement – and later lost a further 30 seconds with a spin. As for Marcus Grönholm, he isn't particularly keen on this event, and his driving style – especially the left-foot braking – doesn't really suit it, so he was erring on the side of caution as well. Worse still, both 206s were struggling with their set-ups. Their road-holding was a long way short of perfect, the Peugeot men having contrived to unsettle a car which is usually so good on tarmac. It took a stern word from Panizzi for them to get it sorted out – and how! – for next time, but of course for Monte Carlo 2002 it was already too late. The three works

New car, new team – same old story on tarmac. Eriksson made a low-profile comeback.

Solberg, equal-best performer with Loeb thanks to five scratches, was very impressive on the tricky going.

206s did finish (Grönholm 5th, Panizzi 7th and Burns 8th), but the French outfit had been really hoping to lay the curse of the Principality to rest. The other unhappy soldier on this day was Didier Auriol. Entered in a Step 2 Toyota Corolla WRC (that's an offshoot of Scuderia Grifone, in charge of Toyota Team Europe supplies) the '94 World Champion struggled from the start with a series of engine cut-outs that saw him retire after the first timed section. In the meantime, it was the 'ironmongers next door', as Peugeot call their friends at PSA, who took centre stage. They were lucky, too, because two of their cars were out very early. Both Philippe Bugalski and Thomas Radström fell victim to engine block failures. The same thing had happened to Loeb's Xsara, but that was in the pre-event shakedown, which meant his mechanics still had time to put in a motor from another production run. Phew! Spared any breakages, the

Mäkinen-Loeb duel intensified on the second leg. Faced with a wily, experienced Finn, a master of strategy and terrain, a great improviser and a clever chooser of tyres– and they were all trump cards on this tricky mix of dry roads, icy roads, wet roads, night driving and ever-changing temperatures – Sébastien countered punch with punch.

Both Colin McRae, who not only had a loose driving seat but an engine running on just three cylinders, and Solberg, who cost himself two minutes with an off that damaged his steering, were losing touch with the two tearaways at the front. The Subaru driver set three scratch times on the Saturday, his rival two. Going flat out, Seb had a spin on the Col de Turini and took 10 seconds or so to get his engine started again, but he had kept the lead with a 28.2 margin over Makinen. The final leg, with just four specal stages – two of them

Loda and Turnini! – promised a thrilling fight to the finish. Sadly, Subaru, sure of their position and certain that Citroën would be penalised (see below), decided to rein in Mäkinen, given that he would end up winning anyway. The four-time World Champion didn't tempt fate in the Turini stage, settling for safety first and making it back to the Principality. He left it to his young lieutenant Petter Solberg to catch the spotlight, and the Norwegian duly did so by setting three out of four possible scratches and leaving one to Loeb, who was hell bent on proving that he was boss. The

Frenchman crossed the line with a 45.9-second lead over Mäkinen, a consistent rather than brilliant Carlos Sainz making up the podium ahead of Colin McRae, Marcus Grönholm and Petter Solberg. With four World Champions in his wake, five scratch times (a record shared with Solberg), the lead at the end of the fourth special stage, and having contained Mäkinen, Sébastien Loeb had pulled off quite a coup. Or so he thought. ■

1._ Bernardini won in 1996, when the event did not count towards the World Championship.

François Duval took the Ford Puma to its first Junior Championship victory.

After getting his fingers burned in that early off, the World Champion decided to be conservative and build up some experience of this unfamiliar terrain.

advantage to be gained, a rule's a rule. All the tyres had to do was get the car to parc fermé and back the following morning for another change in the service park. It seemed like an innocent mistake. Except to certain people... The British teams know the rules inside-out and spend much time not only on their own strategy but also on what their rivals are up to. In this instance, Subaru reported the incident to the stewards, and they decided to hand down a two-minute penalty to Citroën Sport. Though not denying their mistake, the Red Army lodged an appeal in the belief that the penalty was out of all proportion – no-one could imagine they had gained any advantage. The appeal was due to be heard on January 29, but the team wihdrew it four days

after the finish. The rule – as daft as it was clear – allowed for no other interpretation than the penalty. Not only that, but some heavy-handed advertising boasting about Loeb's victory, which appeared in the newspaper L'Equipe the day after the Rally, had got right under the sporting authorities' skins. Nonetheless, FIA President Max Mosley immediately promised a full-scale investigation into WRC regulations. So Subaru and Mäkinen got back the win that Citroën and Loeb had well and truly earned. The Finn, nevertheless, had driven a fabulous rally all round, and his fourth successive win in the great winter classic makes him the giant of the Monte Carlo Rally. It also gave him an outright WRC record with a total of 24 victories. ∎

The battle between Loeb and Mäkinen was a beauty – pity it ended in the stewards' room.

THAT SLIP-UP
Mäkinen on the carpet

So he wasn't part of the podium celebrations. So what, Tommi Mäkinen might ask? Four days after the 2002 Monte Carlo Rally Citroën withdrew their appeal over the decision to hand Sébastien Loeb a two-minute penalty. At a stroke, victory went not to the young man but to the great old hand, with the Frenchman classified second, just in front of Carlos Sainz. Just how had this all come to be?
The supplementary regulations allowed for a short service stop, just

10 minutes, rather than the usual 45 minutes in the service park. The latter, ending the leg, had been put back to the following morning to save teams and crews a late finish after a long day and the back-up crews' slow return from Digne. The idea behind the mini-stop was to get the cars spruced up for their podium appearance in front of all those spectators. Despite pre-event warnings about what was and wasn't permitted on the stop, the Citroën people changed the tyres on Loeb's Xsara, which was specifically forbidden at that time. Although there was no

70th Rallye Automobile Monte Carlo

TOP ENTRIES

1st leg of the 2002 World Rally championship for constructors and drivers. 1st leg of the Junior WRC championship.

Date 17th to 20th January 2002

Route
1461,28 km divided in 3 legs
15 special stages on tarmac roads (388,88 km) but 14 contested (351,65 km)

1st leg
Friday 18 January (06h00-20h00):
Monaco > Digne-Monaco, 704,56 km;
5 special stages (157,70 km) but
4 contested (122,97 km)

2nd leg
Saturday 19th January (08h00-20h40):
Monaco > Monaco, 486,50 km;
6 special stages (131,88 km)

3rd leg
Sunday 20th January (07h30-15h02):
Monaco > Monaco , 270,22 km;
4 special stages (98,80 km)

Entry List - Starters - Finishers:
57 - 55 - 26

Conditions: dry, wet, awash, snow, ice or black ice.

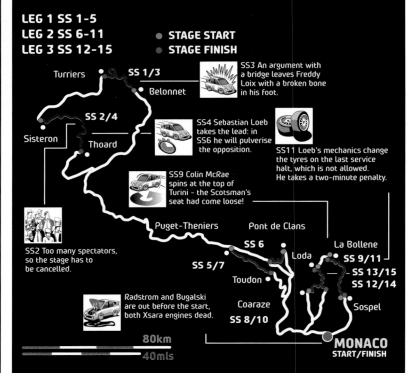

LEG 1 SS 1-5
LEG 2 SS 6-11
LEG 3 SS 12-15

● STAGE START
● STAGE FINISH

Turriers — SS 1/3
Belonnet

SS3 An argument with a bridge leaves Freddy Loix with a broken bone in his foot.

SS 2/4
Sisteron — Thoard

SS4 Sebastian Loeb takes the lead: in SS6 he will pulverise the opposition.

SS11 Loeb's mechanics change the tyres on the last service halt, which is not allowed. He takes a two-minute penalty.

SS9 Colin McRae spins at the top of Turini - the Scotsman's seat had come loose!

Puget-Theniers — Pont de Clans

SS2 Too many spectators, so the stage has to be cancelled.

SS 6
Toudon

La Bollene
SS 9/11
Loda
SS 13/15
SS 12/14

SS 5/7

Radstrom and Bugalski are out before the start, both Xsara engines dead.

Coaraze
SS 8/10

Sospel

80km
40mls

MONACO
START/FINISH

1 Richard BURNS - Robert REID
   Peugeot 206 WRC
2 Marcus GRÖNHOLM - Timo
   RAUTIAINEN Peugeot 206 WRC
3 Gilles PANIZZI - Hervé PANIZZI
   Peugeot 206 WRC
4 Carlos SAINZ - Luis MOYA
   Ford Focus RS WRC 02
5 Colin McRAE - Nicky GRIST
   Ford Focus RS WRC 02
6 Markko MÄRTIN - Michael PARK
   Ford Focus RS WRC 02
7 François DELECOUR - Daniel GRATALOUP
   Mitsubishi Lancer Evolution WRC
8 Alister McRAE - David SENIOR
   Mitsubishi Lancer Evolution WRC
10 Tommi MÄKINEN - Kaj LINDSTRÖM
   Subaru Impreza WRC 2001
11 Petter SOLBERG - Philip MILLS
   Subaru Impreza WRC 2001
14 Kenneth ERIKSSON - Tina THORNER
   Skoda Octavia WRC Evo 2
15 Toni GARDEMEISTER - Paavo LUKANDER
   Skoda Octavia WRC Evo 2
16 Roman KRESTA - Jan TOMANEK
   Skoda Octavia WRC Evo 2
17 Armin SCHWARZ - Manfred HIEMER
   Hyundai Accent WRC[2]
18 Freddy LOIX - Sven MEETS
   Hyundai Accent WRC[2]
20 Thomas RADSTROM - Denis GIRAUDET
   Citroën Xsara
21 Sébastien LOEB - Daniel ELENA
   Citroën Xsara
22 Philippe BUGALSKI - J-P. CHIARONI
   Citroën Xsara
24 Didier AURIOL - Jack BOYERE
   Toyota Corolla WRC
25 Harri ROVANPERÄ - Risto
   MANNISENMÄKI Peugeot 206 WRC
26 Bruno THIRY - Stéphane PREVOT
   Peugeot 206 WRC
27 Armin KREMER - Klaus WICHA
   Ford Focus RS WRC
29 Manfred STOHL - Ilka PETRASKO
   Toyota Corolla WRC
51 Andréa DALLAVILLA - Giovanni
   BERNACCHINI Citroën Saxo VTS
52 Niall McSHEA - Michael ORR
   Opel Corsa Super 1600
53 Giandomenico BASSO - Luigi PIROLLO
   Fiat Punto Super 1600
55 François DUVAL - Jean-Marc FORTIN
   Ford Puma
60 Nicola CALDANI - Sauro FARNOCCHIA
   Peugeot 206 XS
62 Janne TUOHINO - Petri VIHAVAINEN
   Citroën Saxo VTS
64 Gianluigi GALLI - Guido D'AMORE
   Fiat Punto Super 1600
65 Daniel SOLA - David MORENO
   Citroën Saxo VTS
67 Daniel CARLSSON - Per KARLESSON
   Ford Puma
68 Nikolaus SCHELLE - Gerhard WEISS
   Suzuki Ignis
71 David DOPPELREITER - Thomas LETTNER
   Peugeot 206 XS
78 Roger FEGHALI - Nicola ARENA
   Ford Puma

Special Stages Times

SS1 Selonnet - Turriers I (28,73 km)
1.Sainz 17'54"3; 2.Mäkinen +0"9;
3.C. McRae +4"6; 4.Panizzi +6"7;
5.Schwarz +10"1; 6.Kresta +13"1;
Jr. (23) Sola +1'41"4

SS2 Sisteron - Thoard (36,72 km)
Cancelled - Too many spectators

SS3 Selonnet - Turriers II (28,73 km)
1.Solberg 17'15"9; 2.C. McRae +12"6;
3.Mäkinen +12"6; 4.Grönholm +15"8;
5.Loeb +17"4; 6.Sainz +26"1; Jr. (20)
Duval +1'32"7

SS4 Sisteron - Thoard II (36,72 km)
1.Loeb 23'41"1; 2.Grönholm +18"0;
3.C. McRae +21"1; 4.Solberg +22"1;
5.Mäkinen +22"8; 6.Burns +25"8;
Jr (18) Galli +2'36"6

SS5 Puget - Toudon I (26,76 km)
1.Loeb 17'44"7; 2.Panizzi +17"0;
3.Sainz +20"5; 4.Mäkinen +31"4;
5.Grönholm +31"6; 6.C. McRae +37"3;
Jr. (19) Galli +2'07"3

**SS6 Pont de Clans - Villars Sur Var I
(12,07 km)**
1.Solberg 9'44"5; 2.Mäkinen +4"6;
3.C. McRae +5"5; 4.Loeb +5"9;
5.Grönholm +6"2; 6.Sainz +8"9;
Jr. (19) Duval +37"1

SS7 Puget - Toudon I (26,76 km)
1.Loeb 17'30"7; 2.Grönholm +4"8;
3.Mäkinen +10"6; 4.Panizzi +11"0;
5.C. McRae +15"3; 6.Burns +22"4;
Jr. (16) Galli +1'32"4

SS8 Coaraze - Loda I (23,04 km)
1.Mäkinen 15'56"6; 2.Loeb +6"3;
3.Sainz +8"6; 4.C. McRae +14"0;
5.Solberg +14"5; 6.Panizzi +19"4;
Jr. (17) Galli +1'15"4

**SS9 La Bollène - Turini - Moulinet I
(23,46 km)**
1.Mäkinen 15'58"6; 2.Solberg +7"8;
3.Loeb +12"8; 4.Sainz +20"9;
5.Panizzi +22"8; 6.Grönholm +23"2;
Jr. (17) Galli +1'24"0

SS10 Coaraze - Loda II (23,04 km)
1.Loeb 16'08"2; 2.Mäkinen +8"8;
3.Panizzi +23"2; 4.Sainz +25"4;
5.Solberg +26"0; 6.C. McRae +34"3;
Jr. (17) Carlsson +2'10"4

**SS11 La Bollène - Turini-Moulinet II
(23,46 km)**
1.Mäkinen 16'21"4; 2.Loeb +7"5;
3.Solberg +8"4; 4.Panizzi +10"2;
5.Sainz +13"5; 6.Grönholm +20"1;
Jr. (15) Caldani +2'04"7

**SS12 Sospel - Turini - La Bollène I
(32,84 km)**
1.Solberg 22'38"4; 2.Mäkinen +1"0;
3.Sainz +1"2; 4.Panizzi +6"5;
5.C. McRae +7"8; 6.Loeb +10"6;
Jr. (17) Caldani +2'02"6

SS13 Loda - Lucéram I (16,54 km)
1.Loeb 12'03"9; 2.C. McRae +8"2;
3.Sainz +10"3; 4.Panizzi +10"9;
5.Burns +21"8; 6.Grönholm +21"9;
Jr. (17) Duval +1'30"4

**SS14 Sospel - Turini - La Bollène II
(32,84 km)**
1.Solberg 22'02"2; 2.Panizzi +7"0;
3.C. McRae +10"7; 4.Sainz +10"8;
5.Loeb +26"8; 6.Mäkinen +27"8;
Jr. (18) Caldani +2'28"3

SS15 Loda - Lucéram II (16,54 km)
1.Solberg 11'52"7; 2.Panizzi +3"2;
3.Sainz +10"5; 4.Loeb +10"7;
5.Mäkinen +11"0; 6.C. McRae +12"9;
Jr. (17) Carlsson +1'23"1

Results WRC

	Driver/Navigator	Car	Gr.	Time
1	Mäkinen - Lindström	Subaru Impreza WRC 2001	A	3h59'30"7
2	Loeb - Elena	Citroën Xsara		+ 1'14"1
3	Sainz - Moya	Ford Focus RS WRC 02		+ 1'15"7
4	C. McRae - Grist	Ford Focus RS WRC 02		+ 1'58"0
5	Grönholm - Rautiainen	Peugeot 206 WRC		+ 2'07"4
6	Solberg - Mills	Subaru Impreza WRC 2001		+ 2'29"6
7	Panizzi - Panizzi	Peugeot 206 WRC		+ 3'20"1
8	Burns - Reid	Peugeot 206 WRC		+ 4'16"4
9	Delecour - Grataloup	Mitsubishi Lancer Evolution WRC		+ 5'35"7
10	Gardemeister - Lukander	Skoda Octavia WRC Evo 2		+ 6'42"4
17	Duval - Fortin	Ford Puma	Jr.	+ 25'35"5

Leading Retirements (29)

SS.7	Rovanperä - Mannisenmäki	Peugeot 206 WRC	Steering
SS.7	Kresta - Tomanek	Skoda Octavia WRC Evo 2	Off
SS.4	Basso - Pirollo	Fiat Punto Super 1600	Off
SS.4	Schwarz - Hiemer	Hyundai Accent WRC 2	Off
SS.3	Loix - Smeets	Hyundai Accent WRC 2	Off
SS.1	McShea - Orr	Opel Corsa Super 1600	Off
SS.1	Dallavilla - Bernacchini	Citroën Saxo VTS	Off
SS.1	Auriol - Boyère	Toyota Corolla WRC	Engine
SS.1	Radström - Giraudet	Citroën Xsara	Engine
SS.1	Bugalski - Chiaroni	Citroën Xsara	Engine

Performers

	1	2	3	4	5	6
Loeb	5	2	1	2	2	1
Solberg	5	1	1	1	2	-
Mäkinen	3	5	1	1	2	1
Sainz	1	-	5	3	1	2
Panizzi	-	3	1	5	1	1
C. McRae	-	2	4	1	2	3
Grönholm	-	2	-	1	2	3
Burns	-	-	-	-	1	2
Schwarz	-	-	-	-	1	-
Kresta	-	-	-	-	-	1

Event Leaders

SS.1	Sainz
SS.2	Cancelled
SS.3	Mäkinen
SS.4 > SS.15	Loeb

S. Loeb AB–
D. Elena O+

Previous winners

1973	Andruet - "Biche" Alpine Renault A 110
1975	Munari - Mannucci Lancia Stratos
1976	Munari - Maiga Lancia Stratos
1977	Munari - Maiga Lancia Stratos
1978	Nicolas - Laverne Porsche 911 SC
1979	Darniche - Mahé Lancia Stratos
1980	Rohrl - Geistdorfer Fiat 131 Abarth
1981	Ragnotti - Andrié Renault 5 Turbo
1982	Rohrl - Geistdorfer Opel Ascona 400
1983	Rohrl - Geistdorfer Lancia rally 037
1984	Rohrl - Geistdorfer Audi Quattro
1985	Vatanen - Harryman Peugeot 205 T16
1986	Toivonen - Cresto Lancia Delta S4
1987	Biasion - Siviero Lancia Delta HF 4WD
1988	Saby - Fauchille Lancia Delta HF 4WD
1989	Biasion - Siviero Lancia Delta Integrale
1990	Auriol - Occelli Lancia Delta Integrale
1991	Sainz - Moya Toyota Celica GT-Four
1992	Auriol - Occelli Lancia Delta HF Integrale
1993	Auriol - Occelli Toyota Celica Turbo 4WD
1994	Delecour - Grataloup Ford Escort RS Cosworth
1995	Sainz - Moya Subaru Impreza 555
1996	Bernardini - Andrié Ford Escort Cosworth
1997	Liatti - Pons Subaru Impreza WRC
1998	Sainz - Moya Toyota Corolla WRC
1999	Mäkinen - Mannisenmäki Mitsubishi Lancer Evo 6
2000	Mäkinen - Mannisenmäki Mitsubishi Lancer Evo 6
2001	Mäkinen - Mannisenmäki Mitsubishi Lancer Evo 6

Championship Classifications

FIA Drivers (1/14)
1. Tommi Mäkinen — 10
2. Sébastien Loeb — 6
3. Carlos Sainz — 4
4. Colin McRae — 3
5. Marcus Grönholm — 2
6. Petter Solberg — 1

FIA Junior WRC (1/6)
1. François Duval — 10
2. Nicola Caldani — 6
3. Roger Feghali — 4
4. Daniel Carlsson — 3
5. David Doppelreiter — 2
6. Nikolaus Schelle — 1

FIA Constructors (1/14)
1. Subaru — 12
2. Ford — 10
3. Peugeot — 4

Sverige

When it's wintery, Marcus Grönholm fears no-one. With many of his rivals eliminating themselves, the Finn rolled on towards his eighth World Championship win and brought Peugeot their first of the season. And for good measure, last year's winner Harri Rovanpera made it a Peugeot one-two.

WRC
WORLD RALLY
CHAMPIONSHIP

The Subaru engine's temperatures soared after it hit a snow bank, forcing Mäkinen into retirement.

Harri Rovanperä had high hopes of a repeat performance but, unluckily for him, he caught Grönholm on one of his best days.

Finnish prospect Jani Paasonen impressed, eclipsing Delecour and McRae in the same machinery until he broke a wheel and slipped back into the pack.

THE RACE
GRÖNHOLM THE MASTER

The joke's getting a bit long in the tooth, but season after season it stands up to the test of time. That's right: Peugeot should forget the Monte Carlo once and for all and kick off every sporting programme in Sweden. The 206 has won everything, or almost everything, but the most prestigious rally of them all seems still beyond it. Well, too bad about the Monte, and bring on the Scandinavian round. At least this one doesn't play hard to get. Every time the pretty little 206 has taken the start it's won, and the 2002 event did nothing to undermine the tried and trusted saying: snow in Sweden brings a win in February.

Marcus Grönholm gave the little lioness and her team their first World Championship win of 2002. Last year the Finn, as reigning champion, was hampered in his bid for back-to-

back wins with a faulty head gasket, which meant the top step went to Peugeot's star understudy on dirt or snow, the flawless Harri Rovanpera.

But this time nothing and no-one was going to get in the way of the tall man from Espoo. Right at the start, and just to show who was boss, Grönholm set the first scratch time of the day on a special stage that took a fair fall of snow before the start. The early starters, notably Tommi Mäkinen, were in most trouble: the four-time World Champion, handicapped by the wrong choice of tyres, conceded a huge 21 seconds to the quickest men. In those conditions Thomas Radstrom set the second-fastest time, which was briefly reassuring for Citroën, at least where the car was concerned, but not the driver, who lost 40 seconds with a spin on the next stage and a further seven minutes on the third when he planted the Xsara in a snowdrift.

Loix likes the Hyundai more than the Mitsubishi, as shown by this excellent third-fastest time on Granberget 1, broken left foot or no broken left foot.

top spot in the team. However tight a rein you keep on them, boys will be boys and barrack-room brawls will always break out...

In their wake the opposition was starting to find the going hard. First to go, apart from a despairing Radstrom – who did manage to set a scratch time – was Richard Burns.

The Englishman is certainly quick, but maybe he was pushing just a bit too hard to keep pace and match it with his Finnish team mates. On Granberget, the third stage against the clock, he got it wrong, hit a snow bank and was seriously slowed as the engine temperature climbed alarmingly.

Rovanpera hadn't forgotten how to be quick in such conditions and he hit back at Grönholm immediately.

The two of them went at it hammer and tongs on the opening leg, not only for the lead in this rally but because they were slugging it out for

He wasn't the only one to bury it in the snow banks lining the Scandinavian course. On the Fredriksberg stage Tommi Mäkinen did the same thing when he tried to cut it just too fine. Same cause, more serious effects: the dense

snow forced into the intakes caused the Subaru's engine to overheat as the water drained away. There was no way to get liquid in there as it red-lined and the Finn was forced to switch off. And given that he's no longer in the business of running just for the sake of picking up experience, the man who had led the title chase to that point threw in the towel.

That meant the field was spread out as the first leg ended. Grönholm was in front, but just nine-tenths ahead of Rovanpera. Colin McRae, 41.5s back, made up the first three from the astonishing Jani Paasonen, having his first drive in a works Mitsubishi, and a very much on-form Freddy Loix in the Hyundai. It was a great comeback from the likeable Belgian despite the continuing handicap of a broken foot which meant he not only wore a cast from knee to toe but also needed some modifications to the Hyundai with a long brake pedal.

Alister McRae's leading role in the winter pre-season testing helped him fare better than Delecour at the wheel of the tricky Lancer WRC.

Brillant in previous years at this event, Colin McRae was one of the few threats to the Peugeots until he destroyed a wheel on the second stage.

Once the opening shots had been fired, there was no real suspense any more. The big question was whether Rovanpera had the talent – and the balls – to go after Master Marcus.

At the start of the second stage McRae just went for it, as the Scotsman so often does. But despite a first scratch time in the morning, he hit a rock with the left rear wheel of his Focus WRC and broke the rim. He wasn't the only one, either: Paasonen, just up the road from the Ford, had done exactly the same thing at the same place, Radstrom broke a brake disc there and Loeb had ridden his luck, coming out of the day's second stage with a damaged wheel but also with a very handy fifth-fastest time.

At the end of 2001 Burns had claimed he could be a winner in the 206 WRC as early as Sweden. Wrong!

A podium finish for Sainz as Ford bowed to Peugeot pressure as early as the Swedish round.

McRae's misadventures at least meant that the Peugeot folk could relax a little. While there were no team orders, Rovanpera soon realised that it wasn't a question of his employers laying down the law, it was the survival of the fittest. Apart from McRae's success early in the day, Grönholm took all the other Friday scratch times, one of them ahead of the surprising Skoda in the hands of the even more surprising veteran Kenneth Eriksson, still the driving force he always was on his home soil. Sadly he had to give up the next day when his engine overheated.

By the end of the second leg Marcus Grönholm had the rally in the bag. He was 50.1s ahead of his Peugeot teammate, 2m 21.5s in front of the consistent Carlos Sainz. With Rovanpera back in the ranks, he had no need to push it next day, giving Burns the chance to shine. After sorting out the settings on his 206 the Englishman was back in the groove, but despite three best times from a possible five he couldn't quite dislodge Ford's Spaniard from the third step of the podium. Still, his was a fine fourth place and it underlined Peugeot's superiority as they completed a one-two with Grönholm and Rovanpera. It put him ahead of the brothers McRae, Alister (5th) for once ahead of his brother Colin in sixth. Yes, it might be a good thing if Peugeot were to forget all about the Monte-Carlo in future... ■

THE DEBUTANTS
LAURELS FOR LOEB AND DUVAL

It was hard to see exactly why, but the 2002 version of Rally Sweden had the honour of hosting several first-time appearances with a major bearing on the shape of things to come. Apart from Citroën, there to try out the Xsara, its drivers and its teams in the far north, both Sébastien Loeb and Gilles Panizzi were having their first Scandinavian drives in World Championship context, and François Duval his first WRC drive of any kind. And then there was Jani Paasonen, mentioned earlier, a Mitsubishi debutant but a man used to being on snow and ice since his childhood years.

On the team front, it was a sortie into the unknown for the Red Army. Yes, they had done a lot of testing in winter conditions, but how would the Xsara stack up against the

opposition in that configuration? A good car won't lie to you. Radstrom, a former winner of Rally Sweden (back in 1994, when it counted only for the two-litre World Championship and had been spurned by the big guns), went straight on the attack – and left all sense of judgement behind.

First he had a spin on the Rammen stage (40 seconds gone), then it was a smart encounter with a snowdrift on Granberget (another seven minutes lost), and by the end of that third stage the Scandinavian starlet was already nearly eight minutes adrift of the leader.
At the rate he was accumulating silly off-road excursions he would be hitting Karlstad three days after the leader. In the end he set one scratch time, two second-fastests and a third-fastest. The Xsara passed its baptism by ice, and Radstrom had taken it to the limit. And we should remember that a lengthy stop for a turbo change as early as the first stage cost it a lot of time.

Thankfully for Citroën, they have Loeb as well, and the man from Alsace showed that maybe he has more talent than he is given credit for. On the first special stage he surprised all and sundry by matching Mäkinen's time, the two of them having gone out first and been troubled by the layer of fresh snow. Their times weren't outstanding, but being on the same mark as Mäkinen was worth its weight in gold.

Later, without being so handicapped by his position on the road, Loeb set a convincing third-best time on Lejen II, the eighth timed section of the event. Denis Giraudet, who knows a good drive when he sees one, was fulsome in his praise: 'It was right up there with what Jean-Luc Thérier used to do', he insisted, and that is some comparison. The Citroën driver was there to learn, and he showed just what a quick learner he is. He finished up in 17th place, but he had been delayed by

an off and a blocked air intake after the bump.

It wasn't serious – all part of learning by your mistakes. François Duval, for his part, may not be quite as talented, but talented the lad most certainly is. We all thought so, and he confirmed it. He may not have set any Loeb-like times on Lejen, but his rally was as sensible as it was eventful, with countless moments for him and co-driver Jean-Marc Fortin.

A flawless drive culminated in a fine 10th place. Ford boss Malcolm Wilson had had the good sense to warn him not to pay any attention to what his old adversary from the 2001 French Super 1600 championship was getting up to. In the end the two youngsters were separated by eight best times to seven in Loeb's favour, which highlights how good the young Belgian's performance was. And to think that Carlos Sainz set up the diffs on his Ford Focus WRC for him. 'I don't think Carlos will be doing that again!', he quipped later.

The last of the debutants was Gilles Panizzi, who had the last of the front-running 206 WRC cars in Sweden. This is a semi-works car entered alternately for him on gravel or snow and Harri Rovanpera on tarmac by the Bozian team rather than by Scuderia Grifone during the 2001 season.

After a trying first stage as the Frenchman struggled to come to grips with the driving techniques required on Scandinavian tracks, he was more like himself after some set-up changes and his times improved significantly. In fact at times they were better than those of Sebastian Lindholm, who had a virtually identical 206 but a lot more experience. Eventually he was 16th, and while he was far from the star among the first-timers, the 'Tarmac Master' at least got a clear idea of the gap he needs to bridge. ∎

Citroën were banking on Thomas Radstrom, but the Swede made too many mistakes to have any real chance.

A first WRC rally for François Duval – and a first chance to shine with some remarkable times.

Uddeholm International Swedish Rally

2nd leg of the 2002 World Rally Championship for constructors and drivers. 1st leg of FIA Production Car WRC Championship.

Date 31st January to 3rd February 2002

Route
1895,21 km divided in 3 legs
16 special stages on snow covered tracks (381,84 km), 15 contested (358,69 km)

Start
Thursday 31st January (19h00): Karlstad
1st leg
Friday 1st February (06h00-19h15):
Karlstad > Hagfors > Karlstad, 696,74 km; 5 special stages (124,01 km)
2nd leg
Saturday 2nd February (06h00-18h53):
Karlstad > Hagfors > Karlstad, 509,27 km; 6 special stages (129,04 km)
3rd leg
Sunday 3rd February (06h00-16h15):
Karlstad > Hagfors > Karlstad, 509,27 km; 5 special stages and 4 contested (105,64 km)

Entry List - Starters - Finishers:
85 - 75 - 51

Conditions: snow then rain, the surface got progressively soft.

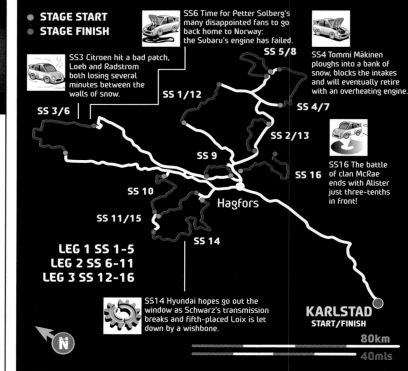

- ● **STAGE START**
- ● **STAGE FINISH**

SS3 Citroen hit a bad patch, Loeb and Radstrom both losing several minutes between the walls of snow.

SS6 Time for Petter Solberg's many disappointed fans to go back home to Norway: the Subaru's engine has failed.

SS4 Tommi Mäkinen ploughs into a bank of snow, blocks the intakes and will eventually retire with an overheating engine.

SS16 The battle of clan McRae ends with Alister just three-tenths in front!

SS14 Hyundai hopes go out the window as Schwarz's transmission breaks and fifth-placed Loix is let down by a wishbone.

SS 1/12
SS 3/6
SS 5/8
SS 4/7
SS 2/13
SS 9
SS 16
SS 10
Hagfors
SS 11/15
SS 14

KARLSTAD START/FINISH

LEG 1 SS 1-5
LEG 2 SS 6-11
LEG 3 SS 12-16

80km
40mls

VARNING!
SVAG IS
CAUTION!
THIN ICE

TOP ENTRIES

1. Richard BURNS - Robert REID
   Peugeot 206 WRC
2. Marcus GRÖNHOLM - Timo RAUTIAINEN Peugeot 206 WRC
3. Harri ROVANPERÄ - Risto PIETILÄINEN Peugeot 206 WRC
4. Carlos SAINZ - Luis MOYA
   Ford Focus RS WRC 02
5. Colin McRAE - Nicky GRIST
   Ford Focus RS WRC 02
7. François DELECOUR - Daniel GRATALOUP
   Mitsubishi Lancer Evo WRC
8. Alister McRAE - David SENIOR
   Mitsubishi Lancer Evo WRC
9. Jani PAASONEN - Arto KAPANEN
   Mitsubishi Lancer Evo WRC
10. Tommi MÄKINEN - Kaj LINDSTRÖM
    Subaru Impreza WRC 2002
11. Petter SOLBERG - Philip MILLS
    Subaru Impreza WRC 2002
14. Kenneth ERIKSSON - Tina THORNER
    Skoda Octavia WRC Evo 2
15. Toni GARDEMEISTER - Paavo LUKANDER
    Skoda Octavia WRC Evo 2
16. Stig BLOMQVIST - Ana GONI
    Skoda Octavia WRC Evo 2
17. Armin SCHWARZ - Manfred HIEMER
    Hyundai Accent WRC
18. Freddy LOIX - Sven SMEETS
    Hyundai Accent WRC
19. Juha KANKKUNEN - Juha REPO
    Hyundai Accent WRC
20. Thomas RADSTROM - Denis GIRAUDET
    Citroën Xsara WRC
21. Sébastien LOEB - Daniel ELENA
    Citroën Xsara WRC
23. Francois DUVAL - Jean-Marc FORTIN
    Ford Focus Rs WRC 01
24. Gilles PANIZZI - Hervè PANIZZI
    Peugeot 206 WRC
31. Sebastian LINDHOLM - Timo HANTUNEN
    Peugeot 206 WRC 7
32. Henning SOLBERG - Cato MENKERUD
    Toyota Corolla WRC
33. Janne TUOHINO - Petri VIHAVAINE
    Ford Focus RS WRC 01
34. Juuso PYKÄLISTÖ - Esko MERTSALMI
    Toyota Corolla WRC
51. Gustavo TRELLES - Jorge DEL BUONO
    Mitsubishi Lancer Evo 6
53. Alessandro FIORIO - Enrico CANTONI
    Mitsubishi Lancer EVO 7
57. Toshihiro ARAI - Tony SIRCOMBE
    Subaru Impreza 555
59. Natalie BARRATT - Roger FREEMAN
    Mitsubishi Lancer Evo 6
66. Dimitar ILIEV - Petar SIVOV
    Mitsubishi Lancer Evo 7
67. Marko IPATTI - Kari KAJULA
    Mitsubishi Lancer Evo 6
69. Bernt KOLLEVOLD - Olav BODILSEN
    Mitsubishi Lancer Evo 6
73. Martin ROWE - Chris WOOD
    Mitsubishi Lancer Evo 6
75. Kristian SOHLBERG - Jukka AHO
    Mitsubishi Lancer Evo 6
113. Tomasz KUCHAR - Maciej SZCEPANIAK
    Toyota Corolla WRC
115. Ioannis PAPADIMITRIOU - Allan HARRYMAN Subaru Impreza 555

Special Stage Times

SS1 Sagen I (14,17 km)
1.Grönholm 7'32"7; 2.Radström +4"2;
3.Rovanperä +5"5; 4.Burns +7"3;
5.Tuohino +9"2; 6.C. McRae +14"0;
FIA Prod. (35) Arai +50"3

SS2 Rammen I (23,15 km)
1.Rovanperä 12'04"5; 2.Grönholm +3"0;
3.Burns +7"0; 4.Paasonen +15"1;
5.Solberg +16"3; 6.Tuohino +16"9;
FIA Prod. (31) Sohlberg +58"3

SS3 Granberget I (40,50 km)
1.Rovanperä 20'50"5;
2.Grönholm +12"6; 3.Loix +14"6;
4.Schwarz +18"4; 5.Sainz +23"5;
6.Kankkunen +25"3;
FIA Prod. (32) Sohlberg +1'39"2

SS4 Fredriksberg I (18,13 km)
1.Radström 10'42"6; 2.Grönholm +0"6;
3.C. McRae +2"9; 4.Solberg +3"9;
5.Paasonen +5"5; 6.Rovanperä +7"5;
FIA Prod. (30) Sohlberg +48"3

SS5 Lejen I (28,06 km)
1.C. McRae 14'04"4; 2.Grönholm +5"3;
3.Burns +7"9; 4.Radström +8"2;
5.Rovanperä +9"1; 6.Loix +9"6;
FIA Prod. (31) Fiorio +1'22"5

SS6 Granberget II (40,50 km)
1.C. McRae 19'59"7; 2.Grönholm +1"3;
3.Rovanperä +6"1; 4.Burns +13"4;
5.Eriksson +20"1; 6.Radström +22"6;
FIA Prod. (32) Sohlberg +1'55"8

SS7 Fredriksberg II (18,13 km)
1.Grönholm 10'15"8;
2.Rovanperä +12"3; 3.Radström +14"8;
4.Sainz +16"6; 5.Loeb +16"8;
6.Burns +17"0;
FIA Prod. (23) Sohlberg +52"1

SS8 Lejen II (28,06 km)
1.Grönholm 13'58"4; 2.Eriksson +4"7;
3.Loeb +7"1; 4.Sainz +10"7;
5.Rovanperä +11"4; 6.C. McRae +11"5;
FIA Prod. (29) Fiorio +1'26"7

SS9 Malta (11,25 km)
1.Grönholm 5'34"9; 2.Radström +4"2;
3.Sainz +5"8; 4.C. McRae +8"5;
5.Burns +8"4; 6.Rovanperä +9"2;
FIA Prod. (31) Trelles +42"4

SS10 Hara (11,90 km)
1.Grönholm 5'59"2; 2.Radström +3"2;
3.Rovanperä +4"3; 4.Burns +6"5;
5.Sainz +7"1; 6.Tuohino +7"3;
FIA Prod. Ipatti +42"0

SS11 Torntop I (19,20 km)
1.Grönholm 10'14"8; 2.Sainz +4"3;
3.Radström +5"4; 4.Rovanperä +6"9
5.C. McRae +5"2; 6.Burns +9"3;
FIA Prod. (27) Ipatti +1'12"9

SS12 Sagen II (14,17 km)
1.Burns 7'20"2; 2.Grönholm +0"4;
3.C. McRae +1"1; 4.Rovanperä +5"8;
5.Sainz+5"9; 6.Duval +6"1;
FIA Prod. (32) Ipatti +46"6

SS13 Rammen II (23,15 km)
Cancelled because of impassible road

SS14 Vargasen (32,43 km)
1.Burns 17'50"1; 2.C. McRae +0"4;
3.Sainz +0"6; 4.Grönholm +0"6;
5.Rovanperä +7"5; 6. Eriksson +14"8;
FIA Prod. (25) Sohlberg +1'25"0

SS15 Torntop II (19,20 km)
1.C. McRae 9'55"7; 2.Burns +2"6;
3.Grönholm +5"4; 4.Radström +8"8;
5.Rovanperä +10"9; 6. Sainz +14"8;
FIA Prod. (27) Ipatti +54"6

SS16 Hagfors 2002 (39,84 km)
1.Burns 19'45"2; 2.Sainz +4"4;
3.Radström +6"6; 4.C. McRae +12"1;
5.Grönholm +15"0; 6.A. McRae +22"9;
FIA Prod. (24) Ipatti +1'54"7

Results — WRC

	Driver/Navigator	Car	Gr.	Time
1	**Grönholm - Rautiainen**	**Peugeot 206 WRC**	**A**	**3h07'28"6**
2	Rovanperä - Pitilainen	Peugeot 206 WRC		+ 1'24"5
3	Sainz - Moya	Ford Focus RS WRC 02		+ 2'25"8
4	Burns - Reid	Peugeot 206 WRC		+ 2'33"9
5	A. McRea - Senior	Mitsubishi Lancer Evo WRC		+ 4'14"7
6	C. McRea - Grist	Ford Focus RS WRC 02		+ 4'15"0
7	Tuohino - Vihavainen	Ford Focus RS WRC 01		+ 4'23"4
8	Kankkunen - Repo	Hyundai Accent WRC		+ 4'36"9
9	Lindholm - Hantunen	Peugeot 206 WRC		+ 4'56"6
10	Duval - Fortin	Ford Focus RS WRC 01		+ 6'33"3
24	**Sohlberg - Aho**	**Mitsubishi Lancer Evo 6**	**Prod.**	**+ 17'57"3**

Leading Retirements (22)

SS.16	Eriksson - Thörner	Skoda Octavia WRC	Overheating engine
SS.15	Gardemeister - Lukander	Skoda Octavia WRC	Off
SS.14	Schwarz - Hiemer	Hyundai Accent WRC	Transmission
SS.14	Loix - Smeets	Hyundai Accent WRC	Suspension
SS.11	Trelles - Del Buono	Mitsubishi Lancer Evo 6	Stopped in SS11
SS.6	Solberg - Mills	Subaru Impreza WRC 2002	Engine
SS.4	Mäkinen - Lindström	Subaru Impreza WRC 2002	Engine

Performers

	1	2	3	4	5	6
Grönholm	6	6	2	-	1	-
Burns	3	1	2	3	1	2
C. McRae	3	1	2	2	1	2
Rovanperä	2	1	3	2	4	2
Radström	1	3	3	2	-	1
Sainz	-	2	2	2	3	1
Eriksson	-	1	-	-	1	1
Loeb	-	-	1	-	1	-
Loix	-	-	1	-	-	-
Paasonen	-	-	-	1	1	-
Solberg	-	-	-	1	1	-
Schwarz	-	-	-	1	-	-
Tuohino	-	-	-	1	1	2
Duval	-	-	-	-	-	1
Kankkunen	-	-	-	-	-	1
A. McRae	-	-	-	-	-	1

Event Leaders

SS.1 > SS.2	Grönholm
SS.3 > SS.4	Rovanperä
SS.5 > SS.16	Grönholm

Previous winners

1973	Blomqvist - Hertz Saab 96 V 4		1988	Alen - Kivimaki Lancia Delta HF 4WD
1975	Waldegaard - Thorszelius Lancia Stratos		1989	Carlsson - Carlsson Mazda 323 4WD
1976	Eklund - Cederberg Saab 96 V 4		1991	Eriksson - Parmander Mitsubishii Galant VR-4
1977	Blomqvist - Sylvan Saab 99 ems		1992	Jonsson - Backman Toyota Celica GT-Four
1978	Waldegaard - Thorszelius Ford Escort RS		1993	Jonsson - Backman Toyota Celica Turbo 4WD
1979	Blomqvist - Cederberg Saab 99 Turbo		1994	Rådström - Backman Toyota Celica Turbo 4WD
1980	Kullang - Berglund Opel Ascona 400		1995	Eriksson - Parmander Mitsubishi Lancer Ev.2
1981	Mikkola - Hertz Audi Quattro		1996	Mäkinen - Harjanne Mitsubishi Lancer Ev.3
1982	Blomqvist - Cederberg Audi Quattro		1997	Eriksson - Parmander Subaru Impreza WRC
1983	Mikkola - Hertz Audi Quattro		1998	Mäkinen - Mannisenmaki Mitsubishi Lancer Ev.4
1984	Blomqvist - Cederberg Audi Quattro		1999	Mäkinen - Mannisenmaki Mitsubishi Lancer Ev.6
1985	Vatanen - Harryman Peugeot 205 T16		2000	Grönholm - Rautiainen Peugeot 206 WRC
1986	Kankkunen - Piironen Peugeot 205 T16		2001	Rovanperä - Pietilainen Peugeot 206 WRC
1987	Salonen - Harjanne Mazda 323 Turbo			

Championship Classifications

FIA Drivers (2/14)
1. Marcus Grönholm — 12
2. Tommi Mäkinen — 10
3. Carlos Sainz — 8
4. Sébastien Loeb — 6
. Harri Rovanperä — 6
6. Colin McRae — 4
7. Richard Burns — 3
8. Alister McRae — 2
9. Petter Solberg — 1

FIA Constructors (2/14)
1. Peugeot — 20
2. Ford — 16
3. Subaru — 12
4. Mitsubishi — 3
5. Hyundai — 1

FIA Production Car WRC (1/8)
1. Kristian Sohlberg — 10
2. Toshihiro Arai — 6
3. Marko Ipatti — 4
4. Alessandro Fiorio — 3
5. Saulius Girdauskas — 2
6. Martin Rowe — 1

FIA Junior WRC (1/6)
1. François Duval — 10
2. Nicola Caldani — 6
3. Roger Feghali — 4
4. Daniel Carlsson — 3
5. David Doppelreiter — 2
6. Nikolaus Schelle — 1

France

The Subarus were the only ones to try, at least for a little while, to resist the Peugeout steamroller in a Tour de Corse that was run in difficult conditions. But the French team scored a superb treble, with Panizz ahead of Grönholm and Burns. Philippe Bugalsk confirmed the PSA group's dominance by finishing fourth for Citroen

Marcus Grönholm is no match for Panizzi on tarmac yet, but he did set a fine second-fastest time.

Citroën gambled by entering their evolution 2002 Xsara through a satellite team, which gave Bugalski the chance to assess its performance on the ground.

THE RALLY
Peugeot crushing in Corsica

It's red, has two silver chevrons on the grille and makes a fine old noise: it's a Xsara WSC. A hell of a thing, whether you treat it as semi-works or semi-privateer – and this was no works car with some namby-pamby bloodline either. Just to show how different it is, its roof is as red as the rest of it, not the white that goes with the prototypes straight off the Satory production line. The official target for this entry from Spain via Piedrafita, the very pragmatic Iberian set-up that runs the national chamionship, was to try out the new car and run it in ahead of entering it on the home front this season. But while they were about it, why not simplify life by putting it in the hands of Philippe Bugalski, rather than whoever might be driving it on the Spanish roads? Nice one, Citroën: the party line was swallowed hook, line and sinker not only by the sporting authorities but also by the media, specialist press included. In fact a quick inquiry on the Tour de Corse soon revealed the truth behind this unexpected entry. Philippe Bugalski's Xsara WRC was none other than the 2002 evolution of the car,

homologated on March 1. Behind this intelligent little tactic was the intention to test it out on the ground before its official appearance in Catalunya, the next round, and see how the improvements, particularly those to its engine, panned out. There is nothing in the rules to prevent a private outfit from giving a car its debut in an event. It also enabled Citroën to honour their pre-season commitment to seven events with Citroën Sport in 2002 and not a single one more. It was pretty clever, and you had to take your hat off to them. Guy Fréquelin's team did it all again later in the season (San Remo, Australia, Great Britain), not for homologation purposes but because race data is so much more instructive. In Corsica it all got under Peugeot's skin, aggrieved as they were to see a Xsara right behind them on tarmac – the car that had eclipsed the 206s in the most recent Monte Carlo Rally and also won on the 'Beautiful Island' last time out! With Bugalski at the wheel, it was a mean-looking machine. Sadly, the sharp-looking new mount had no cutting edge. The start of the event was a disaster as Bug dropped right back to 15th, partly because the driver himself was taking time to find his feet with it, but mostly

because the car wasn't properly set up. Thanks to a fine fightback drive, the three-time French Champion finished fourth without ever threatening the leaders.

And they were – need you ask – Peugeot. With the waywardness of Monte Carlo all sorted out, Gilles Panizzi, the Lion's tarmac ace, did the job he is paid for: setting best time after best time, staying in front and gathering in the points. He went straight to the front on the first stage, set four consecutive scratch times, and left Marcus Grönholm to do the same on the last special stage of the day. That was one up on his Finnish teammate, who did very well to stay within three seconds of the leader. Richard Burns, third at 25.1 seconds, sealed the World Champion team's grip on things. They had had an easy day of it,

Despite the occasionally tricky going, and a car that faltered in the closing stages, Gilles Panizzi put in a flawless performance.

After his remarkable Monte, Solberg was again surprisingly good on the Corsican tarmac. He deserved better than fifth after a small mistake.

Brilliant in the Peugeot not so long ago, Delecour was lacklustre in a Lancer that handled more than tolerably well.

troubled only slightly by the downpour near the end (Ocana-Radicale, SS5) even though the winners on the day were the ones who suffered more in the wet than the earlier starters. Hence Grönholm's scratch time and insignificant gap. In the lionesses' wake, the most explosive man of the day was again Petter Solberg, who caught the eye more than team leader Tommi Mäkinen. But yet again the Norwegian went off, hit hard and broke a rear suspension link. Brought forward to March after a friendly exchange with Cyprus (the Tour de Corse had been scheduled

for mid-April but because of the French school holidays the Cypriot organisers agreed to put their event back), it was the first time the island event had been staged so early in the season. That made for all kinds of meteorological mayhem, with rain forecast but never arriving when and where it was expected to. For proof of that, look no further than the second stage. From the outset the conditions looked hard to get a handle on: wet in parts, dry in others, some absolutely soaked and even covered in mud. When it came to setting an indicative time, there was a wide range of tyre options.

3

Another off for Mäkinen, aquaplaning on stage two in pursuit of the Peugeots.

The latest evolution of the Hyundai Accent, christened WRC3, made a promising debut in Corsica.

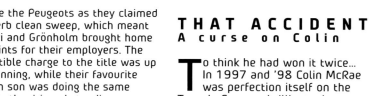

Subaru made the best choice, putting slicks on Solberg's and Mäkinen's cars and seeing them pulverise the times. On a more cautious note the Peugeot drivers (with Panizzi and Grönholm on intermediates) had to suffer in silence, but the Fords, already pretty low-profile, sank without trace. That one stage was enough for the Imprezas to get going again and for the blue team's Finnish star to start threatening Burns. So the day started wet. As the rain swept across the service area, most of the leading drivers went back out on intermediates. No joy for Mäkinen and Solberg: they should have stuck to their slicks, because up on the high ground the roads were much less slippy than foreseen. So once again they were knocked back a long way behind Fortress Peugeot, the latter also suffering a puncture and dropping back a lot further than the former.

There was hardly time to comment on the haphazard way things were turning out before the bad weather came back with a vengeance, this time setting in for good. The last three timed stages of the day took place in steadily worsening conditions. But the Subaru camp were so frustrated that the drivers opted for cut slicks rather than the cut intermediates the others had gone for. It was a dicey decision, so much so that Makinen aquaplaned into retirement with deranged

suspension – but Solberg cleaned the stage! Still, he was brought back to heel by Panizzi who, like any good master of the hunt, was determined not to let anyone else finish off such an amazing day in splendid style. Not only that, but the Norwegian was his usual mix of excellent and execrable and had a puncture at the end of the stage. Thanks to their rather conservative choice, Peugeot ended up with a comfortable lead. Subaru's war effort was undermined by inconsistency in the Anglo-Japanese camp. Now occupying the first three places, with Bugalski almost two minutes behind in fourth, the 206s only had to manage the final stage as best they could.

And they managed it without much trouble, despite a defective anti-roll bar on Panizzi's car at the start of the day. The stage was notable for the attack by Colin McRae, who was hell bent on getting ahead of Bugalski as the latter struggled with a fair degree of understeer. Going for it just a bit too hard, the Scot had a huge off in the second-last stage. Panizzi, logically enough, was given the same time as Grönholm, who had been quickest to that stage, the point being to avoid affecting the outcome of an event which ended with the first clean stage for Bugalski in his last chance of achieving one. The semi-works, semi-privateer car was up and running. It was never in a position to

trouble the Peugeots as they claimed a superb clean sweep, which meant Panizzi and Grönholm brought home 16 points for their employers. The irresistible charge to the title was up and running, while their favourite Finnish son was doing the same thing in the drivers' standings. Dominating the race in trying conditions – an outstanding effort less than two months after their colourless Monte Carlo – and with two drivers working in perfect harmony, the Tour de Corse was literally a one-way event. ■

THAT ACCIDENT
A curse on Colin

To think he had won it twice... In 1997 and '98 Colin McRae was perfection itself on the Tour de Corse, a brilliant winner at the wheel of his Subaru. He seemed to have tamed the traps on this awesome event, much to the joy of the locals. They like nothing better than a bit of showmanship and a dash of flair, two things the Highlander has

Tarmac Master: rally after rally, Gilles Panizzi remains the man they all have to beat on tarmac. Thanks to him and the efforts of Grönholm and Burns, Peugeot claimed a remarkable treble.

Dazzling in Corsica for Subaru, McRae couldn't do it in his Ford, his rally again ending in a nasty accident.

Carlos Sainz nicked three points for Ford on a rally where he was beset by technical problems.

never been short of. But since his move to Ford his island outings have been either anonymous or absolute disasters. In 2000 he had the biggest bucking bronco ride of his life, his Focus flying through the air before coming to a halt on its roof, and it took forever to free him. Strapped into his seat and hanging upside down, he was jammed in by the roll-over hoop which had been dislodged by the violence of the impact. Half-conscious, he was helicoptered straight away to hospital in Bastia, with a bad break to his cheekbone and a punctured lung. A few days later, in the only interview he would give on his big roll, he admiited he had thought he was about to meet his Maker. Soon afterward he underwent microsurgery in Edinburgh to have a plate inserted behind his cheekbone, leaving his face marked

forever by his exertions in Corsica. In 2001 he drove a good event, but for little reward. And once again this year brought a terrible off, right at the end of the rally. His driving in Saturday's rain made up for the shortcomings of the Focus WRC on tarmac, and of his Pirellis. His fine attacking drive saw him managing to dislodge Philippe Bugalski from fourth place come Sunday morning. But once again, on SS15 (Coti Chavari-Pietra Rossa) he got carried way and found himself off the road and a prisoner again in the carcass of his Ford. With just an injury to his left hand, Colin McRae was still able to take part in the Catalunya Rally a fortnight later. Once again the accident put the supposed dangers of the island event firmly in the spotlight. McRae in 2000, Mäkinen last year (he also hit a cow at full tilt), then another one

this year, as well as Fabrice Morel's terrifying plunge into a ravine in 2001: the Tour de Corse can be frightening, and there is no shortage of people who regularly get hot under the collar and demand that it be dropped from the calendar. Thankfully the organisation was spot-on, and attracted warm praise from the very people who had been most vehemently against the event before it even started. Otherwise the future would be bleak for France's round of the World Championship. It remains to be seen how Colin McRae will go about it in future. His other tarmac outings in 2002 were disappointing. The man is obviously not best buddies with the bitumen, you can feel it and see it. Even Highlander takes a long, long time to rebuild his confidence after something like that... ∎

RALLYE DE FRANCE

inmarsat

3ʳᵈ leg of the 2002 World Rally Championship for constructors and drivers. 2ⁿᵈ leg of FIA Production Car WRC Championship.

Date 8ᵗʰ to 10ᵗʰ March 2002

Route
938,03 km divided in 3 legs
16 special stages on tarmac
(357,70 km)

1ˢᵗ leg
Friday 8ᵗʰ March (08h00-16h44):
Ajaccio › Ajaccio, 334,32 km;
5 special stages (95,47 km)

2ⁿᵈ leg
Saturday 9ᵗʰ March (08h00-17h56):
Ajaccio › Ajaccio, 363,34 km; 7 special stages (150,23 km)

3ʳᵈ leg
Sunday 10ᵗʰ March (08h20-14h36):
Ajaccio › Ajaccio, 240,37 km
4 special stages (112 km)

Entry List- Starters - Finishers:
67 - 61 - 37

Conditions: dry, followed by frequent showers, sun on Sunday.

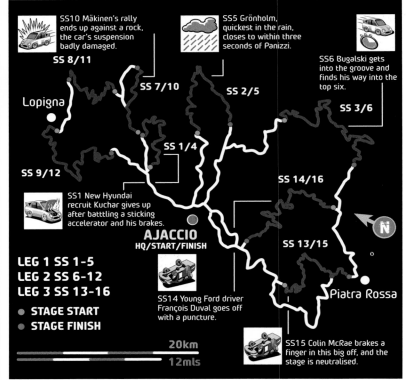

SS10 Mäkinen's rally ends up against a rock, the car's suspension badly damaged.
SS 8/11

SS5 Grönholm, quickest in the rain, closes to within three seconds of Panizzi.

SS6 Bugalski gets into the groove and finds his way into the top six.

Lopigna

SS 7/10

SS 2/5

SS 3/6

SS 1/4

SS 9/12

SS1 New Hyundai recruit Kuchar gives up after batttling a sticking accelerator and his brakes.

SS 14/16

AJACCIO
HQ/START/FINISH

SS 13/15

LEG 1 SS 1-5
LEG 2 SS 6-12
LEG 3 SS 13-16

● STAGE START
● STAGE FINISH

SS14 Young Ford driver François Duval goes off with a puncture.

Piatra Rossa

SS15 Colin McRae brakes a finger in this big off, and the stage is neutralised.

20km
12mls

TOP ENTRIES

1 Richard BURNS - Robert REID
Peugeot 206 WRC

2 Marcus GRÖNHOLM - Timo RAUTIAINEN Peugeot 206 WRC

3 Gilles PANIZZI - Hervè PANIZZI
Peugeot 206 WRC

4 Carlos SAINZ - Luis MOYA
Ford Focus RS WRC 02

5 Colin McRAE - Nicky GRIST
Ford Focus RS WRC 02

6 Markko MÄRTIN - Michael PARK
Ford Focus RS WRC 02

7 Francois DELECOUR - D. GRATALOUP
Mitsubishi Lancer Evo WRC

8 Alister McRAE - David SENIOR
Mitsubishi Lancer Evo WRC

10 Tommi MÄKINEN - Kaj LINDSTRÖM
Subaru Impreza WRC 2002

11 Petter SOLBERG - Philip MILLS
Subaru Impreza WRC 2002

14 Kenneth ERIKSSON - Tina THORNER
Skoda Octavia WRC Evo 2

15 Toni GARDEMEISTER - P. LUKANDER
Skoda Octavia WRC Evo 2

16 Roman KRESTA - Jan TOMANEK
Skoda Octavia WRC Evo 2

17 Armin SCHWARZ - Manfred HIEMER
Hyundai Accent WRC

18 Freddy LOIX - Sven SMEETS
Hyundai Accent WRC

19 Thomas KUCHAR - T. SZCZEPANIAK
Hyundai Accent WRC

23 Francois DUVAL - Jean-Marc FORTIN
Ford Focus RS WRC 01

24 Harri ROVANPERÄ - Risto PIETILÄINEN
Peugeot 206 WRC

25 Philippe BUGALSKI - J.-P. CHIARONI
Citroën Xsara

26 Bruno THIRY - Stèphane PREVOT
Peugeot 206 WRC

27 Achim MÖRTL - Klaus WICHA
Peugeot 206 WRC

32 Stanislav GRIAZINE - Dmitri EREMEEV
Toyota Corolla WRC

33 Benoit ROUSELLOT - Gilles MONDESIR
Subaru Impreza

51 Gustavo TRELLES - Jorge DEL BUONO
Mitsubishi Lancer Evo 7

54 Ramon FERREYROS - Diego VALLEJO
Mitsubishi Lancer Evo 7

58 Luca BALDINI - Marco MUZZARELLI
Mitsubishi Lancer Evo 6

60 Ben BRIANT - Jayson BROWN
Proton Pert Evo 6

65 Beppo HARRACH - Jutta GEBERT
Mitsubishi Lancer Evo 6

66 Dmitri ILIEV - Petar SIVOV
Mitsubishi Lancer Evo 7

69 Bernt KOLLEVOLD - Ola FLOENE
Mitsubishi Lancer Evo 6

71 Stefano MARRINI - Titiana SANDRONI
Mitsubishi Lancer Evo 7

72 Joakim ROMAN - Tina MITAKIDOU
Mitsubishi Lancer Evo 6

73 Martin ROWE - Chris WOOD
Mitsubishi Lancer Evo 6 RS

75 Kristian SOHLBERG - Jukka AHO
Mitsubishi Carisma GT

Special Stage Times

SS1 Cuttoli - Peri I (17,72 km)
1.Panizzi 11'33"3; 2.Solberg +3"8;
3.Grönholm +5"0; 4.Burns +8"5;
5.Mäkinen +9"8; 6.Sainz +12"9;
FIA Prod. (25) Ferreyros +1'09"5

SS2 Ocana - Radicale I (11,65 km)
1.Panizzi 7'26"1; 2.Grönholm +0"3;
3.Solberg +4"4; 4.Burns +5"0;
5.Mäkinen +8"4; 6.Märtin +10"1;
FIA Prod. (25) Al Wahaibi +45"7

SS3 Petreto - Ampaza I (36,73 km)
1.Panizzi 23'45"; 2.Bugalski +6"6;
3.Solberg +7"4; 4.Grönholm +8"2;
5.Burns +9"9; 6.Mäkinen +13"5;
FIA Prod. (25) Ferreyros +2'01"9

SS4 Cuttoli - Peri II (17,72 km)
1.Panizzi 11'33"0; 2.Burns +2"7;
3.Grönholm +2"8; 4.Mäkinen +10"5;
5.C McRae +11"0; 6.Sainz +12"3;
FIA Prod. (22) Ferreyros +1'13"0

SS5 Ocana - Radicale II (11,65 km)
1.Grönholm 7'57"8; 2.Sainz +2"1;
3.Duval +3"1; 4.Schwarz +4"4;
5.CMcRae +5"5; 6.Solberg +6"1;
FIA Prod. (21) Al Wahaibi +24"8

SS6 Petreto - Ampaza II (36,73 km)
1.Solberg 24'29"2; 2.Mäkinen +2"4;
3.Panizzi +12"8; 4.Bugalski +14"5;
5.Duval +16"9; 6.Grönholm +23"4;
FIA Prod. (54) Ferreyros +2'10"2

SS7 Gare de Carbuccia - Gare d'Ucciani I (10,66 km)
1.Panizzi 7'28"2; 2.C. McRae +4"5;
3.Grönholm +5"0; 4.Burns +5"5;
5.Mäkinen +7"2; 6.Bugalski +7"8;
FIA Prod. (20) Al Wahaibi +37"8

SS8 Vero - Pont d'Azzana I (18,28 km)
1.Panizzi 13'01"7; 2.Sainz +3"6;
3.Burns +5"0; 4.Bugalski +6"9;
5.Grönholm +8"0; 6.Mäkinen +12"0;
FIA Prod. (19) Ferreyros +1'12"3

SS9 Lopigna - Sarrola I (27,81 km)
1.Burns 18'11"6; 2.Panizzi +3"8;
3.Sainz +6"8; 4.C McRae +10"1;
5.Bugalski +10"7; 6.Grönholm +11"9;
FIA Prod. (21) Ferreyros +1'53"8

SS10 Gare de Carbuccia - Gare d'Ucciani II (10,66 km)
1.Solberg 7'55"4; 2.Grönholm +1"7;
3.Panizzi +2"4; 4.Schwarz +3"9;
5.Burns +4"8; 6.Duval +5"9;
FIA Prod. (17) Iliev +29"7

SS11 Vero - Pont d'Azzana II (18,28 km)
1.Panizzi 13'11"0; 2.C. McRae +1"1;
3.Grönholm +2"6; 4.Sainz +4"9;
5.Schwarz +9"4; 6.Solberg +10"6;
FIA Prod. (20) Ferreyros +1'32"5

SS12 Lopigna - Sarrola II (27,81 km)
1.Panizzi 18'17"6; 2.C. McRae +0"5;
3.Burns +4"0; 4.Bugalski +4"9;
5.Grönholm +5"1; 6.Sainz +17"5;
FIA Prod. (21) Ferreyros +2'17"7

SS13 Penitencier Coti - Pietra Rossa I (24,21 km)
1.C. McRae 15'11"1; 2.Burns +4"3;
3.Solberg +4"9; 4.Grönholm +4"9;
5.Grönholm +8"1; 6.Duval +8"4;
FIA Prod. (22) Trelles +1'45"8

SS14 Pont de Calzola - Agosta Plage I (31,79 km)
1.Burns 19'23"9; 2.Grönholm +2"6;
3.Bugalski +2"8; 4.Sainz +8"1;
5.Solberg +9"2; 6.Panizzi +12"7;
FIA Prod. (19) Trelles +2'04"2

SS15 Penitencier Coti - Pietra Rossa II (24,21 km)
1.Grönholm 15'10"4 & Panizzi;
3.Solberg +0"8; 4.Bugalski +0"8;
5.Burns +1"3; 6.Sainz +6"8;

FIA Prod. (13=) Trelles +26"8 (same time as Gardemeister)

SS16 Pont de Calzola - Agosta Plage II (31,79 km)
1.Bugalski 19'09"4; 2.Panizzi +2"1;
3.Burns +8"0; 4.Grönholm +11"4;
5.Solberg +12"3; 6.Märtin +17"8;
FIA Prod. (16) Trelles +2'06"2

Résultats

	Driver/Navigator	Car	Gr.	Time
1	**Panizzi - Panizzi**	**Peugeot 206 WRC**	A	3h54'40"3
2	Grönholm - Rautiainen	Peugeot 206 WRC		+ 40"5
3	Burns - Reid	Peugeot 206 WRC		+ 52"4
4	Bugalski - Chiaroni	Citroën Xsara WRC		+ 2'02"2
5	Solberg - Mills	Subaru Impreza WRC 2002		+ 2'28"2
6	Sainz - Moya	Ford Focus RS WRC 02		+ 2'32"8
7	Delecour - Grataloup	Mitsubishi Lancer Evo WRC		+ 5'07"8
8	Märtin - Park	Ford Focus RS WRC 02		+ 5'20"0
9	Loix - Smeets	Hyundai Accent WRC		+ 6'13"8
10	A. McRae - Senior	Mitsubishi Lancer Evo WRC		+ 6'32"5
17	**Ferreyros - Vallejo**	**Mitsubishi Lancer Evo 7**	**Prod.**	+ 22'44"6

Leading Retirements (24)

SS.15	C. McRea - Grist	Ford Focus RS WRC 02	Off
SS.14	Duval - Fortin	Ford Focus RS WRC 01	Off
SS.14	Eriksson - Thorner	Skoda Octavia WRC	Differential
SS.10	Mäkinen - Lindström	Subaru Impreza WRC 2002	Off
SS.10	Thiry - Prevot	Peugeot 206 WRC	Transmission
SS.6	Mörtl - Wicha	Peugeot 206 WRC	Clutch
SS.3	Sohlberg - Aho	Mitsubishi Carisma GT	Off
SS.2	Kuchar - Szczepaniak	Hyundai Accent WRC	Brakes

Championship Classifications

FIA Drivers (3/14)
1. Grönholm 18; 2. Mäkinen, Panizzi 10; 4. Sainz 9; 5. Burns 7;
6. Loeb, Rovanperä 6; 8. C. McRae 4; 9. Solberg, Bugalski 3;
11. A. McRae 2

FIA Constructors (3/14)
1. Peugeot 36; 2. Ford 20; 3. Subaru 16; 4. Mitsubishi 5; 5. Hyundai 1

FIA Production Car WRC (2/8)
1. Sohlberg, Ferreyros 10; 3. Arai, Iliev 6; 5. Rowe 5; 6. Ipatti 4;
7. Fiorio, Trelles 3; 9. Girdauskas, Harrach 2; 11. Marrini 1

FIA Junior WRC (1/6)
1. Duval 10; 2. Caldani 6; 3. Feghali 4; 4. Carlsson 3; 5. Doppelreiter 2;
6. Schelle 1

Performers

	1	2	3	4	5	6
Panizzi	7	2	2	-	-	1
Grönholm	2	3	4	2	3	2
Burns	2	2	3	4	2	-
Solberg	2	2	3	-	2	2
C. McRae	1	3	-	2	2	1
Bugalski	1	2	1	3	1	1
Sainz	-	2	2	1	1	4
Mäkinen	-	1	-	1	3	2
Duval	-	1	-	1	2	
Schwarz	-	-	-	2	1	-
Rovanperä	-	-	-	-	-	1
Märtin	-	-	-	-	-	1

Event Leaders

SS.1 > SS.16	Panizzi

Previous winners

1973	Nicolas - Vial Alpine Renault A 110	1988	Auriol - Occelli Ford Sierra RS Cosworth
1974	Andruet - "Biche" Lancia Stratos	1989	Auriol - Occelli Lancia Delta Integrale
1975	Darniche - Mahé Lancia Stratos	1990	Auriol - Occelli Lancia Delta Integrale
1976	Munari - Maiga Lancia Stratos	1991	Sainz - Moya Toyota Celica GT-Four
1977	Darniche - Mahé Fiat 131 Abarth	1992	Auriol - Occelli Lancia Delta HF Integrale
1978	Darniche Mahé Fiat 131 Abarth	1993	Delecour - Grataloup Ford Escort RS Cosworth
1979	Darniche - Mahé Lancia Stratos	1994	Auriol - Occelli Toyota Celica Turbo 4WD
1980	Thérier - Vial Porsche 911SC	1995	Auriol - Giraudet Toyota Celica GT-Four
1981	Darniche - Mahé Lancia Stratos	1996	Bugalski - Chiaroni Renault Maxi Megane
1982	Ragnotti - Andrié Renault 5 Turbo	1997	McRae - Grist Subaru Impreza WRC
1983	Alen - Kivimaki Lancia Rally 037	1998	McRae - Grist Subaru Impreza WRC
1984	Alen - Kivimaki Lancia Rally 037	1999	Bugalski - Chiaroni Citroën Xsara Kit Car
1985	Ragnotti - Andrié Renault 5 Turbo	2000	Bugalski - Chiaroni Peugeot 206 WRC
1986	Saby - Fauchille Peugeot 205 T16	2001	Puras - Marti Citroën Xsara WRC
1987	Béguin - Lenne BMW m3		

Spain

España

Not only does Gilles 'Tarmac Master' Panizzi have no peer when it comes to that surface, he also had the best car and the best tyres! The Catalunya Rally was one-way traffic as Panizzi and Richard Burns did a superb double and forced the opposition into surrender.

4

Catalonia brought major disappointment for Citroën. The French team (this is Bugalski) came to win but couldn't get near Peugeot.

THE RACE
Gracias, Gilles!

With Auriol gone, Delecour at Mitsubishi, Citroën in torment, Grönholm not quite there yet, Burns still on a bit of a learning curve and Ford and Subaru on Pirellis, who elese was going to do the trick on the Spanish tarmac than Gilles Panizzi? And not just by default, either: the little man is always quicker and stronger than all of his rivals put together when they all have the same equipment to play with. In fact since his Lion-branded reign as 'Tarmac Master' began, the only one who's ever been quicker is the wise old owl from Millau, and that's not a lot. So when the opposition is prey to all the misfortunes listed above, there really is no-one fit to lace the Menton maestro's bootstraps. That's just the way it is, and so much the better for him. And so the 38th Catalonia-Costa Brava Rally was over before it began, and it was only

ever going to go one way. That was the brothers' way: Gilles and Hervé Panizzi were in the lead from the first special stage that actually took place (the second, in fact, because the opening stage at Ruidecanyes had to be cancelled because of crowd congestion) and they were still there three days later at the end of the last one. They had not been toppled for a moment, not even seriously threatened. Just to get the statistics that tell the full story of their dominance out of the way, their 206 WRC set 10 out of 15 possible fastest times (three special stages were cancelled, all for the same reason), six of them in a row. Once they had opened up a big enough gap, Gilles and Hervé had no need to push their luck: they just free-wheeled it to the end. Game over. So was there really a Catalonia race this year? Well, yes, but it wasn't one to set the world on fire. But they all lined up behind the unbeatable lioness, and quite a few of them came to the start line

After his accident in Corsica, Colin McRae had to drive with a broken little finger on his left hand.

Carlos Sainz's rally was brought to a halt by his own fans! Caught out by a badly-parked car, he spun on the second stage and hit a rock.

For the first time this season Richard Burns was ahead of Marcus Grönholm in similar 206's. It wouldn't happen often...

feeling justifiably optimistic. Take Citroën: they had had a superb Monte Carlo, despite the penalty handed down to moral victor Loeb, they had an improved and newly-homologated car, drivers with a good tarmac reputation such as Loeb himself, Bugalski and Puras – all the right ingredients, on paper at least. Bang! The Red Army fell over their own feet and fiddled around from start to finish. And yet it had all been so carefully set up: the 2002 homologation Xsara had made its debut in Corsica, the majority of the development changes coming on the engine front. A lighter flywheel, modifications to exhaust manifold and waste-gate, improved priming ... all little things, but important ones. And they had all been used on the Beautiful Island under cover of a semi-works entry with Bugalski's Piedrafita Xsara. There was no rule that said Citroën couldn't do that, i.e. put out a car with a non-works label in order to deal as discreetly as they could with any teething troubles. But sadly the Citroën's fine balance was gone, as if by magic:

chewing its tyres a lot faster than before, and all in a muddle, the tarmac terror no longer held any terrors for anyone. Like Peugeot on the Monte-Carlo, their PSA cousins had managed to unsettle a car that had been working perfectly well. Incredibly enough, the Satory firm managed to bag just one scratch time and had to make do with third place for Bugalski, with Loeb fourth till just before the finish when an ill-timed roll put an end to his race, and Puras plagued by unfathomable problems in his brakes.

If Citroën couldn't give Peugeot a run for their money, the spectators were certainly banking on local hero Carlos Sainz and the king of the freeskaters, Colin McRae, to put some life into proceedings. Not only has the Scot fallen out of love with tarmac since his terrible off on the 2000 Tour de Corse, he was also driving with a broken little finger sustained in Corsica – where else? – in 2002. He was a pale imitation of his real self. As for Carlos Sainz, who had Marc Marti as his co-driver in the absence of Luis Moya following an accident in private testing, he put in a completely lacklustre drive, giving up during the second leg because of a spot of bother with the crowd. What happened was that he had to make a sudden change of direction to avoid a badly-parked spectator car. The Focus went into a spin and ripped the right rear wheel off. Not Citroën, not Ford... so who else? Surprisingly it was Subaru, especially Solberg. Mäkinen got himself in a mess again, went off in SS6 and damaged an engine that had been overheating since the start of the second leg. Exit one Finn. But the Norwegian set two scratch times which were entirely his doing and couldn't mask the shortcomings of the machinery. The Impreza, not on

the same level as the PSA cars, also runs on Pirelli tyres, known to be less competitive than the Michelins. The same Michelins, of course, as used by Mitsubishi, Skoda and Hyundai, three constructors who are off the pace but who had a good scrap for the lesser placings in Catalonia. The latest evolution Octavia gave Gardemeister the chance to shine, and it took all Delecour's class from days gone by to fight off his attacks and those of Freddy Loix and earn his team the point for sixth place.

But this was all happening light years away from what the Panizzis were doing. Richard Burns was the only one who looked, for a while at least, as if he could go head to head with them. But the Englishman isn't as much at home on tarmac yet as the Frenchman, in fact he's a long way off it, even if he put in a big effort before the event both to bring the 206 to heel and to polish his own driving. With second place and two scratch times, he proved to Peugeot that if the Frenchman ever leaves, and despite the fact that Auriol is already gone, he could still make them a force on the bitumen.

And of course he won his own little private war! For the first time this season he finished a rally in front of Marcus Grönholm, and he beat him fair and square. For three long days the Finn, who had been so much in control in Corsica the last time out, had to contend with a soft brake pedal and its inevitable consequence: inadequate braking. Maybe it all stemmed from his driving style on this particular surface. Nonetheless, fourth place inherited right at the death through Loeb's late retirement meant Marcus kept his World Championship lead, though just a point ahead of Panizzi. With their third one-two in four events, Peugeot had an iron grip on thee title, the French marque's points tally being double that of second-placed Ford.

Before heading off for four tricky gravel rallies, the WRC caravan packed away its tarmac things and left us with one memorable image. Just for fun and for the benefit of thousands of spectators packed in around the best spot on the Catalunya Rally, the freeway bridge on the Villadrau special stage – Gilles Panizzi flung his 206 into a superb doughnut, shrouding it in a blanket of smoke from its shrieking tyres and sending the onlookers into a frenzy. It may have cost him 10 seconds, but it was a warm, spontaneous gesture and it will have its own little place in rally history. Gracias, Gilles! ∎

Gardemeister, Loix and Delecour fought it out for the sixth constructors' point, which just went to the Frenchman.

In the points again, Solberg was gaining unaccustomed status at Subaru and putting maestro Mäkinen himself in the shade.

A moment that will go down in rally history: Gilles Panizzi, ever the showman, treated the Catalan crowd to a superb 360 – just for fun, right in the thick of the rally!

THE YOUNGER BRIGADE
Sola right at home

Grab your cars and let's get into it again! In Catalunya the Junior WRC – a rather more appealing name than 2001's Super 1600 – made its own second appearance on the calendar. And it turned out to be a lot more interesting and instructive where the two-litre, two-wheel drive cars were concerned than the Monte Carlo, the first date on their calendar. The classic winter test had provided just too many pitfalls and too many restrictions for these cars with their independent transmissions. A few key facts have appeared this year. One is that winner Sébastien Loeb has gone to the next level. He has a factory

Spain's Sola, in a PH Sport-entered Saxo, wasn't about to let anyone else win the Junior Championship event on his home soil.

drive with World Rally Car, the promotion which is this competition's raison d'être. Then there are some new cars, more or less works-entered: the Opel Corsa, MG ZR and Suzuki Ignis. David Richards, the

driving force of the discipline, would like to see the class become a spring-board for the young drivers and also give the constructors a few ideas as well. It's an interesting initiative, but we shall have to wait and see if it's the right one. But we should point out the withdrawal of the 'official' Peugeot and Citroën teams over a disagreement with the FIA about the proposed calendar. That means that the Saxo and 206 entries are entirely privateers, even if the factories are giving their customers some back-up.
While there are some leading lights from last season at the wheel, 2001 runner-up Dallavilla, Duval, Basso, Stenshorne, Galli and McShea among them, there are some new faces up

at the front and one of them belongs to the promising Spaniard Daniel Sola.
He doesn't do things by half, either. Enjoying a high reputation in his native Catalonia, he is backed by the all-powerful RACC, the organising club of Spain's World Championship round. On top of that, with the Saxo and the PH Sport team having done the business for Loeb the previous year, Sola also turned to that highly efficient package. And since he was born near Vic, he was pretty much at home on these roads too. Monte Carlo winner and hot favourite François Duval saw his progress interrupted in Catalonia by a series of wearing mechanical misfortunes: brake balance, engine down on power,

water leak, power steering failure, gearbox and two punctures! The Belgian made it home in sixth place in class, keeping the Championship lead, but the Puma is still not a very reliable car. The other Fords – Carlsson, Galanti, Rowe and co. all suffered the same relative anonymity.
In fact, as in 2001, at the end it all came down to a Saxo-Punto duel. But – again like 2001 – it worked out in favour of the drivers of the little French machine. In the early stages Dallavilla, a refugee from Fiat to Citroën this year, took charge for a while before Sola, after a little bump, got the upper hand in the special stages around Vic. Four stages from the end, though, the Catalan had a puncture and ended up on a rim. Coming out of the next service stop where his gearbox was changed, he was second and 24.3s down on Dallavilla. But then it was the Italian's turn to have a puncture on the last special stage, and Sola just made it home in front.
And where were the Fiats? The Puntos didn't seem at all at ease on tarmac and Basso, who ended up third, was never a threat to the Saxos. He was ahead of another Transalpine car in the hands of Galli, who was himself classified in front of another Saxo, this one Tuohino's. Duval was sixth and at least salvaged something from the wreckage for the Blue Oval.
At this early stage of the year it was obvious that there are some cars that have a clear edge and are also being driven by the best of the younger brigade. The Suzuki Ignis machines showed a reasonable turn of speed but were obviously short on reliability. The rest were even worse off: Nial McShea, third in the 2001 standings, didn't make it past the second special stage in his Opel Corsa. The same thing happened to Katajamaki's Volkswagen Polo. Last but not least, Gwyndaf Evans's little MG was off the pace. Back to the drawing-board for some... ∎

38th Spanish Rally - Catalunya

4th leg of the 2002 World Rally Championship for constructors and drivers. 2nd leg of WRC Junior Championship.

Date 21st to 24th March 2002

Parcours
1948,95 km divided in 3 legs
18 special stages on tarmac (394,84 km) and 15 contested (348,01 km)

1st leg
Friday 22nd March (05h30-21h51):
Lioret de Mar > Salou > Lioret de Mar, 936,21 km; 6 special stages scheduled (176,66 km) and 5 contested (164,01 km)

2nd leg
Saturday 23rd March (08h00-20h00):
Lioret de Mar > Manlleu > Lioret de Mar, 513,12 km; 6 special stages scheduled (111,94 km) et 4 contested (77,76 km)

3rd leg
Sunday 24th mars (06h15-17h15):
Lioret de Mard > Manlleu > Lioret de Mar, 499,62 km; 6 special stages (106,24 km)

Entry List - Starters - Finishers:
74 - 68 - 41

Conditions: fine and dry.

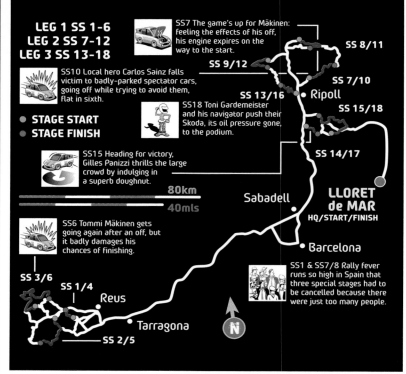

LEG 1 SS 1-6
LEG 2 SS 7-12
LEG 3 SS 13-18

SS7 The game's up for Mäkinen: feeling the effects of his off, his engine expires on the way to the start.

SS10 Local hero Carlos Sainz falls victim to badly-parked spectator cars, going off while trying to avoid them, flat in sixth.

● STAGE START
● STAGE FINISH

SS18 Toni Gardemeister and his navigator push their Skoda, its oil pressure gone, to the podium.

SS15 Heading for victory, Gilles Panizzi thrills the large crowd by indulging in a superb doughnut.

SS6 Tommi Mäkinen gets going again after an off, but it badly damages his chances of finishing.

SS1 & SS7/8 Rally fever runs so high in Spain that three special stages had to be cancelled because there were just too many people.

80km
40mls

SS 8/11
SS 9/12
SS 7/10
Ripoll
SS 13/16
SS 15/18
SS 14/17
Sabadell
LLORET de MAR
HQ/START/FINISH
Barcelona
SS 3/6
SS 1/4
Reus
Tarragona
SS 2/5
N

TOP ENTRIES

1   Richard BURNS - Robert REID
    Peugeot 206 WRC
2   Marcus GRÖNHOLM - Timo RAUTIAINEN
    Peugeot 206 WRC
3   Gilles PANIZZI - Hervé PANIZZI
    Peugeot 206 WRC
4   Carlos SAINZ - Luis MOYA
    Ford Focus RS WRC 02
5   Colin McRAE - Nicky GRIST
    Ford Focus RS WRC 02
6   Markko MÄRTIN - Michael PARK
    Ford Focus RS WRC 02
7   François DELECOUR - Daniel GRATALOUP
    Mitsubishi Lancer Evo WRC
8   Alister McRAE - David SENIOR
    Mitsubishi Lancer Evo WRC
10 Tommi MÄKINEN - R.MANNI-SENMÄKI
    Subaru Impreza WRC 2002
11 Petter SOLBERG - Philip MILLS
    Subaru Impreza WRC 2002
14 Kenneth ERIKSSON - Tina THORNER
    Skoda Octavia WRC Evo 2
15 Toni GARDEMEISTER - Paavo LUKANDER
    Skoda Octavia WRC Evo 2
16 Stig BLOMQVIST - Ana GONI
    Skoda Octavia WRC Evo 2
17 Armin SCHWARZ - Manfred HIEMER
    Hyundai Accent WRC3
18 Freddy LOIX - Sven SMEETS
    Hyundai Accent WRC3
20 Thomas RADSTROM - Denis GIRAUDET
    Citroën Xsara
21 Sébastien LOEB - Daniel ELENA
    Citroën Xsara
22 Philippe BUGALSKI - J.-P. CHIARONI
    Citroën Xsara
23 Harri ROVANPERÄ - R. PIETILÄINEN
    Peugeot 206 WRC
24 Bruno THIRY - Stèphane PREVOT
    Peugeot 206 WRC
25 Jésus PURAS - Carlos DEL BARRIO
    Citroen Xsara
26 Achim MÖRTL - Klaus WICHA
    Peugeot 206 WRC
27 Miguel CAMPOS - Carlos MAGALHAES
    Peugeot 206 WRC
32 Gabriel POZZO - Daniel STILLO
    Skoda Octavia WRC Evo 1
33 Stanislav GRIAZINE - Dmitri EREMEEV
    Toyota Corolla WRC
34 Armin KREMER - D. SCHNEPPENHEIM
    Ford Focus WRC
65 Daniel SOLA - Alex ROMANI
    Citroën Saxo VTS
51 Andréa DALLAVILLA - Giovanni BERNACCHINI Citroën Saxo VTS
53 Giandomenico BASSO - Luigi PIROLLO
    Fiat Punto Kit
55 François DUVAL - Jean-Marc FORTIN
    Ford Puma
60 Nicola CALDANI - Sauro FARNOCCHIA
    Peugeot 206 XS
62 Janne TUOHINO - Petri VIHAVAINEN
    Citroën Saxo VTS
64 Gianluigi GALLI - Guido D'AMORE
    Fiat Punto
65 Daniel SOLA - David MORENO
    Citroën Saxo VTS
78 Roger FEGHALI - Nicola ARENA
    Ford Puma

Special Stage Times

ES1 Riudecanyes I (12,65 km)
Cancelled – too many spectators

ES2 Pratdip I (27,64 km)
1.Panizzi 16'37"8; 2.Burns +7"7;
3.Grönholm & Solberg +15"4;
5.Loeb +15"9; 6.Bugalski +19"4;
Jr. (24) Sola +1'36"4

ES3 Escaladei I (48,04 km)
1.Panizzi 29'19"6; 2.Burns +3"6;
3.Bugalski +14"2; 4.Loeb +20"2;
5.C. McRae +20"4; 6.Sainz +22"9;
Jr. (18) Dallavilla +2'07"8

ES4 Riudecanyes II (12,65 km)
1.Panizzi +8'32"4; 2.Burns +2"2;
3.Grönholm +4"4; 4.Loeb +4"7;
5.Bugalski +5"3; 6.Solberg +5";
Jr. (25) Sola +42"1

ES5 Pratdip II (27,64 km)
1.Panizzi +16'44"2; 2.Bugalski +1"6;
3.Burns +4"2; 4.Grönholm 6"7;
5.Loeb 7"1; 6.Solberg +12"8;
Jr. (25) Dallavilla +1'27"6

ES6 Escaldei II (48,04 km)
1.Panizzi 29'19"6; 2.Bugalski +4'2;
3.Burns +8"4; 4.Loeb +22"5;
5.C. McRae +26"2; 6.Grönholm +28"6;
Jr. (22) Dallavilla +2'16"7

ES7 Coll de Bracons I (19,65 km)
Cancelled – too many spectators

ES8 Valfogona II (14,53 km)
Cancelled – too many spectators

ES9 Les Llosses-Alpens I (21,79 km)
1.Panizzi 13'19"9; 2.Loeb +3"7;
3.Burns +5"2; 4.Bugalski +7"6;
5.Solberg +8"2; 6.Grönholm +9"5;
Jr. (20) Sola +58"3

ES10 Col de Bracons II (19,65 km)
1.Solberg 12'44"3; 2.Panizzi +0"2;
3.Burns +0"8; 4.Loeb +4"9;
5.Grönholm +5"4; 6.Bugalski +6"0;
Jr. (20) Sola +59"0

ES11 Valfagona II (14,53 km)
1.Panizzi 8'30"3; 2.Burns +0"9;
3.Bugalski +1"5; 4.Loeb +3"5;
5.Solberg +4"2; 6.Grönholm +4"3;
Jr. (19) Duval +35"7

ES12 Les Llosses-Alpens II (21,79 km)
1.Panizzi 13'20"4; 2.Bugalski +2"1;
3.Grönholm +4"5; 4.Loeb +4"9;
5.C. McRae +9"1; 6.Solberg +9"7;
Jr. (20) Duval +1'02"0

ES13 La Trona I (12,89 km)
1.Burns/Panizzi 8'18"8; 3.Puras +1"2;
4.Grönholm +1"5; 5.Bugalski +2"1;
6.Solberg +4"9; Jr. (20) Sola +36"4

ES14 La Roca I (5,05 km)
1.Puras 3'02"1; 2.Solberg +0"3;
3.Grönholm +1"2; 4.Märtin +1"2;
5.Mörtl +1"6; 6.Burns +1"8;
Jr. (20) Sola +14"7

ES15 Viladrau I (35,18 km)
1.Burns 21'14"9; 2.Grönholm +5"7;
3.Bugalski +8"4; 4.Panizzi +10"7;
5.Solberg +12"8; 6.Puras +13"4;
Jr. (20) Dallavilla 1'51"4

ES16 La Trona II (12,89 km)
1.Panizzi 8'17"9; 2.Solberg +1"1;
3.Grönholm +1"2; 4.Burns +3"9;
5.Bugalski +5"5; 6.Puras +5"9;
Jr. (19) Sola +36"9

ES17 La Roca II (5,05 km)
1.Panizzi/Märtin 3'04"6;
3.Grönholm +0"6; 4.Loix +0"9;
5.Solberg +1"1; 6.Delecour +1"2;
Jr. (18) Sola +13"3

ES18 Viladrau II (35,18 km)
1.Solberg 21'23"7; 2.Panizzi +5"8;
3.Burns +6"0; 4.Grönholm +8"6;
5.Rovanperä +8"9; 6.Bugalski +10"2;
Jr. (18) Sola 1'30"5

Résultats — WRC

	Driver/Navigator	Car	Gr.	Time
1	**Panizzi - Panizzi**	**Peugeot 206 WRC**	**A**	**3h34'09"9**
2	Burns - Reid	Peugeot 206 WRC		+ 37"3
3	Bugalski - Chiaroni	Citroën Xsara WRC		+ 1'13"5
4	Grönholm - Rautiainen	Peugeot 206 WRC		+ 1'42"7
5	Solberg - Mills	Subaru Impreza WRC 2002		+ 2'01"6
6	C. McRae - Grist	Ford Focus RS WRC 02		+ 3'27"3
7	Rovanperä - Pietilainen	Peugeot 206 WRC		+ 3'40"1
8	Märtin - Park	Ford Focus RS WRC 02		+ 3'43"9
9	Delecour - Grataloup	Mitsubishi Lancer Evo WRC		+ 5'28"6
10	Loix - Smeets	Hyundai Accent WRC 3		+ 5'30"6
11	Gardemeister - Lukander	Skoda Octavia WRC Evo 2		+ 5'35"2
12	Puras - Del Barrio	Citroën Xsara WRC		+ 7'18"9
13	A. McRae - Senior	Mitsubishi Lancer Evo WRC		+ 8'21"8
14	Mörtl - Wicha	Peugeot 206 WRC		+ 9'38"9
18	**Sola - Romani**	**Citroën Saxo**	**Jr.**	**+ 18'02"5**

Leading Retirements (26)

SS.14	Loeb - Elena	Citroën Xsara WRC	Suspension damage after roll
SS.10	Sainz - Moya	Ford Focus RS WRC 02	Off
SS.9	Thiry - Prévot	Peugeot 206 WRC	Clutch
SS.7	Blomqvist - Goni	Skoda Octavia WRC Evo 2	Alternator
SS.7	Mäkinen - Linström	Subaru Impreza WRC 2002	Engine
SS.6	Pozzo - Stillo	Skoda Octavia WRC Evo 1	Engine
SS.6	Radström - Giraudet	Citroën Xsara WRC	Off

Performers

	1	2	3	4	5	6
Panizzi	11	2	-	1	1	1
Burns	2	4	5	1	-	1
Solberg	2	2	1	-	4	4
Puras	1	-	1	-	-	2
Märtin	1	-	1	-	-	-
Bugalski	-	3	3	1	3	3
Grönholm	-	1	6	3	1	3
Loeb	-	1	-	6	2	-
Loix	-	-	1	-	-	-
C. McRae	-	-	-	-	3	-
Rovanperä	-	-	-	-	1	-
Mörtl	-	-	-	-	1	-
Sainz	-	-	-	-	-	1
Delecour	-	-	-	-	-	1

Event Leaders

SS.1 > SS.16   Panizzi

Championship Classifications

FIA Drivers (4/14)
1. Grönholm 21; 2. Panizzi 20; 3. Burns 13; 4. Mäkinen 10; 5. Sainz 9;
6. Bugalski 7; 7. Loeb 6; 8. Rovanperä 6; 9. C. McRae, Solberg 5;
11. A. McRae 2

FIA Constructors (4/14)
1. Peugeot 52; 2. Ford 25; 3. Subaru 20; 4. Mitsubishi 6; 5. Hyundai 1

FIA Production Car WRC (2/8)
1. Sohlberg, Ferreyros 10; 3. Arai, Iliev 6; 5. Rowe 5; 6. Ipatti 4;
7. Fiorio, Trelles 3; 9. Girdauskas, Harrach 2; 11. Marrini 1

FIA Junior WRC (2/6)
1. Duval 11; 2. Sola 10; 3. Caldoni, Dallavilla 6; 5. Feghali, Basso 4;
7. Carlsson, Galli 3; 9. Doppelreiter, Tuohino 2; 11. Schelle 1

Previous winners

1991	Schwarz - Hertz Toyota Celica GT-Four	1997	Mäkinen - Harjanne Mitsubishi Lancer Ev.4
1992	Sainz - Moya Toyota Celica Turbo 4WD	1998	Auriol - Giraudet Toyota Corolla WRC
1993	Delecour - Grataloup Ford Escort RS Cosworth	1999	Bugalski - Chiaroni Citroën Xsara Kit Car
1994	Bertone - Chiapponi Toyota Celica Turbo 4WD	2000	C. McRae - Grist Ford Focus WRC
1995	Sainz - Moya Subaru Impreza	2001	Auriol - Giraudet Peugeot 206 WRC
1996	McRae - Ringer Subaru Impreza		

Cyprus

Another Peugeot one-two, Grönholm heading home Burns – this epic event was as remarkable for some further lapses by Colin McRae as it was for the capricious weather that made it a real thriller.

WRC
WORLD RALLY
CHAMPIONSHIP

5

He could – should – have threatened Grönholm and the Peugeot, but moderation isn't the McRae hallmark and late in the rally he threw away a promising start.

THE RACE
SUSPENSE ALL THE WAY

Thank goodness we still have rallies! If motor racing all boiled down to marking time behind red cars from Italy we'd all go off and shoot ourselves from boredom. But there is still road-based racing, and amen to that. The World Championship, coming off a Catalan event that was as predictable as the local coffee – delicious, but utterly unexciting – gave us a gem of a rally, perhaps THE event of the season. A little scene-setting first, then. Cyprus: an island in the Mediterranean, an island split in two, its inhabitants as charming as its sea-front sites are disfigured and its

mountains stripped bare. Cyprus, the most arid of lands – except in spring, when depression follows depression across the wide blue yonder out to the east, the clouds unleashing splendid storms as the humid mass hits the high mountains and the heat. There are those who would have you believe it was all the Corsicans' fault that the 2002 Cyprus event suffered so much at the hands of the weather. Not a bit of it. True, the event took place on the dates originally set for the Tour de Corse, but the FIA had overlooked one little detail in drawing up the calendar for the season: the April school holidays in metropolitan France would have a big impact on accommodation on the Beautiful

The old lion was back with Hyundai, but he thrashed the Accent and retired with a broken crankcase.

Island. The Cypriots are generous folk, and they agreed to swap dates with the French round. Hence the World Championship squad arrived in Limassol in fine fettle for their first crack at a gravel start for the year on Friday April 19.

The first leg came and went at the pace of a debs' ball. Colin McRae claimed the first scratch time, and with it the lead, but he was immediately ousted from that purely honorary position by one of the young bloods from his own stable, François Duval. Not only was it the latter's first fastest time in the World Championship, it was also the first time in his short career he had shown up in the lead in a top-flight rally. And here in Cyprus the young Belgian was taking part in only his second event in a World Rally Car, a Ford Focus of course. But the fiery youngster then had a spin on the next stage, handing both the scratch and the lead to Markko Märtin, another of the Ford youngsters. And while we are on the subject of youth, let's cut straight away to Solberg

and his winning time on stage four. Colin McRae got back down to business in second place and stayed there to the end of the first leg.

The Scot must have taken a long, hard look at the time sheets at that point. They would have shown him the young cubs baring their teeth, though that was all a bit of a flash in the pan; but they would also have shown him some handy times set by a rather more dangerous lion, one by the name of Marcus Grönholm. To the Finn fell the thankless task of running first on the Cyprus road, the honour reserved for the man leading the drivers' standings at the start of each rally. So all day long, on dry roads, the bold Marcus did the sweeper's job, though he still managed to give away no more than 6.9 seconds to McRae after the six scheduled stages. It took some talent to overcome such an obvious handicap. Some will argue that the Ford driver, Cyprus winner in 2001, went off just six cars after the Peugeot, but that was enough to set the line and set it very clearly.

Back in Limassol that evening it was clear that the fight for victory was going to come down to those two. Behind them, the pursuing pack had either thinned out or been left well behind. Sainz had had problems with his transmission first, then his power steering; the brilliant Solberg had lost four minutes after breaking the shaft of his throttle pedal; Mäkinen had got his settings wrong, and his tyre choice as well; Rovanpera was another to get the tyres wrong, while Burns's main concern was the heat. The Englishman hates the hot weather and can't stand having to drive in overheating cockpits. He was pretty well out of it, though not as obviously as Juha Kankkunen's Hyundai, laid low by a burst crankcase, or the Alister McRae and Francois Delecour Mitsubishis with their fragile transmissions.

After one classic leg, the Cyprus Rally now took on truly epic proportions. The day began with

mark you, were on tyres they had chosen three hours earlier, when they couldn't have foreseen how heavy the rain would be. Thus most of them had opted for tyres that hadn't been too heavily re-cut, so that they wouldn't simply fall apart on the dry roads. The Peugeot drivers, their Subaru counterparts, Carlos Sainz and Markko Märtin had all put on re-cut tyres that were hardly cut at all. Colin McRae is a big gambler: he could have opted for caution and gone the same way as his most serios rival, Marcus Grönholm, but not our Colin – he went for narrow Pirellis that had been cut to the quick! On the river of mud the road had become, he was the only one with boots on while the rest were all in joggers. In those dreadful conditions, the retirements simply piled up: Alister McRae after a minor off, Bruno Thiry with suspension trouble, Freddy Loix with broken gearbox control, Roman Kresta with an off of his own. As for

Not a single scratch time – but he won it all the same. Grönholm was well on top, his driving making up for the handicap of running first on the road at the start.

Given a hard time by Solberg in the Subarus, Mäkinen made it on to the podium after losing out in his face-off with Burns.

Ford have got their hands on one of the stars of tomorrow: by the end of the second stage Duval was in front, then had a spin on the next.

A very disappointing rally for Mitsubishi, the Lancers plagued by driveshaft problems: no fewer than five broke on Alister McRae's car, seen here in action.

nothing more noteworthy than a series of super-quick times. Grönholm and McRae weren't messing about, and the flying Solberg was coming back at the front men with all guns blazing. The first drops fell on SS10 between Prastio and Pachna, after the leaders went through. On the next, Platres-Saittas, Solberg was the only one to beat the rain which caught out Rovanpera as he rolled, though without serious consequences. Up to that point everything was fine. Up to that point... On the 18-mile 12th stage between Foini and Koilinia the clouds came together in a violent storm and the heavens opened. The crews,

Delecour and Gardemeister, they were running minus wipers and Märtin's demister system wasn't working.
Solberg, the only one who went through between downpours, set the scratch time, but McRae in second place could put no more than 15 seconds on the flying Grönholm. At the end of the second day, when the Scot could – and should – have opened up a gap on the way to Koilinia, he was only 26.2 ahead of his main rival, with Mäkinen third but 1m44s away. So the race was far from run: the third leg promised five special stages with a total of 50 miles against the clock.

Suffering in the heat, the World Champion was overshadowed by teammate Marcus Grönholm.

Grönholm and Burns made it a fourth consecutive Peugeot 1-2 since the season started. To think they said the 206 was fragile...

constructor: with a margin of 41 points over second-equal Ford and Subaru, 68-27, Peugeot were walking away with the constructors' title. What's more, they also had the happy sight of three Peugeot drivers – Grönholm, Panizzi and Burns – sitting atop the drivers' standings. Oh, that wretched man McRae... ■

UNLUCKY FOR SOME
Solberg sparkles

So near and yet so far! That's how Petter Solberg finished round five of the 2002 World Championship. The Norwegian was the unluckiest man on the rally. But for one little thing he would at last have won his first WRC rally to put the seal of victory on his formidable talent. Saint

Theodore clearly hadn't taken him under his wing – it was on the Agios Theodoros special that the Subaru's throttle pedal broke, a bad enough handicap and one made worse by problems with the diffs. That cost the usually happy chappie four minutes and all chance of a good result. Once his Impreza was repaired, he flung himself into a frenzied fightback that was all the more remarkable as he was often the first man on the road. Just ask Grönholm what he thinks of that 'advantage'"'

Still, fortune favours the brave and Solberg got through the second leg unscathed. Heading off first on stages 11 and 12, he missed the downpours – twice – and the apocalyptic rain on the second. His progress up the leader-board was impressive

Right at the outset Ford made a hideous mistake with their time signalling. Phil Short, the man who did so much to help Mäkinen win for Mitsubishi and gave McRae a big helping hand a year earlier, held out a board with a highly encouraging '-1' on it. In fact, rather than being a second ahead of Grönholm at that halfway point in the stage, McRae was nine seconds down on him and the board should have read '+9'. Not pushing it at all, McRae only realised his mistake at the halt: Grönholm had taken 12.6s off him. Every lover of a single malt knows the fire and spirit that flows through it. Well, it's the same with McRae. A frustrated and angry Highlander threw himself into an attack that was as big-hearted as it was crazy. During the next stage he put the Focus into a very impressive roll, presenting his Finnish opponent with another 19 seconds and the rally lead.

Just to add spice to the closing stages, the rain swept back in. McRae

rolled up his sleeves again, but made a mess of a braking manoeuvre which he started in fifth in the mud, and sent the Focus skyward again. He could have consolidated second place, but why settle for that when you think you're the Master of the Rolls? Not quite mastering his landing technique, he destroyed his wipers, a small point maybe but one that meant he had to stop to clean his screen. You could hear Marcus Grönholm saying, 'See you later, thanks a lot' as he headed off to the finish.

The search was on for a runner-up, McRae having fallen back to sixth. There was a hell of a scrap going on between Mäkinen and Burns, comfortable at last now the rain had come. But after setting the scratch in the penultimate stage Mäkinen then spun in the last one, giving Burns the chance to bring Peugeot yet another one-two finish, their fourth in four events. No need to point out how happy that made the French

Diff and brake problems dropped Eriksson down the order after an encouraging start.

indeed. But then his fire got the better of him and he rolled on the last bend of the last stage, a second-gear right-hander, between Lageia and Kavalasos (SS17). Still, that was only a minor incident given the number of rolls we had seen in Cyprus this year. Panizzi, Alister McRae, Rovanpera, Märtin and of course – twice – Colin McRae had all shown a curious penchant for the cylindrical manoeuvre and its pear-shaped consequences. In the end Petter Solberg made it to the finish in fifth place, no mean feat as he garnered an outstanding six scratch times to better teammate Tommi Mäkinen's five. To say the Subarus had a tough time of it would be putting it lightly.

As for the likeable Norwegian, he knows that what goes around comes around, rally wins included... ∎

No doubt about it, Colin McRae is the Master of the Rolls! Pity, because a fine rally deserved second rather than sixth. But such artistry...

Solberg missed the fierce storms on the second stage and set some remarkable times. He must have been cursing the loss of so much time the day before with a throttle problem.

Rally Cyprus 2002

5th leg of the 2002 World Rally Championship for constructors and drivers. 3rd leg of FIA Production Car WRC Championship.

Date 18th to 21st April 2002

Route
1306,21 km divided in 3 legs.
20 gravel special stages scheduled (324,13 km) and 19 special stages contested (294,26 km).

1st leg
Friday 19th April (08h00-17h05):
Limassol > Limassol, 356,80 km;
6 stages (96,30 km)
2nd leg
Saturday 20th April (06h00-20h18):
Limassol > Limassol, 640,29 km;
8 special stages scheduled (145,95 km) and 7 special stages contested (116,08 km)
3rd leg
Sunday 21st April (08h00-16h30):
Limassol > Limassol, 309,12 km;
6 stages (81,88 km)

Entry List - Starters - Finishers:
66 - 60 - 32

Conditions: dry first day, then changeable with showers on several stages.

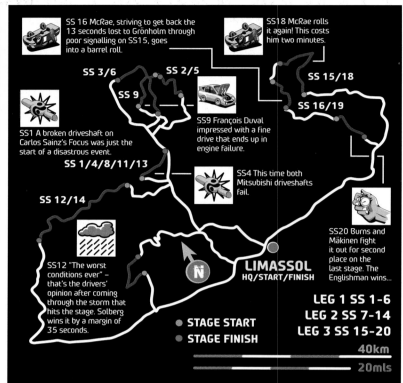

SS 16 McRae, striving to get back the 13 seconds lost to Grönholm through poor signalling on SS15, goes into a barrel roll.

SS18 McRae rolls it again! This costs him two minutes.

SS 3/6

SS 2/5

SS 15/18

SS 9

SS 16/19

SS1 A broken driveshaft on Carlos Sainz's Focus was just the start of a disastrous event.

SS9 François Duval impressed with a fine drive that ends up in engine failure.

SS 1/4/8/11/13

SS4 This time both Mitsubishi driveshafts fail.

SS 12/14

SS20 Burns and Mäkinen fight it out for second place on the last stage. The Englishman wins...

SS12 "The worst conditions ever" – that's the drivers' opinion after coming through the storm that hits the stage. Solberg wins it by a margin of 35 seconds.

LIMASSOL HQ/START/FINISH

● STAGE START
● STAGE FINISH

LEG 1 SS 1-6
LEG 2 SS 7-14
LEG 3 SS 15-20

40km
20mls

TOP ENTRIES

1   Richard BURNS - Robert REID
    Peugeot 206 WRC
2   Marcus GRÖNHOLM - Timo RAUTIAINEN
    Peugeot 206 WRC
3   Harri ROVANPERÄ - Risto MANNISENMÄKI Peugeot 206 WRC
4   Carlos SAINZ - Luis MOYA
    Ford Focus RS WRC 02
5   Colin McRAE - Nicky GRIST
    Ford Focus RS WRC 02
6   Markko MÄRTIN - Michael PARK
    Ford Focus RS WRC 02
7   Francois DELECOUR - Daniel GRATALOUP
    Mitsubishi Lancer Evo WRC
8   Alister McRAE - David SENIOR
    Mitsubishi Lancer Evo WRC
9   Jani PAASONEN - Arto KAPANEN
    Mitsubishi Lancer Evo WRC
10 Tommi MÄKINEN - Kaj LINDSTRÖM
    Subaru Impreza WRC 2002
11 Petter SOLBERG - Philip MILLS
    Subaru Impreza WRC 2002
14 Kenneth ERIKSSON - Tina THORNER
    Skoda Octavia WRC Evo 2
15 Toni GARDEMEISTER - Paavo LUKANDER
    Skoda Octavia WRC Evo 2
16 Roman KRESTA - Jan TOMANEK
    Skoda Octavia WRC Evo 2
17 Armin SCHWARZ - Manfred HIEMER
    Hyundai Accent WRC 3
18 Freddy LOIX - Sven SMEETS
    Hyundai Accent WRC 3
19 Juha KANKKUNEN - Juha REPO
    Hyundai Accent WRC 3
23 Gilles PANIZZI - Hervè PANIZZI
    Peugeot 206 WRC
24 Francois DUVAL - Jean-Marc FORTIN
    Ford Focus RS WRC 02
25 Bruno THIRY - Stèphane PREVOT
    Peugeot 206 WRC
26 Achim MÖRTL - Klaus WICHA
    Peugeot 206 WRC
27 Tomasz KUCHAR - Maciej SZCEPANIAK
    Hyundai Accent WRC 02
28 Gabriel POZZO - Daniel STILLO
    Skoda Octavia WRC Evo 1
29 Janne TUOHINO - Petri VIHAVAINEN
    Ford Focus RS WRC 01
30 Manfred STOHL - Ilka PETRASKO
    Ford Focus RS WRC 01
31 Juuso PYKÄLISTÖ - Esko MERTSALMI
    Toyota Corolla WRC
32 Ioannis PAPADIMITRIOU - A. HARRIMAN
    Subaru Impreza 555
51 Gustavo TRELLES - Jorge DEL BUONO
    Mitsubishi Lancer Evo 7
54 Ramon FERREYROS - Diego VALLEJO
    Mitsubishi Lancer Evo 7
57 Toshihiro ARAI - Tony SIRCOMBE
    Subaru Impreza WRX
58 Luca BALDINI - Marco MUZZARELLI
    Mitsubishi Lancer Evo 6
66 Dmitri ILIEV - Petar SIVOV
    Mitsubishi Lancer Evo 7
73 Martin ROWE - Chris WOOD
    Mitsubishi Lancer Evo 6 RS
74 Karamjit SINGH - Allen OH
    Proton Pert
75 Kristian SOHLBERG - Jukka AHO
    Mitsubishi Carisma GT

Special Stage Times

SS1 Katos Amiantos I (11,60 km)
1.C. McRae 9'20"8; 2.Solberg +0"6;
3.Grönholm +2"9; 4.Märtin +4"8;
5.Loix +5"2; 6.Eriksson +5"3;
FIA Prod. (28) Singh +48"5

SS2 Lagoudera - Kapouras I (15 km)
1.Duval 14'18"5; 2.Märtin +2"6;
3.Grönholm +6"9; 4.C. McRae +9"0;
5.Loix +11"7; 6.Stohl +11"9;
FIA Prod. (25) Ligato +1'07"9

SS3 Aghios Theodoros I (21,55 km)
1.Märtin 20'16"6; 2.Kankkunen +1"0;
3.Eriksson +2"6; 4.C. McRae +4"2;
5.Grönholm +4"5; 6.Mäkinen +7"1
FIA Prod. (21) Ferreyros 1'15"2

SS4 Kato Amiantos II (11,60 km)
1.Solberg 9'21"7; 2.C. McRae +1"4;
3.Duval +7"7; 4.Rovanperä +8"3;
5.Grönholm +8"8; 6.Mäkinen +8"9
FIA Prod. (26) Manfrinato +48"6

SS5 Lagoudera - Kapouras I (15 km)
1.Mäkinen 14'11"7; 2.Grönholm +0"2;
3.Solberg +0"7; 4.Duval +2"7;
5.C. McRae +6"9; 6.Loix +9"8;
FIA Prod. (21) Manfrinato +1'11"9

SS6 Aghios Theodoros II (21,55 km)
1.C. McRae 19'51"5; 2.Märtin/Solberg
+2"8; 4.Grönholm +5"1; 5.Rovanperä
+11"2; 6.Duval +13"2;
FIA Prod. (21) Manfrinato +1'23"4

SS7 Prastio - Pachna I (10,92 km)
1.Sainz 6'29"0; 2.Grönholm +0"4;
3.C. McRae +2"0; 4.Burns/Rovanperä
+5"0; 6.Solberg +7"0
FIA Prod. (25) Manfrinato +43"4

SS8 Platres - Saittas I (11,25 km)
1.Sainz 9'21"2; 2.C. McRae +6"4;
3.Rovanperä +8"0; 4.Burns 8"8;
5.Grönholm +9"5; 6.Solberg +14"4
FIA Prod. (21) Singh +53"4

SS9 Kourdali - Spilia (30,62 km)
1.Mäkinen 29'21"8; 2.Solberg +7"0;
3.Sainz +12"3; 4.Rovanperä +12"7;
5.Grönholm 14"4; 6.Burns +15"1
FIA Prod. (23) Singh +3'42"7

SS10 Prastio - Pachna II (10,92 km)
1.Solberg 6'14"3; 2.Rovanperä +1"9;
3.Burns/Mäkinen +2"5; 5.Sainz +3"7;
6.Loix +4"0;
FIA Prod. (23) Trelles +44"1

SS11 Platres - Saittas II (11,25 km)
1.Solberg 9'02"7; 2.C. McRae +17"2;
3.Delecour +20"8; 4.Burns +21"2;
5.Mäkinen +22"2; 6. Schwarz +24"4;
FIA Prod. (24) Singh +1'41"3

SS12 Foini - Koilinia I (29,87 km)
1.Solberg 29'31"3; 2.C. McRae +35"0;
3.Grönholm +50"5; 4.Schwarz +1'11"8;
5.Burns +1'22"6; 6.Eriksson +1'23"8
FIA Prod. (15) Girdauskas +5'18"0

SS13 Platres - Saittas III (11,25 km)
1.Solberg 9'24"6; 2.Burns +7"5;
3.Rovanperä +8"7; 4.Sainz +16"0;
5.C. McRae +16"9; 6.Eriksson +17"2
FIA Prod. (18) Singh +1'33"4

SS14 Foini - Koilinia II (29,87 km)
Cancelled because of poor road
conditions

SS15 Mandra Kambiou I (19 km)
1.Rovanperä 16'34"9; 2.Burns +0"7;
3.Grönholm +1"1; 4.Mäkinen +5"1;
5.Märtin +6"6; 6.Solberg +13"6;
FIA Prod. (17) Trelles +1'45"4

SS16 Agioi Vavatsinas I (12,80 km)
1.Mäkinen 10'55"8; 2.Rovanperä +0"3;
3.Burns +1"7; 4.Grönholm +3"0;
5.Panizzi +8"7; 6.Solberg +9"7;
FIA Prod. (17) Trelles +1'30"9

SS17 Lageia - Kalavasos I (9,14 km)
1.Mäkinen 7'41"0; 2.Burns +2"2;
3.Grönholm +2"4; 4.Rovanperä +7"3;
5.Schwarz +9"9; 6.Panizzi +12"2;
FIA Prod. (12) Trelles +46"7

SS18 Mandra Kambiou II (19 km)
1.Solberg 17'02"1; 2.Panizzi +1"0;
3.Gardemeister +5"2; 4.Delecour
+12"6; 5.Rovanperä +13"7; 6.Sainz
+16"7; FIA Prod. (18) Trelles +2'42"9

SS19 Agioi Vavatsinias II (12,80 km)
1.Mäkinen 11'16"7; 2.Solberg +0"4;
3.Burns +5"2; 4.Rovanperä +6"2;
5.Sainz +9"6; 6.C. McRae +13"1;
FIA Prod. (18) Harrach +2'06"7

SS20 Lageia - Kalavasos II (9,14 km)
1.Burns 7'37"3; 2.Rovanperä +3"7;
3.Mäkinen +3"8; 4.C. McRae +6"0;
5.Märtin +6"5; 6.Solberg +9"9;
FIA Prod. (17) Singh +53"7

Results ⊔ᴖᴈᴄ

	Driver/Navigator	Car	Gr.	Time
1	Grönholm - Rautianen	Peugeot 206 WRC	A	4h21'25"7
2	Burns - Reid	Peugeot 206 WRC		+ 56"8
3	Mäkinen - Lindström	Subaru Impreza WRC 2002		+ 59"0
4	Rovanperä - Pietilainen	Peugeot 206 WRC		+ 1'18"7
5	Solberg - Mills	Subaru Impreza WRC 2002		+ 2'17"9
6	C. McRae - Grist	Ford Focus RS WRC 02		+ 2'45"5
7	Schwarz - Hiemer	Hyundai Accent WRC 3		+ 2'47"4
8	Märtin - Park	Ford Focus RS WRC 02		+ 4'22"6
9	Eriksson - Parmander	Skoda Octavia WRC Evo 2		+ 6'17"7
10	Panizzi - Panizzi	Peugeot 206 WRC		+ 8'12"2
17	Singh - Oh	Proton Pert	Prod.	+ 30'52"2

Leading Retirements(28)

SS.15	Stohl - Petrasko	Ford Focus RS WRC 02	Off
SS.12	Thiry - Prévot	Peugeot 206 WRC	Collapsed suspension
SS.12	Loix - Smeets	Hyundai Accent WRC 3	Gearbox control
SS.12	Kresta - Tomaneko	Skoda Octavia WRC Evo 2	Off
SS.12	A. McRae - Senior	Mitsubishi Lancer Evo WRC	Transmission
SS.9	Duval - Fortin	Ford Focus RS WRC 02	Oil pump
SS.8	Paasonen - Kapanen	Mitsubishi Lancer Evo WRC	Steering, off
SS.4	Kankkunen - Repo	Hyundai Accent WRC 3	Burst sump
SS.4	Pykalisto - Mertsalmi	Toyota Corolla WRC	Gearbox
SS.3	Mortl-Wicha	Peugeot 206 WRC	Engine

Performers

	1	2	3	4	5	6
Solberg	6	4	1	-	-	5
Mäkinen	5	-	2	1	1	2
Sainz	2	-	1	1	2	1
C. McRae	1	4	1	3	2	1
Burns	1	3	3	3	1	1
Rovanperä	1	3	2	5	2	-
Märtin	1	2	-	1	2	-
Duval	1	-	1	1	-	1
Grönholm	-	2	5	2	4	-
Panizzi	-	1	-	-	1	1
Kankkunen	-	1	-	-	-	-
Delecour	-	-	1	1	-	-
Eriksson	-	-	1	-	-	3
Gardemeister	-	-	1	-	-	-
Schwarz	-	-	-	1	1	1
Loix	-	-	-	-	2	2
Stohl	-	-	-	-	-	1

Event Leaders

SS.1	C. McRae
SS.2	Duval
SS.3	Märtin
SS.4 > SS.15	C. McRae
SS.16 > SS.20	Grönholm

Previous winners

2000	Sainz - Moya	2001	C. McRae - Grist
	Ford Focus WRC		Ford Focus RS WRC 01

Championship Classifications

FIA Drivers (5/14)
1. Grönholm 31; 2. Panizzi 20; 3. Burns 19; 4. Mäkinen 14;
5. Sainz, Rovanperä 9; 7. Bugalski, Solberg 7; 9. Loeb, C. McRae 6;
11. A. McRae 2

FIA Constructors (5/14)
1. Peugeot 68; 2. Ford 27; 3. Subaru 7; 4. Mitsubishi 6; 5. Hyundai 2

FIA Production Car WRC (3/8)
1. Sohlberg, Ferreyros & Singh 10; 4. Iliev, Trelles 9; 6. Arai 6;
7. Rowe 5; 8. Ipatti, Ballldini & Girdauskas 4; 11. Fiorio 3;
12. Harach 2; 13. Marrini, Kollevold 1

FIA Junior WRC (2/6)
1. Duval 11; 2. Sola 10; 3. Caldoni, Dallavilla 6; 5. Feghali, Basso 4;
7. Carlsson, Galli 3; 9. Doppelreiter, Tuohino 2; 11. Schelle 1

Argentina

Marcus Grönholm came out on top on the road after a superb fight with Tommi Mäkinen, but was disqualified. So the win went to Richard Burns, only for him to be excluded in his turn. As a terrific rally degenerated into the absurd, Carlos Sainz emerged as its unlikely winner.

Marcus the accursed: he should have been the winner. He was the best, he was set for victory – and then a mistake by his team brought disqualification right at the death.

THE RACE
GRÖNHOLM WINS IT-ON THE TRACK

Marcus Grönholm is bound to know the famous song, "Don't Cry for me Argentina". He won't forget the words in a hurry, either, after being the one with most to cry about in the land of the gaucho. And yet it all started so well for the World Championship leader. Just this once, having to run first on the road wasn't such a terrible thing, with the loose South American surfaces evening things up. He immediately set the first scratch time on the second special stage (the first had been cancelled as the crowds flocked in), and again on the next two as Mäkinen, Burns (delayed by a broken plug) and Solberg all tried to hang on to his coat-tails. With his Cyprus antics probably still firmly in mind, Colin McRae was quick to have another spin, which cost him vital seconds. Forcing the pace, Peugeot's Finnish ace almost threw it away on the super-special held midway through the leg, his 206 careering wildly on two wheels. It was right at the end of the opening day that things took a surprising turn. Dense fog came down on SS8 between La Cumbre and Agua de Oro, and spread to the laneways of the final section from Ascochinga to La Cumbre. That meant there were 33 miles blanketed in the thickest fog imaginable. Though he has always hated running in such conditions, Grönholm promptly annihilated the opposition, in the process depriving the World Championship's sixth round of any interest it might have had. In all he opened up a gap of 1m40s,

running an incredible three seconds a mile faster than his rivals. Timo Rautiainen stared so hard at the time sheets it hurt his eyes – this the man who had just had an operation so that he could put away his customary little specs. Marcus was the one with the sharpest eyes of the lot! He wasn't the only one to shine: Freddy Loix set the fastest time in his Hyundai on the stage back to La Cumbre, something he hadn't managed since January 2001, while on the previous stage Gilles Panizzi was third and Gardemeister's Skoda came up with a stunning fourth-fastest time in the last one. Tommi Mäkinen, on the other hand, found himself unable to put up much of a fight when his gearbox stuck in fourth. As for Richard Burns, whose reputation was so

firmly built in the British fog, he was all at sea, conceding 45 seconds to his teammate in SS8. 'I'm no Marcus,' he admitted. Needless to say, as the next leg got under way they were all thinking about the minor placings after the slap in the face administered by Grönholm the day before. It didn't turn out that way. Scarcely had his 206 got into the first special stage of the second leg than it came to a halt with its hydraulic pressure dropping like a stone. The leader stopped, disconnected the electronic throttle, went back to the good old mechanical ways and got his stricken car going again, its diffs and other things also affected. That little escapade cost him 1m24s before he got to the first service stop at the end of the opening two

Märtin's mission was to make it to the finish first time on this rally. He did so admirably, finishing fourth.

stages. The Peugeot mechanics duly changed the gearbox and hydraulic pump and the Finn was back on the attack. But by now Mäkinen had recovered his equilibrium, and the confidence boost he got from his arch-rival's mishaps saw him setting off on a charge of his own. He claimed four scratches, finally knocked the unfortunate Grönholm off top spot and had the narrowest of leads, some half a second, by the end of the second leg. There had been some thinning of the ranks behind them. Francois Delecour was already gone the day before, barrel-rolling twice after misjudging a severe jump; Panizzi went the same way on the Saturday, his engine overheating wildly. Markko Martin was in strife with his brakes as a result of a broken rim that had split a line, this before a moronic

spectator threw a rock at his windscreen. Solberg lost precious seconds when his gearbox went into safety mode and then a diff gave up the ghost. Which all meant that the fight to the finish would be between Mäkinen and Grönholm, with Burns, now 34.7s behind, looking to pick up the crumbs from the rich men's table.

For some time now the Argentine Rally has concluded over some of the loveliest and most lethal stages in the World Championship. This time things were even more apocalyptic as the fog descended once more. Both at the end of the El Condor stage and after Giulio Cesare, Mäkinen had met his master, for Grönholm was quicker on both and went into a 5.5s lead. But Tommi knows how to handle the pressure, and just go for it, and

Gardemeister was good in the fog, but the rest of his rally was a disappointment.

Loix has always been outstanding in peasoupers, setting his first scratch time for Hyundai on La Cumbre.

Mäkinen is a consummate showman: determined to chase down Grönholm, he barrel-rolled spectacularly near the end of the rally.

here he gave us further proof of that fact, albeit it in the sound and fury of a rather second-hand Subaru Impreza. On the last bend of the second-last special, ending up at Cienaga de Allende, his beautiful blue machine took off and barrel-rolled seven times at high speed. Some people swore the Subaru had gone into orbit. 'No doubt about it, that was the most impressive accident of my entire career,' mused Mäkinen afterwards, his left eye looking as though he'd been in the ring with Mike Tyson.

That meant Grönholm was leading again, with Burns delighted to pick up second place, once more thanks to Mäkinen. Third-placed man Carlos Sainz had finally got the better of the dashing Solberg, who gave himself a hell of a fright by overshooting in the fog, then had brake failure. All of which calmed him down and saw him settle for a fine fourth place. So that was it, another double – the fifth – for Peugeot. All good stuff. ∎

Argentina might have brought Richard Burns his first victory in a 206, but an illegal flywheel meant otherwise.

A COLD BATH
Penalty for Peugeot

A few hours later, Peugeot saw it all disappear: the one-two finish, the 16 points.
It all went back to the moment they were leaving parc fermé at the start of the third leg. Marcus Grönholm's 206 fired up, then fell silent. No way it would start again. Driver and co-driver pushed the car to a halt 10 metres beyond the 'End Zone' board to try and carry out repairs. Near the car were three of the Lion's engineers, including the head of the technical, Michel Nandan. The threesome gave the crew advice, though not coming to their physical assistance.

Eventually the engine fired up, the car gave itself a shake and set off for the service paddock about 60 miles further up the road. Peugeot didn't see any problem, their star was back in the race. But that's not how everyone saw it, especially not one George Donaldson, the Subaru sporting director. A wily fox if if ever there was one, knows his way around the rule-book better than anyone else. The previous day he had notified the FIA stewards that Peugeot's engineers had given Gilles Panizzi some advice when he was trying to get some water into his engine on the way out of a service area. Not on! In fact, the rule is crystal clear: article 12.2.2 explains that no team member may come within one kilometre of a car except on special stages, when the cars are queuing up at a service area or are regrouping, or to provide a spare battery, or when the rally route crosses the service route, and so on. In fact there should have been no-one in a blue shirt near Panizzi's car; he was

For a while, the Argentinian crisis threatened the event and its somptuous and colourful background.

With a bit of luck, Eriksson (in action) and Gardemeister' Skodas brought back five points.

They under-performed in cmparison with Peugeot and Subaru, but Ford scooped the pool with Sainz in the stewards' room.

immediately on notice of exclusion but officially gave up with engine trouble. And of course the same went for Marcus Grönholm. And all the more so in the eyes of Donaldson and his employers, whose lead driver Tommi Mäkinen was having a fantastic rally. The whisper that the fastest of the Peugeot boys was disqualified grew louder as the third leg went on, and his exclusion became official at the last service area, before the podium ceremony in Cordoba itself.

With Grönholm out (Peugeot decided it was wiser not to appeal, as Burns would also have been excluded given that the engineers who had come to Grönholm's aid were also of course within the famous one-kilometre radius of the number.1 206), Richard Burns thought he had picked up the win, an undeserved one but a win nevertheless.

But he didn't stay winner for long. Four hours after the finish he too was hit by a bolt from the blue: the Burns-Reid crew were disqualified in their turn! This time the reason was even more straightforward. The car had been declared illegal after the post-race technical checks, its flywheel 20 grams under weight. It had been Peugeot's mistake to fit the part on the Englishman's car when it had already been picked up as being too light back at Velizy. But a breakdown in internal communications had seen it slip through again accidentally, though it certainly had no effect on the car's performance.

What should have been a triumphant return turned into a rather crestfallen trip home. Burns was rightly disappointed, but not as much as Grönholm. It will be a while before the star of the rally forgets this disqualification, after all the effort he put into that stunning winning drive. It may even have been the best of his career. In the end Carlos Sainz was declared the winner from Solberg and Colin McRae. But the well-bred Spaniard did not dwell on his 24th World Championship success, merely accepting the ten points that came with it. ∎

Justifiably disappointed, Marcus Grönholm kept the lead in the Drivers' Championship.

If he hadn't lost the head-to-head with Sainz, Petter Solberg could have pulled off a surprise win!

22ⁿᵈ Rally of Argentina

6ᵗʰ leg of the 2002 World Rally Championship for constructors and drivers. 4ᵗʰ leg of FIA Production Car WRC Championship.

Date 16ᵗʰ to 19ᵗʰ May 2002

Route
1456,00 km divided in 3 legs
22 gravel special stages scheduled (381,45 km), 21 contested (358,43 km)

1ˢᵗ leg
Friday 17ᵗʰ May (06h40-18h42):
Villa Carlos Paz > La Cumbre > Villa Carlo Paz, 479,17 km; 9 special stages scheduled (153,79 km) and 8 contested (130,77 km)

2ⁿᵈ leg
Saturday 18ᵗʰ May (06h40-18h42):
Villa Carlo Paz > La Cumbre > Villa Carlo Paz, 477,97 km; 9 special stages (153,79 km)

3ʳᵈ leg
Sunday 19ᵗʰ May (06h00-15h33):
Villa Carlo Paz > Mina Clavero > Cordoba's Stadium, 498,86 km; 4 special stages (73,87 km)

Entry List - Starters - Finishers:
81 - 68 - 29

Conditions: Friday morning dry, later rain and fog. Changeable thereafter.

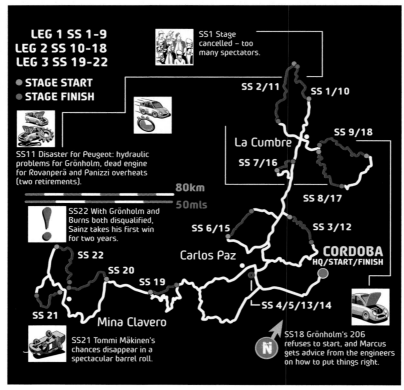

LEG 1 SS 1-9
LEG 2 SS 10-18
LEG 3 SS 19-22

● STAGE START
● STAGE FINISH

SS1 Stage cancelled – too many spectators.

SS11 Disaster for Peugeot: hydraulic problems for Grönholm, dead engine for Rovanperä and Panizzi overheats (two retirements).

SS22 With Grönholm and Burns both disqualified, Sainz takes his first win for two years.

SS21 Tommi Mäkinen's chances disappear in a spectacular barrel roll.

SS18 Grönholm's 206 refuses to start, and Marcus gets advice from the engineers on how to put things right.

80km
50mls

La Cumbre
SS 2/11
SS 1/10
SS 9/18
SS 7/16
SS 8/17
SS 6/15
SS 3/12
SS 22
SS 20
SS 19
Carlos Paz
CORDOBA HQ/START/FINISH
SS 4/5/13/14
SS 21
Mina Clavero

Special Stage Times

SS1 Capilla del Monte I (23,02 km)
Cancelled - too many spectators

SS2 San Marcos Sierra I (26,96 km)
1.Grönholm 15'38"7; 2.Mäkinen +6"6;
3.Solberg +16"5; 4.Rovanperä +14"5;
5.Burns +23"5; 6.C. McRae/Kankkunen
+26"8; FIA Prod. (18) Arai +1'33"5

SS3 Cosquin I (19,19 km)
1.Grönholm 13'20"9; 2.Burns +6"6;
3.Mäkinen +8"5; 4.Rovanperä +8"6;
5.Solberg +17"9; 6.Märtin +18"5;
FIA Prod. (17) Ligato +1'15"8

SS4 Pro-Racing Lane A I (3,44 km)
1.Grönholm 2'10"5; 2.Solberg +1"4;
3.Burns +1"6; 4.C. McRae +2"4;
5.Sainz +2"5; 6.Märtin +2"6;
FIA Prod. (18) Ligato +11"4

SS5 Pro-Racing Lane B I (3,44 km)
1.Mäkinen 2'10"2; 2.Sainz +0"3;
3.Burns/Rovanperä +0"7;
5.Solberg +0"9; 6.Märtin +1"1;
FIA Prod. (18) Ligato +10"0

SS6 Tanti I (16,06 km)
1.Burns 8'27"3; 2.Mäkinen +1"8;
3.Rovanperä +2"1; 4.Grönholm +2"2;
5.Loix +5"0; 6.Sainz +5"2;
FIA Prod. (18) Ligato +47"5

SS7 La Falda-Vila Giardino I (9,36 km)
1.Grönholm 6'36"7; 2.Mäkinen +0"4;
3.Burns +0"6; 4.Solberg +4"1;
5.Sainz +4"9; 6.Rovanperä +8"8;
FIA Prod. (17) Ligato +41"1

SS8 La Cumbre I (23,45 km)
1.Grönholm 20'38"9; 2.Burns +45"1;
3.Panizzi +55"3; 4.Sainz +59"8;
5.Solberg +1'03"7; 6.Mäkinen +1'20"9;
FIA Prod. (16) Ligato +3'54"5

SS9 Ascochinga I (28,82 km)
1.Loix 20'18"6; 2.Grönholm +16"0;
3.Mäkinen +18"9; 4.Gardemeister
+28"5; 5.Sainz +39"6; 6.Solberg +39"7;
FIA Prod. (8) Arai +56"3

SS10 Capilla del Monte II (23,02 km)
1.Burns 17'10"0; 2.Mäkinen +2"8;
3.Märtin +9"0; 4.Sainz +10"5;
5.Solberg +13"3; 6.C. McRae +16"1;
FIA Prod. (12) Arai +1'25"6

SS11 San Marcos Sierra II (26,96 km)
1.Mäkinen 15'13"3; 2.Burns +3"9;
3.C. McRae +9"6; 4.Solberg +9"7;
5.Märtin +17"8; 6.Sainz +23"6;
FIA Prod. (13) Singh +1'52"4

SS12 Cosquin II (19,19 km)
1.Mäkinen 13'16"7; 2.Grönholm +3"5;
3.Märtin +4"0; 4.Burns +4"2;

SS13 Pro-Racing A II (3,44 km)
1.Burns 2'12"7; 2.Kankkunen +0"5;
3.Grönholm/Märtin +0"7;
5.Sainz/Mäkinen +1"3;
FIA Prod. (13) Arai +11"9

SS14 Pro-Racing B II (3,44 km)
1.C. McRae 2'12"2; 2.Mäkinen +0"6;
3.Panizzi +0"9; 4.Burns/Märtin +1"1;
6.Grönholm +1"2;
FIA Prod. (14) Arai +12"0

SS15 Tanti II (16,06 km)
1.Mäkinen 8'22"7; 2.Burns +2";
3.Grönholm +3"8; 4.C. McRae +6"7;
5.Sainz +7"6; 6.Solberg +8"8;
FIA Prod. (14) Arai +56"3

SS16 La Falda II (9,36 km)
1.C. McRae 6'35"9; 2.Sainz +0"3;
3.Mäkinen +0"4; 4.Burns +1"7;
5.Solberg +3"0; 6.Grönholm +3"7;
FIA Prod. (14) Ligato +43"6

SS17 La Cumbre II (23,45 km)
1.Mäkinen 19'49"4; 2.Grönholm +8"1;
3.Burns +8"2; 4.Sainz +10"4;
5.Solberg +13"7; 6.Kankkunen +14"1;
FIA Prod. (13) Ferreyros +1'56"2

5.C. McRae +6"1; 6.Solberg +6"9;
FIA Prod. (14) Ferreyros +1'17"5

SS18 Ascochinga II (28,82 km)
1.Mäkinen 18'39"2;
3.Grönholm +2"0; 4.Solberg +5"6;
5.Märtin +6"1; 6.Sainz +5"1;
FIA Prod. (13) Arai +1'35"1

SS19 El Condor-Copina (16,77 km)
1.Grönholm 13'52"6; 2.Mäkinen +1"9;
3.Sainz +8"4; 4.Burns +12"8;
5.Märtin +13"5; 6.C. McRae +17"1;
FIA Prod. (13) Ligato +1'12"8

SS20 Giulo Cesare (22,81 km)
1.Grönholm 18'35"0; 2.Mäkinen +4"1;
3.Sainz +16"8; 4.Solberg +17"9;
5.Burns +27"9; 6.Märtin +28"5;
FIA Prod. (13) Ferreyros +1'42"1

SS21 Cura Brochero (13,63 km)
1.Grönholm 6'43"1; 2.Sainz/Solberg
+3"2; 4.Kankkunen +8"3; 5.Burns +8"4;
6.C. McRae +12"3;
FIA Prod. (12) Ligato +45"2

SS22 El Mirador (20,64 km)
1.Burns 11'30"8; 2.Solberg +0"2;
3.Sainz +5"8; 4.Grönholm +6"2;
5.C. McRae +13"8; 6.Kankkunen +16"4;
FIA Prod. (11) Ligato +58"0

Results — WRC

	Driver/Navigator	Car	Gr.	Time
1	Sainz - Moya	Ford Focus RS WRC 02	A	4h08'09"1
2	Solberg - Mills	Subaru Impreza WRC 2002		+ 4"0
3	C. McRae - Grist	Ford Focus RS WRC 02		+ 2'19"1
4	Märtin - Park	Ford Focus RS WRC 02		+ 2'52"4
5	Gardemeister - Lukander	Skoda Octavia WRC Evo 2		+ 5'18"8
6	Eriksson - Parmander	Skoda Octavia WRC Evo 2		+ 6'16"6
7	Kankkunen - Repo	Hyundai Accent WRC 3		+ 9'03"3
8	A. McRae - Senior	Mitsubishi Lancer Ev.o WRC		+ 8'49"6
9	Pozzo - Stillo	Skoda Octavia WRC Evo 2		+ 13'58"9
10	Ferreyros - Vallejo	Mitsubishi Lancer Evo 7	Prod.	+ 24'18"5

Leading Retirements (37)

CH22B	(1) Grönholm - Rautiainen	Peugeot 206 WRC	Disqualified
CH22B	(1) Burns - Reid	Peugeot 206 WRC	Disqualified
SS.21	Mäkinen - Lindström	Subaru Impreza WRC 2002	Off
SS.17	Panizzi - Panizzi	Peugeot 206 WRC	Engine
SS.10	Loix - Smeets	Hyundai Accent WRC 3	Accelerator
SS.10	Rovanperä - Pietilainen	Peugeot 206 WRC	Engine
SS.9	Schwarz - Hiemer	Hyundai Accent WRC 3	Fuel pressure
SS.7	Delecour - Grataloup	Mitsubishi Lancer Evo WRC	Off

Championship Classifications

FIA Drivers (6/14)
1. Grönholm 31; 2. Panizzi 20; 3. Burns, Sainz 19; 5. Mäkinen 14;
6. Solberg 13; 7. C. McRae 10; 8. Rovanperä 9; 9. Bugalski 7;
10.Loeb 6; 11. Märtin 3; 12. A. McRae, Gardemeister 2; 14. Eriksson 1.

FIA Constructors (6/14)
1. Peugeot 68; 2. Ford 41; 3. Subaru 33; 4. Mitsubishi 6; 5. Skoda 5;
6. Hyundai 3.

FIA Production Car WRC (4/8)
1. Ferreyros 20; 2. Singh 14; 3. Arai, Trelles 12; 5. Sohlberg 10;
6. Iliev 6; 7. Rowe 5; 8. Ipatti, Baldini & Girdauskas 4; 11. Fiorio 3;
12. Ligato, Harrach, Marrini 2; 15. Kollevold 1.

FIA Junior WRC (2/6)
1. Duval 11; 2. Sola 10; 3. Caldani, Dallavilla 6; 5. Feghalli, Basso 4;
7. Carlsson, Galli 3; 9. Doppelreiter, Tuohino 2; 11. Schelle 1.

Performers

	1	2	3	4	5	6
Grönholm	9	3	2	2	-	2
Mäkinen	5	7	4	-	1	1
Burns	5	4	4	4	3	-
C. McRae	2	-	1	2	2	4
Loix	1	-	-	-	1	-
Sainz	-	3	3	3	5	3
Solberg		3	1	4	6	3
Kankkunen	1	-	1	-	3	
Märtin	-	3	1	3	4	
Rovanperä	-	2	2	-	1	
Panizzi	2	-	-	-	-	
Gardemeister	-	-	1	-	-	

Event Leaders

SS.1	Cancelled
SS.2 > SS.16	Grönholm
SS.17 > SS.18	Mäkinen
SS.19 > SS.22	Grönholm

Previous winners

1980	Rohrl - Geistdorfer Fiat 131 Abarth		1994	Auriol - Occelli Toyota Celica Turbo 4WD
1981	Fréquelin - Todt Talbot Sunbeam Lotus		1995	Recalde - Christie Lancia Delta HF Integrale
1983	Mikkola - Hertz Audi Quattro		1996	Mäkinen - Harjanne Mitsubishi Lancer Ev.3
1984	Blomqvist - Cederberg Audi Quattro		1997	Mäkinen - Harjanne Mitsubishi Lancer Ev.4
1985	Salonen - Harjanne Peugeot 205 T16		1998	Mäkinen - Mannisenmäki Mitsubishi Lancer Ev.5
1986	Biasion - Siviero Lancia Delta S4		1999	Kankkunen - Repo Subaru Impreza WRC
1987	Biasion - Siviero Lancia Delta HF Turbo		2000	Burns - Reid Subaru Impreza WRC 2000
1988	Recalde - Del Buono Lancia Delta Integrale		2001	C. McRae - Grist Ford Focus RS WRC 01
1989	Ericsson - Billstam Lancia Delta Integrale			
1990	Biasion - Siviero Lancia Delta Integrale 16v			
1991	Sainz - Moya Toyota Celica GT4			
1992	Auriol - Occelli Lancia Delta HF Integrale			
1993	Kankkunen - Grist Toyota Celica Turbo 4WD			

PIRELLI competizioni

Acropolis

Colin McRae picked up a win that seemed destined to go to a sparkling Markko Märtin, ahead of Marcus Grönholm, the latter handicapped by having to run first on the road. The result meant the Finn and his Peugeot team tightened their grip on the Championship as it reached the halfway stage.

A Mitsubishi and a Subaru in the same shot on the same stage: this was rallying in video arcade mode...

THE RACE
McRAE IS BACK!

To win this year's Acropolis you needed to be in a Ford and not to be too well up in the World Championship standings. The Focus WRCs have always shown impressive reliability on the Championship's most testing ground – Cyprus, Greece, the Safari – even if the 206 WRC, whose ultra-reliable evolution 2002 made its debut in Greece, has come a long way in that area. The starting order, which goes by the drivers' standings before each event, remains controversial, but it all amounts to nothing because no-one has come up with a better solution.

But let's get back to rallies, the Acropolis in particular. Its gravel tracks are among the most punishing

Handicapped by his starting position early in the event, the best Carlos Sainz could hope for was a podium finish.

for the unfortunate souls who have to run on them first, and the 2002 version was no exception to that rule. On the opening stages, Marcus Grönholm, still runaway World

Handicapped by his starting position early in the event, the best Carlos Sainz could hope for was a podium finish.

Championship leader despite his Argentinian misadventures (see previous rally report), used all his very special talent to limit the damage. His efforts against such a handicap put you in mind of Tommi Mäkinen's when he was at his peak and, for years on end, put up uncomplainingly – at least in public – with the same thing. It took all the considerable style of Richard Burns, who complained about it when he was temporary leader of the 1999 Championship, to see that you need to be quite a driver to reduce that handicap. In other words, Marcus, 2002 model, is what Tommi was in 1996, 1997, 1998 and 1999: a giant.

But every giant is hamstrung by his very stature. On the fourth stage, the 206 spun (the only driving mistake he was scheduled to make for the entire year) and the Peugeot driver ended the first leg seventh, 1m16s behind the leader. And who was that? Why, Markko Märtin of course! It was the first time Martin had enjoyed a real chance of winning a World Championship rally, but he

Well might Märtin have his head in the clouds - he made a blinding start, but then his chances disappeared with a puncture in the middle of the second stage.

One scratch, then gone: to think that Citroën felt they had a world-class gravel specialist on their hands...

looked as assured as somebody who had been doing it for years.

Tenth in the Championship, the Estonian had set off from that very favourable starting position. There were other advantages as well: he has a Focus WRC to play with, but he also plays with his head. Well aware of that state of affairs, the young fellow went on the attack in a bid to get as far up the order as possible and start the next two days from an even better position. And he did the job admirably, playing every trump card in his hand right from the word go. As a result, on the first evening the Estonian had the rally in the palm of his hand thanks to four scratch times which put him 50.7s ahead of second-placed man Freddy Loix. The Belgian, an even later starter, had also had a good day, actually bringing Hyundai a scratch time as they improve with every outing. Those two were followed by a lacklustre but patient Colin McRae. Waiting to pick up the pieces as those three fought it out was Petter Solberg, but his lapses – two spins and a little tap that left his Subaru slightly skewiff – limited his success.

Behind them, the rest of the pack covered the spectrum from faint hope to utter disillusion. Thomas Radstrom took a scratch in the Xsara on the Karoutes stage (the first time a Xsara had set a fastest time on gravel) ; Sebastien Loeb had brake problems and couldn't find the right settings; Harri Rovanpera upset his 206's balance when he hit a rock and had a puncture; Makinen was fighting brakes, accelerator, and a power steering problem before he hit a rock and broke the suspension, and pulled out right away.

Carlos Sainz had to make the best of his starting place (3rd), as did a seemingly off-form Richard Burns. As the second leg began, then, Märtin had every reason to be happy with himself. He had a sniff of a first World Championship win, which would only be right and proper after his previous day's performance when he was quickest, fair and square. The first two timed sections went very well for him as Loix slipped back down the order.

But on the Elatia stage (SS9) one of his Pirellis started to unravel, forcing the youngster to stop and change the wheel, which cost him a heart-breaking three minutes. "I didn't hit anything," he despairingly told his team. Sure enough, he hadn't felt a bump any harder than normal, but his uncompromising driving style does mean the car suffers a lot more stress. Unlike Ford's Sainz or McRae, Märtin doesn't slalom between the big rocks, and his is always the Focus whose nether regions suffer most.

This time it was a tyre that started it all, which was a pity, because not only had he led the pack a merry dance, he had also dominated his famous stablemates. Slipping back to ninth, the Estonian was virtually inconsolable.

Up front it was Ford in pursuit of Ford, and the man scooping the pool was Colin McRae, finding some form again after his terrible lapses in

7

A spin, then a tap: Petter Solberg was marking time in mid-season.

No easy place, Greece, for a Swede. What do you think, Mr Eriksson?

Argentina. The Scot was in better shape even if not quite back to his best. He was getting the job done, but the panache, the usual spark of genius, wasn't there. Still, sometimes that's no bad thing if it curbs his excesses.

Meanwhile Solberg and Märtin were swapping scratch times, the former peeved with himself over his previous day's efforts and wrestling with a loose steering wheel – though he still set second fastest time on the Drosohori stage! – and the latter determined to show that the blow-up was just a racing incident. That left little room for the rest in pure performance terms, and Burns was the only other driver to set a fastest time. The result, at the end of the second leg, was that McRae was 32.6 ahead of his fellow-Brit and 42.3 in front of Grönholm, still assiduously sweeping the roads despite an oversteering 206. Märtin wasn't the only one who had had a hard day, with the punctures coming thick and fast: Radstrom, Juha Kankkunen, Rovanperä, Toni Gardemeister, Kenneth Eriksson, Toshihiro Arai, Armin Schwarz...

In the end the last leg was a formality for Colin McRae. He had no need to push, Burns quickly retiring with a broken rear ball pin and Grönholm a long way back. But he still thrashed the Focus, having a nasty coming-together with a tree after a misunderstanding over his notes. Second at the finish, Peugeot's Finnish star had also been quickest on the day with three best times, leaving the last scratch to compatriot Rovanpera, decidedly off-colour throughout an event where he managed to finish fourth just behind the hard-working Sainz.
Solberg – the only non-Ford or Peugeot driver – and Märtin snaffled the last points on offer. Everyone else had found the Acropolis hard going, not least Citroën (Loeb 7th, Radstrom 8th) whose hard-charging Xsara was woefully short of

development on gravel. When Thomas Radstrom is your resident expert it shows how much you can expect... It was all very well for Citroen boss Guy Fréquelin and his men to bemoan their lack of preparation, they had only themselves to blame. It seems there's a little balding chap over Millau way who's still laughing about it, though maybe on the other side of his face. Hyundai, Mitsubishi and Skoda were all operating at a lower level, Loix's eye-catching exploits in the early stages owing much to circumstances.

In the Junior World Championship, incidentally, victory went to Finland's Tuohino in his Saxo from Dallavilla's, followed by Caldari's Punto. Sola, fourth in another Saxo, underlined his leadership of the Championship after a gruelling rally for the front-wheel drive cars, not at all at home on the gravel roads of Greece. ■

THE SEASON SO FAR
SUPERSTARDOM FOR PEUGEOT

Once again the Greek round brings the World Championship season to its halfway point. The strengths and weaknesses are there for all to see, since the cars have run on tarmac, on snow and gravel.

The first point to make is that, as expected, Peugeot have steam-rollered their way to the front. The French team management can't fall back on the excuse of having less experience than their rivals any more. The Vélizy team seems to have reached full bloom: four one-two finishes, one of them a 1-2-3, in seven races help to put the latest Monte Carlo disappointment to the back of their minds and ease the pain of the problems in Argentina. Peugeot were right to point out that the changes to the

calendar played to their strength, particularly with Corsica coming at the start of the year and Portugal being dropped to give an extra tarmac rally.
It was still a convincing demonstration. Now virtually bullet-proof, the 206 WRC has virtually no weaknesses. Not only

Another retirement for Mäkinen, this time with a wheel ripped off. Prior to that he had been brilliant.

Peugeot's Finn managed to stay ahead of Subaru's Norwegian. Just for a moment, Rovanperä got up to fourth.

Even for a giant like Grönholm the handicap of opening the road on the first stage was just too much. But a frustrating rally ended with second place.

At last, Colin was back to the real McRae! The Scot rediscovered all his flair and nous to claim his first win of 2002.

that, but at its wheel Peugeot had the cream of the driving talent: Grönholm in supreme form, Panizzi with no equal on tarmac, the perfect gravel stand-in in Rovanperä and also Burns, whose learning-curve in the car was going beautifully. Solid stuff. After the 2001 Acropolis the French team were 22 points adrift of Ford (based on replacing Portugal with Corsica). This season, they were 22 in front...

Once again Ford was their main rival. Two wins, including the rather far-fetched success in Argentina, and consistent front-running meant Malcolm Wilson's team had kept

things in check. But the Focus pays the price for its poor performances on tarmac, while one of its drivers, McRae, can't stand the stuff and their Pirellis aren't always up to the task. Same thing for Subaru, a team that has two major handicaps to contend with: the incredible number of off-road excursions and other terminal mistakes from Tommi Mäkinen, under pressure from Solberg, and the blue cars' chronic lack of reliability. Mitsubishi, drifting along with their new Lancer WRC, Hyundai, steadily improving in performance if not in reliability, and Skoda, as under-resourced as ever, are in a different league.

So at the mid-season mark no-one doubts that Peugeot will carry off their third successive title. In the drivers' standings, the French team's pilots are also grabbing... the lion's share.

The redoubtable Grönholm has obviously matured: with a rock-solid 206 in his hands, unlike 2001, the Finn really has no opposition and has toyed with

Burns, whose invasion of 'his' team simply acted as a spur. Second-placed Sainz, his turn of speed tempered by the passing of time, has benefited from his sheer consistency. Panizzi owes his third place entirely to his performances on tarmac (two wins) while McRae, running equal with the little man, has scored six times from a possible seven. Burns has now settled in at Peugeot and lies fifth. In the same car, the Englishman isn't quite a match for Grönholm.

At Subaru, Solberg is enjoying new status, easily outdoing Mäkinen, the latter incredibly lucky not to have injured himself in all those frightening flights off road. Whatever happened to the great Tommi? Seeing him break Impreza after Impreza puts you in mind of his crazy days of the early Nineties. Most of all, the first half of the year gave us a clear picture of the new threat to the old guard of the World Championship, as evidenced by Solberg. The new boys, Martin, Loeb and Duval among them, are baring their teeth, so the others had better look out... ∎

49th Acropolis Rally

7th leg of the 2002 World Rally Championship for constructors and drivers. 3rd leg of WRC Junior Championship.

Date 13rd to 16th June 2002

Parcours
1197,85 km divided in 3 legs.
16 gravel stages scheduled (391,50 km) and 15 contested (374,16 km)

1st leg
Friday 14th June (08h00-18h47):
Lilea Parnassos > Lilea Parnassos, 427,53 km; 6 special stages (136,35 km)
2nd leg
Saturday 15th June (07h15-18h29):
Lilea Parnassos > Lilea Parnassos, 429,27 km; 6 special stages scheduled (158,76 km) et 5 contested (141,42 km)
3rd leg
Sunday 16th June (08h00-16h04): Lilea Parnassos > Itea, 241,05 km; 4 special stages (96,39 km)

Entry List - Starters - Finishers:
89 - 84 - 35

Conditions: fine and warm, roads clearing as cars went through.

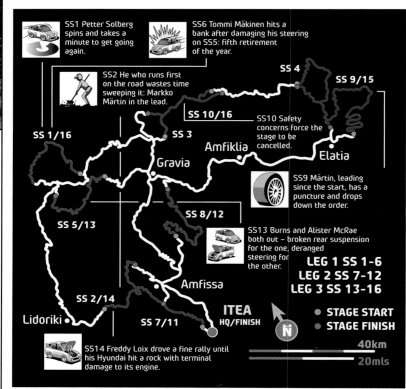

SS1 Petter Solberg spins and takes a minute to get going again.

SS2 He who runs first on the road wastes time sweeping it: Markko Märtin in the lead.

SS6 Tommi Mäkinen hits a bank after damaging his steering on SS5: fifth retirement of the year.

SS10 Safety concerns force the stage to be cancelled.

SS9 Märtin, leading since the start, has a puncture and drops down the order.

SS13 Burns and Alister McRae both out – broken rear suspension for the one, deranged steering for the other.

SS14 Freddy Loix drove a fine rally until his Hyundai hit a rock with terminal damage to its engine.

LEG 1 SS 1-6
LEG 2 SS 7-12
LEG 3 SS 13-16

● STAGE START
● STAGE FINISH

40km
20mls

TOP ENTRIES

1   Richard BURNS - Robert REID
    Peugeot 206 WRC
2   Marcus GRÖNHOLM - Timo
    RAUTIAINEN Peugeot 206 WRC
3   Harri ROVANPERÄ - Risto
    PIETILÄINEN Peugeot 206 WRC
4   Carlos SAINZ - Luis MOYA
    Ford Focus RS WRC 02
5   Colin McRAE - Nicky GRIST
    Ford Focus RS WRC 02
6   Markko MÄRTIN - Michael PARK
    Ford Focus RS WRC 02
7   Francois DELECOUR - Daniel
    GRATALOUP Mitsubishi Lancer Evo WRC
8   Alister McRAE - David SENIOR
    Mitsubishi Lancer Evo WRC
10 Tommi MÄKINEN - Kaj LINDSTRÖM
    Subaru Impreza WRC 2002
11 Petter SOLBERG - Philip MILLS
    Subaru Impreza WRC 2002
12 Toshihiro ARAI - Tony SIRCOMBE
    Subaru Impreza WRC 2002
14 Kenneth ERIKSSON - Tina THORNER
    Skoda Octavia WRC Evo 2
15 Toni GARDEMEISTER - Paavo
    LUKANDER Skoda Octavia WRC Evo 2
16 Stig BLOMQVIST - Ana GONI
    Skoda Octavia WRC Evo 2
17 Armin SCHWARZ - Manfred HIEMER
    Hyundai Accent WRC 3
18 Freddy LOIX - Sven SMEETS
    Hyundai Accent WRC 3
19 Juha KANKKUNEN - Juha REPO
    Hyundai Accent WRC 3
20 Thomas RADSTRÖM - Denis
    GIRAUDET Citroën Xsara
21 Sébastien LOEB - Daniel ELENA
    Citroën Xsara
23 Gilles PANIZZI - Hervè PANIZZI
    Peugeot 206 WRC
24 Bruno THIRY - Stèphane PREVOT
    Peugeot 206 WRC
25 Armin KREMER - Dieter
    SCHNEPPENHEIM Ford Focus WRC
26 Ioannis PAPADIMITRIOU - Allan
    HARRYMAN Ford Focus WRC 01
32 Gabriel POZZO - Daniel STILLO
    Skoda Octavia WRC
33 Armodios VOVOS - EM EL
    Ford Focus WRC
34 Tomasz KUCHAR - Maciej SZCEPANIAK
    Toyota Corolla WRC
35 Abdullah BAKHASHAB - Bobby WILLIS
    Toyota Corolla WRC
51 Andréa DALLAVILLA - Giovanni
    BERNACCHINI Citroën Saxo Super 1600
53 Giandomenico BASSO - Luigi PIROLLO
    Fiat Punto Kit
55 François DUVAL - Jean-Marc FORTIN
    Ford Puma
60 Nicola CALDANI - Dario D'ESPOSITO
    Fiat Punto
62 Janne TUOHINO - Petri VIHAVAINEN
    Citroën Saxo VTS
64 Gianluigi GALLI - Guido D'AMORE
    Fiat Punto Kit
65 Daniel SOLA - David MORENO
    Citroën Saxo
78 Roger FEGHALI - Nicola ARENA
    Ford Puma

Special Stage Times

www.acropolisrally.gr
www.wrc.com

SS1 Pavliani I (24,45 km)
1.Märtin 19'32"1; 3.Grönholm +13"8;
3.Rovanperä +14"5; 4.C. McRae +14"7;
5.Mäkinen & Schwarz +19"3;
Jr. (28) Duval +2'17"0

SS2 Karoutes I (18,88 km)
1.Radström 11'56"5; 2.Loix +0"6;
3.Schwarz +1"6; 4.Solberg +2"2;
5.Märtin +3"8; 6.Loeb +7"9;
Jr. (26) Carlsson +1'12"8

SS3 Paleohori I (20,52 km)
1.Loix 13'54"9; 2.Burns +6"4;
3.Märtin +6"8; 4.Grönholm +7"2;
5.C. McRae +9"8; 6.Rovanperä +10"9;
Jr. (29) Duval +1'59"4

SS4 Rengini I (25,04 km)
1.Märtin 19'38"1; 2.Schwarz +5"3;
3.Mäkinen +15"3; 4.Rovanperä +16"4;
5.Eriksson +16"6; 6.Loix +17"1;
Jr. (29) Duval +2'15"8

SS5 Inohori I (23 km)
Märtin 18'04"8; 5.C. McRae +5"0;
3.Loix +6"8; 4.Loeb +9"6;
5.Sainz +10"5; 6.Radström +10"7;
Jr. (29) Martin 1'55"7

SS6 Pavliani II (24,45 km)
1.Solberg 19'37"4; 2.C. McRae +5"7;
3.Märtin +7"2; 4.Rovanperä +7"5;
5.Grönholm +10"1; 6.Loeb +11"
Jr. (25) Duval +2'35"5

SS7 Bauxites I (23,45 km)
1.Solberg 14'00"4; 2.C. McRae +7"4;
3.Burns +8"3; 4.Märtin +9"5;
5.Grönholm +10"9; 6.Rovanperä +17"2;
Jr. (24) Sola +1'37"7

SS8 Drosohori I (28,68 km)
1.Märtin 23'27"2; 2.Solberg +4"7;
3.Sainz +5"8; 4.C. McRae +6"2;
5.Burns +7"4; 6.Panizzi +8"4;
Jr. (24) Tuohino +2'24"7

SS9 Elatia I (37,15 km)
1.Burns 24'12"6; 2.C. McRae +0"6;
3.Solberg +0"7; 4.Grönholm +16"7;
5.Sainz +22"7; 6. Loix +29"3;
Jr. (24) Tuohino +3'36"4

SS10 Mendenitsa I (17,34 km)
Cancelled - Badly-parked cars

SS11 Bauxites II (23,45 km)
1.Solberg 13'44"8; 2.Grönholm +4"7;
3.Märtin +7"4; 4.C. McRae +7"8;
5.Burns +12"7; 6.Rovanperä +13"6;
Jr. (23) Sola +1'47"0

SS12 Drosohori II (28,68 km)
1.Märtin 23'07"8; 2.Solberg +3"1;
3.Grönholm +10"1; 4.C. McRae +12"7;
5.Panizzi +16"5; 6.Burns +20"2;
Jr. (23) Valimaki +3'01"1

SS13 Inohori II (23 km)
1.Grönholm 17'35"2; 2.Märtin +1"9;
3.Solberg +3"5; 4.Rovanperä +6"8;
5.C. McRae +8"2; 6.Sainz +10"6;
Jr. (22) Sola +2'05"4

SS14 Karoutes II (18,88 km)
1.Grönholm 11'39"9; 2.Solberg +4"9;
3.Rovanperä +5"9; 4.C. McRae +6"5;
5.Sainz +7"8; 6.Loeb +9"8;
Jr. (19) Caldani +1'33"2

SS15 Elatia II (37,15 km)
1.1.Grönholm 23'59"9; 2.McRae +0"4;
3.Solberg +1"8; 4.Sainz +11";
5.Rovanperä +12"9; 6.Märtin +14"3;
Jr. (20) Caldani +3'53"4

SS16 Mendenitsa II (17,34 km)
1.Rovanperä 11'04"; 2.Solberg +1"6;
3.Grönholm +4"9; 4.C. McRae +7"6;
5.Sainz +8"7; 6.Märtin +14"8;
Jr. (19) Dallavilla +2'03"8

Résultats — WRC

	Driver/Navigator	Car	Gr.	Time
1	C. McRae - Grist	Ford Focus RS WRC 02	A	4h27'43"8
2	Grönholm – Rautiainen	Peugeot 206 WRC		+ 24"5
3	Sainz - Moya	Ford Focus RS WRC 02		+ 1'45"6
4	Rovanperä - Pietilainen	Peugeot 206 WRC		+ 1'57"6
5	Solberg - Mills	Subaru Impreza WRC 2002		+ 1'58"6
6	Märtin - Park	Ford Focus RS WRC 02		+ 2'40"1
7	Loeb - Elena	Citroën Xsara WRC		+ 3'45"8
8	Radström – Giraudet	Citroën Xsara WRC		+ 5'08"7
9	Schwarz - Hiemer	Hyundai Accent WRC 3		+ 5'41"0
10	Gardemeister - Lukander	Skoda Octavia WRC Evo 2		+ 7'17"4
11	Delecour - Grataloup	Mitsubishi Lancer Evo WRC		+ 7'21"6
12	Thiry - Prévot	Peugeot 206 WRC		+ 9'20"1
19	Tuohino - Vihavainen	Citroën Saxo VTS	Jr.	+ 36'44"0

Leading Retirements (49)

SS.14	Loix - Smeets	Hyundai Accent WRC 3	Engine
SS.14	Panizzi - Panizzi	Peugeot 206 WRC	Gearbox
SS.13	Burns - Reid	Peugeot 206 WRC	Suspension
SS.13	A. McRae - Senior	Mitsubishi Lancer Evo WRC	Steering
SS.9	Kankkunen -Repo	Hyundai Accent WRC 3	Turbo
SS.8	Duval - Fortin	Ford Puma	Wheel studs
SS.6	Pozzo - Stillo	Skoda Octavia WRC Evo 2	Over time
SS.6	Kremer - Schneppenheim	Ford Focus WRC	Off
SS.6	Mäkinen - Lindström	Subaru Impreza WRC 2002	Wheel torn off

Championship Classifications

FIA Drivers (7/14)
1. Grönholm 37; 2. Sainz 23; 3. C. McRae, Panizzi 20; 5. Burns 19;
6. Solberg 15; 7. Mäkinen 14; 8. Rovanperä 12; 9. Bugalski 7;
10. Loeb 6; 11.Märtin 4; 12. A. McRae, Gardemeister 2;
14. Eriksson 1

FIA Constructors (7/14)
1. Peugeot 77; 2. Ford 55; 3. Subaru 35; 4. Mitsubishi 6; 5. Skoda 5;
6. Hyundai 4

FIA Production Car WRC (4/8)
1. Ferreyros 20; 2. Singh 14; 3. Arai, Trelles 12; 5. Sohlberg 10;
6. Iliev 9; 7. Rowe 5; 8. Ipatti, Baldini & Girdauskas 4; 11. Fiorio 3;
12. Ligato, Harrach, Marrini 2; 15. Kollevold 1

FIA Junior WRC (3/6)
1. Sola 13; 2. Tuohino, Dallavilla 12; 4. Duval 11; 5. Caldani 10;
6. Feghali, Basso 4; 8. Carlsson, Galli 3; 10. Doppelreiter, Rowe 2;
12. Schelle, Foss 1

Performers

	1	2	3	4	5	6
Märtin	5	1	3	1	1	2
Solberg	3	4	3	1	-	-
Grönholm	3	2	2	2	2	-
Burns	1	1	1	-	2	1
Loix	1	1	1	-	-	2
Rovanperä	1	-	2	3	1	3
Radström	1	-	-	-	-	-
C. McRae	-	5	-	6	2	-
Schwarz	-	1	1	-	1	-
Sainz	-	-	1	1	4	1
Mäkinen	-	-	1	-	1	-
Loeb	-	-	-	1	-	3
Panizzi	-	-	-	-	1	1
Gardemeister	-	-	-	1	-	-

Event Leaders

SS.1 > SS.8	Märtin
SS.9 > SS.16	C. McRae

Previous winners

1973	Thérier - Delferrier Alpine Renault A110		1988	Biasion - Siviero Lancia Delta Integrale
1975	Rohrl - Berger Opel Ascona		1989	Biasion - Siviero Lancia Delta Integrale
1976	Kallstrom - Andersson Datsun 160J		1990	Sainz - Moya Toyota Celica GT4
1977	Waldegaard - Thorszelius Ford Escort RS		1991	Kankkunen - Piironen Lancia Delta Integrale 16v
1978	Rohrl - Geistdorfer Fiat 131 Abarth		1992	Auriol - Occelli Lancia Delta Integrale
1979	Waldegaard - Thorszelius Ford escort RS		1993	Biasion - Siviero Ford Escort RS Cosworth
1980	Vatanen - Richards Ford Escort RS		1994	Sainz - Moya Subaru Impreza
1981	Vatanen - Richards Ford Escort RS		1995	Vovos - Stefanis Lancia Delta Integrale
1982	Mouton - Pons Audi Quattro		1996	McRae - Ringer Subaru Impreza
1983	Rohrl - Geistdorfer Lancia Rally 037		1997	Sainz - Moya Ford Escort WRC
1984	Blomqvist - Cederberg Audi Quattro		1998	McRae - Grist Subaru Impreza WRC
1985	Salonen - Harjanne Peugeot 205 T16		1999	Burns - Reid Subaru Impreza WRC
1986	Kankkunen - Piironen Peugeot 205 T16		2000	C. McRae - Grist Ford Focus WRC
1987	Alen - Kivimaki Lancia Delta HF Turbo		2001	C. McRae - Grist Ford Focus RS WRC 01

Kenya

Colin McRae's rally can
be summed up as a win
for tactics and common
sense. Once Tommi
Makinen was out, the
Scot went serenely on
to his third victory in
Kenya and his 25th in
the World
Championship, an
outright record. It was
also Ford's third win in
as many events

8

Experience is essential on the Safari – and McRae has it aplenty, taking a masterly third win in Kenya.

Delecour, on only his second Safari, had to come to terms with the trials of Africa and mechanical woes. He was out with an overheating engine on only the second stage.

THE RACE
LIONTAMER McRAE

But for the fact that he's a born competitor, Marcus Grönholm would have been glad to get out of the Safari Rally so soon. This is one event he hates, probably because he has never quite figured out how to set about it. Obviously it's one for the specialist, but paradoxically the last few winners have also been the best sprinters of the last few years: Colin McRae, Tommi Mäkinen and Richard Burns. Just a little more mental effort, and the Finn will soon work it out. But this year his race ended less than 12 miles from the start of the first section as the 206 WRC's 4-cylinder turbo suddenly downed tools. His Safari had lasted a whole eight

minutes! The World Championship leader's name was the first on a long list. Freddy Loix (clutch) didn't make it to the end of the first section either; Armin Schwarz (alternator) didn't start the second; Toni Gardemeister ripped a wheel off in the third; Francois Delecour's engine expired at the end of the same one and Peter Solberg's on the fourth and last of the first day.

Marcus the great doesn't like this event – and it seems to be mutual. He was out after 10 miles with a dead engine.

The Kenyan rally route might well have been revamped and reformatted with a significant reduction in length and a much more concentrated geographical spread, but this one-off event still retained its own peculiar identity. We've got into the habit of saying that any driver who finishes will finish in the points, and for all the increase in the number of works cars in recent times, the old saying still held good.

On that Friday July 12 the event quickly resolved itself into a duel between Mäkinen and McRae, both former winners, with Carlos Sainz hanging around to pick up any pieces

despite being slowed by damper troubles. Richard Burns, on the other hand, admitted he didn't think his 206 was all that well suited to this event and was unsure of its stability at speed on the very quick local tracks. The first fastest time went to Subaru's Makinen, 21 seconds ahead of the surprising Thomas Radstrom and 1m15s in front of Märtin.

Mäkinen, like Radstrom, for that matter, had given his all. No holding back, and no thoughts of sparing the machinery either. Setting off at a smoother rhythm, McRae then hit back on the next section, giving the lie to his pre-rally pretence of

The Skoda seems to be made for Africa! After a good start, and with a podium finish in sight, Eriksson had to retire with a broken transmission on the second leg.

wishbone and had more than his fair share of punctures as his shockers seized up; Radstrom lost a wheel and covered the 25 miles to the service area with Giraudet in the boot to balance things up; Gilles Panizzi blew hot and cold, with second-fastest time on the third section but a broken rear arm that had to be fixed on the road and then a dreadful slump that came about when dust got into the car and the exhausted Frenchman had to be given oxygen; an unwell Burns broke a damper and also had to stop to nip a fire in the bud. In short, typical African stuff.

Was Mäkinen trying too hard? Maybe, but the first-day leader was definitely out on CS8 between Kerrerie and Seyabei. With the front left wishbone gone he was unable to carry on. Shame, really, he had been having a lot of fun, claiming to have gone through an African stage the previous day faster than he had ever done before, with the old familiar war-cry of 'Flat out'. It may be useful to point out that before the section began the Finn had already lost the lead to McRae as a result of a shock absorber that broke before the day's first section started.

The Scot was really looking after his Focus, driving superbly on tracks that alternate between ultra-quick and dead slow, where touch and instinct are the order of the day. As he explained, 'To win in Kenya, you must always get your speed right when you're approaching whatever difficulty is ahead.' And given that the lie of the land changes each year with the rainfall or as unmaintained roads come into play, knowing the place inside out is not all that much help. Leaving aside his showmanship, McRae has always known how to drive the right way at the right time. And just as Harri Rovanperä was

starting to threaten towards the end of the rally, he knew it was time to put his foot down again. Last but not least, helped by those improving Pirellis and now as solid as a Sherman tank, his Focus was absolutely perfect for those conditions. The winner's only problem was a single damper failure.

It was the right result, but it was a very well managed result as well. Harri Rovanperä finished second again (thanks no doubt to his talents

as a mechanic) and did the most important job for the team, bringing home six precious World Championship points. Still, they fell a long way short of one of the targets they made most noise about at the start of the year – a victory in Kenya.

With fourth place for Märtin, making his debut in a place he hated to start with but warmed to as the miles went by, Ford addded another 14 points to their Championship tally, but the tricolor team still had a

playing a waiting game. Mäkinen did the trick again in the third, and McRae in the fourth. Two scratch times apiece and no half-measures from either man. But then, on the last stage, Mäkinen, who was getting no information at all on his rival's progress, let too much time slip away and his lead, which had been 2m30s, dwindled to just 16 seconds by the end of the opening day – a mere gazelle's breath in the wide open spaces of East Africa.

Retirements apart, and there were plenty, a number of others were going from bad to worse in their wake. Sebastien Loeb bent a

Broken clutch, turbo and engine – and you expect to make it all the way to the end? Not Solberg...

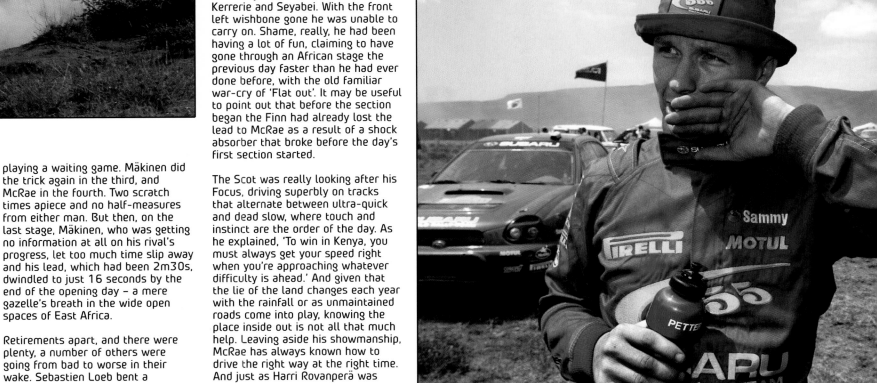

Mäkinen has a liking for this one-off rally, but the maestro's latest trip to Africa in a Subaru met with no success.

substantial advantage following the eighth round on the calendar. Radstrom in third, Loeb (5th) and Panizzi (6th) were the other worthy points-scorers.

So there were a few big names missing from the results. Sainz, who had been third, then second, had been unlucky to come across a fragile Focus – yes, they do exist – and was out midway through the second leg (oil pump). As for Burns, he had swallowed his fill of African dust. Just when he had given himself a shot in the arm with the scratch time on the seventh section, the Englishman broke his 206's left front suspension on the next. Making it to the service area, set in an indescribable dustbowl where the sand was so fine that dust was exactly what it had turned into, Burns put his foot down, both to get up the access ramp at a decent lick but more so to avoid getting stuck.

The wheel couldn't take the load and the studs immediately gave way, the car coming to a halt on three wheels exactly where they didn't want it to. For 30 minutes, i.e. the maximum before exclusion, the no.1 206's crew strove to do the impossible. They put a spare wheel under the right front to try and find some traction, they lowered the tyre pressures, they slid rocks under the wheels, even tried sponsors' banners, but it was no good.

The cloud of dust enveloping the brave duo was all the harder to swallow as the other competitors swept past on their way to the service park. After a half-hour of trying, there was nothing for it but to retire. It was hard to stomach, not

Badly delayed in the early stages, Panizzi drove a sensible rally to a well-deserved sixth place.

There's nothing like the Safari, as the choppers open the road. Kenya first-timer Märtin went about it intelligently.

McRae wins, Sainz retires: Lady Luck had decided which Ford driver she would smile on, and it wasn't the Spaniard.

Sébastien Loeb takes your breath away with every new outing. He knew just how to go about this rally, and with three scratch times he was the joint best performer with the winner.

Third place, after an intelligent race helped in no small part by wise counsel from Denis Giraudet, helped Radstrom redeem his shaky start to his season with Citroën.

only for the lads and the team, but also as far as world-class standards were concerned.

The Safari Rally is a one-off, and the better for it, but putting a service area there was unforgivable. It was a terrible pity for an event that already has so much going against it, economic arguments first and foremost, an event for which some disgruntled souls who can't stand the fact that it IS different have really got the knives out. The Burns affair was a little thing, trivial in the context of the political, economic and sporting context, but it was another instance of the Safari shooting itself in the foot. It's happened so often that the Kenyan event won't be on the 2003 calendar. ∎

What an end to Richard Burns's rally! All their brave efforts were to no avail as he and navigator Robert Reid strove to dig their 206 WRC out of the dustbowl beside the service park.

THE FIRST-TIMERS
STRONG SHOWING BY CITROËN

First time out for Citroën Sport on the Safari Rally – and two Xsara WRC cars in the points, one of them on the podium. Not a bad start on such unique, tricky terrain as East Africa. The French team did their job well, first in the preparation, with a car that was specifically thought out, had reliability very carefully built into it and came with one significant trait in the shape of long suspension travel. They had set about testing on the spot very early, too.

And then they had thought through the team's accommodation and facilities, creating their own bivouac in the service park and saving most of them the long drag from Nairobi, which meant an extra four hours' rest a day. Citroën had drawn heavily on their vast rally-raid experience to get themselves as ready as they could for the Safari. Of course the event itself brought its own share of surprises and lessons learned. First of all they had a terrible problem with overheating shock absorbers, blowing more than their fair share of oil reservoirs, and they had to redo the offending parts on the spot, which meant that some of their mechanics had to make do with three hours' sleep in 72.
The drivers also made the best possible use of the equipment at their disposal. Thomas Radstrom had never competed in Kenya, but before his Citroën days he had tested there and he put in a sterling drive, ably supported by Denis Giraudet. Didier Auriol's one-time navigator tried to instil some of the Millau man's philosophy in the Swede, for while he may never have won it he always

went about it exactly the right way. 'I tried to communicate some of Didier's thinking to Thomas,' the co-driver later wrote, 'and in a sense it went against the grain for a rally driver: use your head, remember it's easier to do a scratch time on the Safari than it is to look after the car.' The crew's journey was not without incident, though. On the second section a steering link gave way, losing them a wheel and then the whole suspension.

As a counterbalance, Giraudet endured 25 miles in the boot, wedged between two spare wheels and getting multiple bruises and a cracked rib for his trouble. The driver then made his way as best he could through the dustbowl that put paid to Burns next day in similar circumstances. The consistent Radstrom, in big trouble with those dampers, managed to claim third place. Loeb was brilliant. After a tricky first section (bent wishbone,

The only Skoda driver to finish, the young Czech brought his employers three points for seventh place.

With Grönholm and Burns gone, Rovanperä was Peugeot's last chance – and he did the job by finishing in second place.

multiple punctures, seized shocks which meant major backache), the newcomer set a total of three scratch times – the same number as the winner – once his Xsara's damping was sorted. But for his early woes, the young Frenchman might have made it on to the podium. His performance would certainly have been a promising one – if the Safari had kept its spot on the calendar. Given all that work, and the Satory stable's fondness for Africa, the event's exclusion from the World Championship must have made them really unhappy.

Citroën (this is Radstrom) had put a lot of work into this rally. It was encouraging for 2003 – until the FIA decided that the Safari would have no place on the World Championship calendar any more!

Another win for Malaysia's Karamjit Singh in the Proton gave him the lead in the Production Championship.

Last word to Hyundai. Like Citroen, the Anglo-Koreans were making their Kenya debut. But they hadn't done any specific development – probably banking on that 2003 exclusion! – except for a bull-bar, raised suspension and an air intake. Needless to say, the Accent proved fragile in the extreme, Freddy Loix and Armin Schwarz withdrawing early on. Kankkunen, on the other hand, ably supported by talented, motivated mechanics, brought his home eighth and helped his employers pocket two points. ■

Kankkunen and Africa go well together. His experience helped him bring the sole surviving Hyundai home, earning the Korean marque two precious points.

Inmarsat Safari Rally of Kenya

8th leg of the 2002 World Rally Championship for constructors and drivers. 5th leg of FIA Production Car WRC Championship.

Date 11th to 14th July 2002

Route
2485 km divided in 3 legs.
12 gravel tests (1010,80 km) scheduled and 11 contested (936,05 km)

1st leg
Friday 12th July (06h00-18h13):
Nairobi > Suswa > Nairobi, 822 km;
4 special stages (336,78 km)

2nd leg
Saturday 13th July (04h45-19h03):
Nairobi > Suswa > Nairobi, 983 km;
5 special stages scheduled (410,87 km)
and 4 contested (336,12 km)

3rd leg
Sunday 14th July (04h45-16h15):
Nairobi > Suswa > Nairobi, 679 km;
3 special stages (263,15 km)

Entry List - Starters - Finishers:
49 - 48 - 11

Conditions: fine and warm.

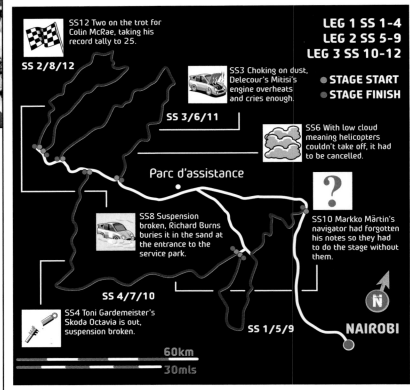

SS12 Two on the trot for Colin McRae, taking his record tally to 25.

SS 2/8/12

SS3 Choking on dust, Delecour's Mitisi's engine overheats and cries enough.

SS 3/6/11

SS6 With low cloud meaning helicopters couldn't take off, it had to be cancelled.

Parc d'assistance

SS8 Suspension broken, Richard Burns buries it in the sand at the entrance to the service park.

SS10 Markko Märtin's navigator had forgotten his notes so they had to do the stage without them.

SS 4/7/10

SS4 Toni Gardemeister's Skoda Octavia is out, suspension broken.

SS 1/5/9

NAIROBI

60km
30mls

LEG 1 SS 1-4
LEG 2 SS 5-9
LEG 3 SS 10-12

● STAGE START
● STAGE FINISH

TOP ENTRIES

1 Richard BURNS - Robert REID
   Peugeot 206 WRC
2 Marcus GRÖNHOLM - Timo
   RAUTIAINEN Peugeot 206 WRC
3 Harri ROVANPERÄ - Risto
   PIETILÄINEN Peugeot 206 WRC
4 Carlos SAINZ - Luis MOYA
   Ford Focus RS WRC 02
5 Colin McRAE - Nicky GRIST
   Ford Focus RS WRC 02
6 Markko MÄRTIN - Michael PARK
   Ford Focus RS WRC 02
7 Francois DELECOUR - Daniel
   GRATALOUP Mitsubishi Lancer Evo WRC
8 Alister McRAE - David SENIOR
   Mitsubishi Lancer Evo WRC
10 Tommi MÄKINEN - Kaj LINDSTRÖM
   Subaru Impreza WRC 2002
11 Petter SOLBERG - Philip MILLS
   Subaru Impreza WRC 2002
14 Kenneth ERIKSSON - Tina THORNER
   Skoda Octavia WRC Evo 2
15 Toni GARDEMEISTER - Paavo
   LUKANDER Skoda Octavia WRC Evo 2
16 Roman KRESTA - Jan TOMANEK
   Skoda Octavia WRC Evo 2
17 Armin SCHWARZ - Manfred HIEMER
   Hyundai Accent WRC 3
18 Freddy LOIX - Sven SMEETS
   Hyundai Accent WRC 3
19 Juha KANKKUNEN - Juha REPO
   Hyundai Accent WRC 3
20 Thomas RADSTRÖM - Denis
   GIRAUDET Citroen Xsara
21 Sébastien LOEB - Daniel ELENA
   Citroen Xsara
23 Gilles PANIZZI - Hervè PANIZZI
   Peugeot 206 WRC
32 Frederic DOR - Didier BRETON
   Subaru Impreza WRC 2002
52 Marcos LIGATO - Ruben GARCIA
   Mitsubishi Lancer Evo 6
53 Alessandro FIORIO - Vittorio
   BRAMBILLA Mitsubishi Lancer Evo 6
57 Toshihiro ARAI - Tony SIRCOMBE
   Subaru Impreza WRX
71 Stefano MARRINI - Tiziana SANDRONI
   Mistubishi Lancer Evo IV
74 Karamjit SINGH - Allen OH
   Proton Pert
100 Rory GREEN - Orson TAYLOR
   Subaru Impreza

Special Stage Times

SS1 Ngema - Kedong (73,63 km)
1.Mäkinen 36'47"8; 2.Radström +21"1;
3.Märtin +1'15"9; 4.Eriksson +1'19"0;
5.Sainz +1'20"1;
6.Gardemeister +1'24"3;
FIA Prod. (17) Ligato +13'53"3

SS2 Seyabei - Kerrerie (81,84 km)
1.C. McRae 37'13"1; 2.Solberg +14'6";
3.Loeb +15"4; 4.Mäkinen +27"9";
5.Rovanperä +47"4; 6.Panizzi +56"8;
FIA Prod. (19) Ligato +10'18"9

SS3 Nailongilok - Il Damat (74,75 km)
1.Mäkinen 44'23"6; 2.Panizzi +1'00"7;
3.A. McRae +1'11"2;
4.C. McRae +1'38"; 5.Märtin +1'39"6;
6.Sainz +2'16"3;
FIA Prod. (18) Singh 16'13"6

SS4 Ntulele - Kedong (106,56 km)
1.C. McRae 51'00"2;
2.Rovanperä +31"0; 3.Sainz +51"8;
4.Mäkinen +2'14"8; 5.Märtin +2'33"2;
6.Loix +3'03"1;
FIA Prod. (14) Ligato +11'57"7

SS5 Kedong - Ngema (73,93 km)
1.Loeb 37'30"6; 2.Sainz +10"8;
3.Rovanperä +19"3; 4.Eriksson +22"3;
5.C. McRae +45"2; 6.Burns +1'15"3;
FIA Prod. (14) Arai +12'48"8

**SS6 Il Damat - Nailongilok
(74,75 km)**
Cancelled - With low cloud meaning
helicopters couldn't take off, it had to be
cancelled.

SS7 Kedong - Ntulele (106,59 km)
1.Burns 51'11"1; 2.C. McRae +16"5;
3.Rovanperä +50"1; 4.Märtin +1'04"1;
5.Panizzi +1'04"2;
6.Radström +1'44"3;
FIA Prod. (14) Arai +14'46"9

SS8 Kerrerie - Seyabai (81,67 km)
1.Panizzi 37'22"4; 2.Loeb +5"1;
3.Rovanperä +43"1; 4.Burns +1'02"8;
5.Radström +1'12"6;
6.C. McRae +1'14"8;
FIA Prod. (10) Singh +9'21"1

SS9 Kedong - Ngema (73,93 km)
1.Loeb 36'36"6; 2.Panizzi +44"0;
3.Rovanperä +1'01"3; 4.C. McRae
+1'31"6; 5.Radström +1'33"0; 6.Märtin
+2'20"1; FIA Prod. (10) Ligato +9'54"6

SS10 Ntulele - Kedong (106,56 km)
1.C. McRae 51'32"1; 2.Rovanperä
+44"1; 3.A.McRae +1'27"2;
4.Loeb +2'04"2; 5.Radström +3'13"7;
6.Panizzi +3'54"7;
FIA Prod. (57) Arai +8'20"9

**SS11 Nailongilok - Il Damat
(74,75 km)**
1.Panizzi 45'26"6; 2.Märtin +1'25"0;
3.C. McRae +1'26"2; 4.Rovanperä
+2'06"3; 5.Radström +3'34"6;
6.Kresta +6'31"5;
FIA Prod. (10) Singh +18'23"7

SS12 Seyabai - Kerrerie (81,84 km)
1.Loeb 36'35"1; 2.Märtin +57"9;
3.Panizzi +1'54"9; 4.Rovanperä
+3'25"7; 5.Kankkunen +3'39"2;
6.Radström +3'44"0;
FIA Prod. (10) Singh +8'40"8

Results

WRC

	Driver/Navigator	Car	Gr.	Time
1	C. McRae - Grist	Ford Focus RS WRC 02	A	7h58'28"
2	Rovanperä - Pietilainen	Peugeot 206 WRC		+ 2'50"9
3	Radström - Giraudet	Citroën Xsara WRC		+ 18'38"6
4	Märtin - Park	Ford Focus RS WRC 02		+ 21'28"0
5	Loeb - Elena	Citroën Xsara WRC		+ 21'48"1
6	Panizzi - Panizzi	Peugeot 206 WRC		+ 34'41"0
7	Kresta - Tomanek	Skoda Octavia WRC Evo 2		+ 54'38"1
8	Kankkunen - Repo	Hyundai Accent WRC 3		+ 1h11'31"5
9	A. McRae - Senior	Mitsubishi Lancer Evo WRC		+ 1h17'13"2
10	Singh - Oh	Proton Pert	Prod.	+ 2h29'27"2

Leading Retirements (37)

SS.8	Burns - Reid	Peugeot 206 WRC	Stuck in sand
SS.8	Sainz - Moya	Ford Focus RS WRC 02	Oil pressure
SS.8	Mäkinen - Lindström	Subaru Impreza WRC 2002	Suspension
SS.7	Eriksson - Thörner	Skoda Octavia WRC Evo 2	Transmission
SS.4	Solberg - Mills	Subaru Impreza WRC 2002	Engine
SS.4	Gardemeister - Lükander	Skoda Octavia WRC Evo 2	Suspension
SS.3	Delecour - Grataloup	Mitsubishi Lancer Evo WRC	Engine
SS.1	Schwarz - Hierner	Hyundai Accent WRC 3	Engine
SS.1	Loix - Smeets	Hyundai Accent WRC 3	Clutch
SS.1	Grönholm - Rautiäinen	Peugeot 206 WRC	Engine

Championship Classifications

FIA Drivers (8/14)
1. Grönholm 37; 2. C. McRea 30; 3. Sainz 23; 4. Panizzi 21;
5. Burns 19; 6. Rovanperä 18; 7. Solberg 15; 8. Mäkinen 14; 9. Loeb 8;
10. Bugalski, Märtin 7; 12. Radström 4; 13. A. McRae, Gardemeister 2;
15. Eriksson 1

FIA Constructors (8/14)
1. Peugeot 83; 2. Ford 69; 3. Subaru 35; 4. Skoda 8; 5. Mitsubishi 7;
6. Hyundai 6

FIA Production Car WRC (5/8)
1. Singh 24; 2. Ferreyros 20; 3. Arai, Trelles 12; 5. Sohlberg 10;
6. Iliev 9; 7. Rowe 5; 8. Ipatti, Baldini & Girdauskas 4; 11. Fiorio 3;
12. Ligato, Harrach & Marrini 2; 15. Kollevold 1

FIA Junior WRC (3/6)
1. Sola 13; 2. Tuohino, Dallavilla 12; 4. Duval 11; 5. Caldani 10;
6. Feghali, Basso 4; 8. Carlsson, Galli 3; 10. Doppelreiter, Rowe 2;
12. Schelle, Foss 1

Performers

	1	2	3	4	5	6
C. McRae	3	1	1	2	1	1
Loeb	3	1	1	2	-	1
Panizzi	2	2	1	-	1	2
Mäkinen	2	-	-	2	-	-
Burns	1	-	-	1	-	1
Rovanperä	-	2	4	2	1	-
Märtin	-	2	1	1	2	1
Sainz	-	1	1	-	1	1
Radström	-	1	-	-	4	2
Solberg	-	1	-	-	-	-
A.McRae	-	-	2	-	-	-
Eriksson	-	-	-	2	-	-
Kankkunen	-	-	-	-	1	-
Kresta	-	-	-	-	-	1
Gardemeister	-	-	-	-	-	1

Event Leaders

SS.1 > SS.4	Mäkinen
SS.5 > SS.12	C. McRae

Previous winners

1973	Mehta - Drews Datsun 240 Z	1988	Biasion - Siviero Lancia Delta Intégrale
1974	Singh - Doig Mitsubishi Colt Lancer	1989	Biasion - Siviero Lancia Delta Integrale
1975	Andersson - Hertz Peugeot 504	1990	Waldegaard - Gallagher Toyota Celica GT-Four
1976	Singh - Doig Mitsubishi Colt Lancer	1991	Kankkunen - Piironen Lancia Delta Integrale
1977	Waldegaard - Thorszelius Ford Escort RS	1992	Sainz - Moya Toyota Celica Turbo 4WD
1978	Nicolas - Lefebvre Peugeot 504 v6 Coupé	1993	Kankkunen - Piironen Toyota Celica Turbo 4WD
1979	Metha - Doughty Datsun 160 J	1994	Duncan - Williamson Toyota Celica Turbo 4WD
1980	Metha - Doughty Datsun 160 J	1995	Fujimoto - Hertz Toyota Celica Turbo 4WD
1981	Metha - Doughty Datsun Violet GT	1996	Mäkinen - Harjanne Mitsubishi Lancer EV.3
1982	Metha - Doughty Datsun Violet GT	1997	McRae - Grist Subaru Impreza WRC
1983	Vatanen - Harryman Opel Ascona 400	1998	Burns - Reid Mitsubishi Carisma GT
1984	Waldegaard - Thorzelius Toyota Celica Turbo	1999	Colin Mc Rae - Nicky Grist Ford Focus WRC
1985	Kankkunen - Gallagher Toyota Celica Turbo	2000	Burns - Reid Subaru Impreza WRC
1986	Waldegaard - Gallagher Toyota Celica Turbo	2001	Mäkinen - Mannisenmäki Mitsubishi Lancer EVO
1987	Mikkola - Hertz Audi 200 Quattro		

Finland

Suomi-Finland

Richard Burns and Harri Rovanperä both made excellent starts, but they paid dearly for their mistakes and eventually had to give best to Marcus Grönholm. Peugeot and the Finn took an iron grip on the event.

THE RACE
GRÖNHOLM OWES ONE TO BURNS

Gloom and doom all round. Quite a few drivers had hoped to shake up the now-established order as they headed for familiar, classic territory. And Peugeot had faltered over the three previous events, handing Sainz the Argentine win, fighting in vain against the Ford tide in Greece and letting storm force McRae blow through the Safari, but it was all just a mirage.

The 206 has always been a formidable force up here in the land of the Finns – in three previous attempts it had been beaten just once, by its own newness, back in 1999. Up here reliability isn't a factor, and the frailty that dogged the car for so long has never played it any tricks on the tracks and over the bumps around Jyväskylä. And it wasn't about to start, given that Michel Nandan and his inspired gang of engineers had put so much of their recent effort into giving the car bullet-proof reliability to match its bullet-like speed.

So it was just tough luck for any driver who couldn't strap himself into one of the Lionesses – the rest were fighting for scraps on the slippery Finnish slopes.
Just by way of a change, the curtain-raiser for the ninth round of the 2002 World Championship was a super-special on the Thursday evening. Whizzing around the Jyväskylä racecourse, Richard Burns served notice that he was a man on a mission, setting the fastest time and, for the first time in any rally this year, going into the lead. But that happy state of affairs for the Englishman didn't last long. By next day, when they got on the hard stuff, Grönholm took control again. The reigning World Champion has given proof enough that

Once again Freddy Loix made a fine start – and once again the Accent's reliability cut it short, its handling and brakes dropping off as the rally progressed.

he has what it takes to become only the third non-Scandinavian, after Sainz and Auriol, to win in Finland. The Englishman took full advantage of the starting order, going off fifth as opposed to his Finnish arch-rival who went first, and gave an excellent account of himself on a first leg blessed by balmy weather. In fact Burns grabbed five scratch times on the nine stages on this first real day of the rally, leaving two to Grönholm, who was delayed near day's end by a broken damper, one to Harri Rovanperä and the last to an astonishing Carlos Sainz, as combative as ever.

Reading between the lines of the results, it was easy to see that try though he might Rovanperä would

Sainz had decided to spare no effort in his bid to be the first non-Peugeot finisher. But he had to concede to Solberg after a 10-second penalty for a jump start on the third leg.

have a hard job staying with his stablemates. Good old Harri is quick, but he wasn't as clever as Burns at making his position on the road count. Yes, he did end up second on the leg, 12 seconds adrift of the Englishman, but his days were numbered.

Behind the untouchable trio at the front, consternation reigned. Tommi Mäkinen, outdriven by Petter Solberg, was concerned about a down-on-power engine. The Fords were fighting hard, but they were such a long way back. And the rest? Well, it was a rout: all day long Kenneth Eriksson was plagued by mysterious mechanical woes on his Skoda, then gave up after the beginnings of a fire. Towards the end, Francois Delecour and Francois Duval also laid down their arms, with a damaged engine cradle and broken suspension, the Frenchman having also had trouble with his power steering. But what was most striking was the air of resignation hanging over all the non-Peugeot teams. Even the privateer 206's were quicker than the other works cars!

Among them, outstanding prospect Juuso Pykälistö, a protégé of Marcus Grönholm, ran fourth for a while before retiring, leading Sébastien Lindholm, a cousin of the self-same Marcus. His race may have been cut short, but the young fellow's potential was there for all to see. One of the things Marcus Grönholm – Marcus the agent, not Marcus the driver – will take most pleasure from this season is the official Peugeot contract Pykälistö put his name to soon after. For the time being, though, the Finn and his Lion had a race to finish and an Englishman to lay low. For Burns was starting to make a nuisance of himself, refusing to lie down.

Not only that, he stretched his lead on the first special stage of the second day. But Finland has its pitfalls, and he hasn't figured all the traps out yet. The one that mattered was a very well-known bump on the equally famous Ouuninpohja stage. In previous years, driving his Subaru, Richard Burns didn't need to negotiate it, he just jumped it and came back down on all four wheels. But the 206 is no Impreza, this lioness landing heavily on her nose before the driver caught it up and kept it on the road. But the damage was done: a turbo pipe was broken, which left the World Champion to make his way slowly to the stop and the service area, where his mechanics had just a little bit of work to do.
Engine cradle, front suspension, radiator and intercooler were all changed, to say nothing of the pipes

Sebastian Lindholm never misses his home rally in his privateer 206 WRC. Grönholm's happy-go-lucky cousin came home seventh this time.

113

Harri Rovanperä gave everything in the attempt to win but broke his suspension midway through the second leg while in the lead.

A podium finish beckoned, but sadly McRae's Ford went up in smoke right at the end – a pity, as he had driven a very intelligent rally.

and cables destroyed by the impact. Unable to complete their mechanical tour de force in the allotted 20 minutes, Burns was late out and also picked up a 20-second penalty. No matter: by that stage his race was run and lost. 'Just when I was starting to think I could beat the Finns on their own turf,' he said. It really was a shame, because Burns' brilliance would have forced Grönholm into a major effort of his own. While the Englishman trod water, Rovanperä took over the field-marshal's baton. But then, on the next stage, he hit a rock as he went in too deep and punctured his own 206's front right tyre. He did finish the stage, but with broken suspension and another stage to come before the service area he wasn't going any further than that. So in the space of two stages Marcus Grönholm regained a lead he would hang on to until the next day's finish. 'I'd rather Harri had kept going,' he said determinedly, 'because I was going to win anyway!' On the technical side, he had opted to start the rally with the much talked-about hydraulic anti-roll bars, already a standard part of the 206's make-up on tarmac. But he found it a little unsettling on gravel, had them replaced by the older system and it gave him a real burst of energy. Rovanperä probably wouldn't have been able to hold him off for long.

In fact it was a very well put-together win. On the first day, Grönholm never dropped his bundle despite the disadvantage of the running order. That helped him put pressure on his team mates on day two, while he avoided making their mistakes – due no doubt in part to that same pressure. So the Finn had no real worries about the eventual outcome, pocketing his third successive home win after the final leg. The real interest lay with the fight for the minor placings. While Burns set about consolidating second place with more scratch times, Colin McRae and Carlos Sainz were keeping a wary eye on troublemakers Petter Solberg and Markko Märtin as they steamed up behind them in the closing stages.

The Scot ran first of the non-Peugeots for quite a while but had to retire two stages from the finish with his Focus on fire. As for the Spaniard, he couldn't contain the fiery Norwegian as he swept past to third place on the podium, but he did manage to stay ahead of Märtin, this time not quite the same man who had such a huge Finnish Rally in 2001.

But hordes of his supporters had come in from his Estonian homeland, separated from Norway by a narrow strip of the Baltic Sea. Sixth place went to a vexed Tommi Mäkinen. It's not so long ago that the four-time World Champion was the benchmark where Finland was concerned. How times change... ∎

Finland's not easy in a WRC, as Sébastien Loeb found out, but he still managed a top-ten finish.

Burns's mishaps, then Rovanperä's, made life easier for Marcus Grönholm, unbeaten in his home rally since 2000.

WHAT WAS NEW
THERE'S STILL SOME WORK TO DO...

To think that only yesterday the Mitsubishi Lancer was being called the Ferrari of the rally scene: quick, strong, beautifully driven, the car and its star driver used to monopolise the wins. Mitsubishi brought in a Lancer WRC in 2001 that didn't work. Now Mäkinen is driving for Subaru and Marlboro, sponsor in those halcyon days, is getting ready to go. But the Japanese marque brought a major evolution of their car to Finland in the shape of the eagerly anticipated Lancer WRC Step 2.

Before the event got under way the drivers and technicians were waxing lyrical about the new machine and the potential it had shown in testing. But that was before we got going... The

engine had had a major overhaul, with changes to intercooler, manifold and turbo, but so had the aerodynamics, the weight distribution and the suspension. They all seemed to be steps in the right direction. The aim was to start bridging the gap to the other teams, but it soon became obvious that that was some way off. The feistiest of the three drivers entered was Jaani Paasonen, who overshadowed both Francois Delecour and Alister McRae on his way to an eventual eighth place behind Lindholm's privateer 206.

Mitsubishi's Frenchman fought like a tiger, easily staying ahead of Alister McRae before retiring at the end of the first leg with a problem on the engine cradle. As for McRae Junior, he suffered a string of mechanical misfortunes and gave up with suspension broken and the Lancer on fire.

For the first time Mitsubishi brought out their Step 2 Lancer WRC, but the end result was as disappointing for Alister McRae, in action here, as it was for Delecour and Paasonen.

Good news for Petter Solberg's supporters: not only does he love them back, he also claimed an outstanding third place, to the detriment of Carlos Sainz.

The other evolution we were waiting to see came from Skoda. For budgetary reasons, the Octavia WRC has scarcely developed since its World Championship debut, its last homologation dating back to September 2000.

Here too it was the engine that had been the in-house mechanics' main priority (intake manifold, exhaust redesign, turbo, cooling and therefore the aerodynamics too), but the Finnish results showed the Skodas still lagging a long way behind the other works cars. Eriksson was forced into early retirement while Gardemeister was 12th, though he could have got himself into the top ten but for a time penalty picked up for being late after stopping to make his own repairs to a fuel injection sensor. So, Herr Volkswagen, when are you going to give your Czech team some serious funding? After all, nothing seems too much for those Audis in endurance racing...

Citroën were also making their first appearance in Finland. The French team set out to learn the lie of the land, banking on their Swedish star to set the sparks flying.

It didn't happen: as was the case in Greece, the Xsara was clearly short of gravel preparation. One question kept coming up: why on earth had they gone for Radstrom ahead of Auriol? The Scandinavian put in a decent enough first leg but then fell victim to his old demons, going off near the end while fighting for ninth place. Will we ever know why they really took Radstrom instead of Auriol? As for Sébastien Loeb, he consistently ran ahead of his teammate and finished 10th in a place he was seeing for the first time and in a car that wasn't really up to the job. Making consistent progress, Loeb set a number of very encouraging times midway through and once again, of all the newcomers, Loeb was the one who really caught the eye. ∎

Neste Rally of Finland

9th leg of the 2002 World Rally Championship for constructors and drivers.6th leg of FIA Production Car WRC Championship.

Date 8th to 11th August 2002

Parcours
1703,22 km divided in 3 legs.
22 special stages on dirt roads
(410,52 km)

1st leg
Friday 9th August (08h00-21h31):
Jyvaskyla > Jyvaskyla, 565,72 km;
9 special stages (130,63 km)

2nd leg
Saturday 10th August (06h00-21h11):
Jyvaskyla > Jyvaskyla, 774,83 km;
6 special stages (185,55 km)

3rd leg
Sunday 11th August (07h20-17h00):
Jyvaskyla > Jyvaskyla, 362,77 km;
6 special stages (94,34 km)

Entry List - Starters - Finishers:
83 - 77 - 30

Conditions: dry, with dry roads clearing as cars went through.

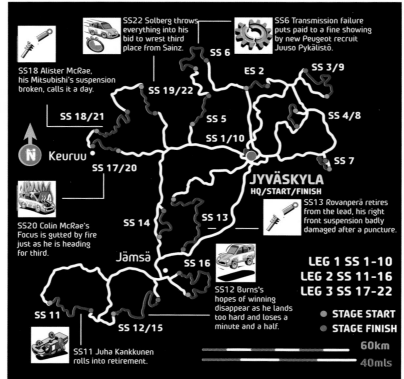

SS22 Solberg throws everything into his bid to wrest third place from Sainz.

SS6 Transmission failure puts paid to a fine showing by new Peugeot recruit Juuso Pykälistö.

SS18 Alister McRae, his Mitsubishi's suspension broken, calls it a day.

SS20 Colin McRae's Focus is gutted by fire just as he is heading for third.

SS13 Rovanperä retires from the lead, his right front suspension badly damaged after a puncture.

SS12 Burns's hopes of winning disappear as he lands too hard and loses a minute and a half.

SS11 Juha Kankkunen rolls into retirement.

Keuruu

JYVÄSKYLA
HQ/START/FINISH

Jämsä

LEG 1 SS 1-10
LEG 2 SS 11-16
LEG 3 SS 17-22

● STAGE START
● STAGE FINISH

60km
40mls

TOP ENTRIES

1	Richard BURNS - Robert REID	Peugeot 206 WRC
2	Marcus GRÖNHOLM - Timo RAUTIAINEN	Peugeot 206 WRC
3	Harri ROVANPERÄ - Voitto SILANDER	Peugeot 206 WRC
4	Carlos SAINZ - Luis MOYA	Ford Focus RS WRC 02
5	Colin McRAE - Nicky GRIST	Ford Focus RS WRC 02
6	Markko MÄRTIN - Michael PARK	Ford Focus RS WRC 02
7	François DELECOUR - D.GRATALOUP	Mitsubishi Lancer Evo WRC 2
8	Alister MCRAE - David SENIOR	Mitsubishi Lancer Evo WRC 2
9	Jani PAASONEN - Arto KAPANEN	Mitsubishi Lancer Evo WRC 2
10	Tommi MÄKINEN - Kaj LINDSTRÖM	Subaru Impreza WRC 2002
11	Petter SOLBERG - Philip MILLS	Subaru Impreza WRC 2002
14	Kenneth ERIKSSON - Tina THORNER	Skoda Octavia WRC Evo 3
15	Toni GARDEMEISTER - P. LUKANDER	Skoda Octavia WRC Evo 3
17	Armin SCHWARZ - Manfred HIEMER	Hyundai Accent WRC 3
18	Freddy LOIX - Sven SMEETS	Hyundai Accent WRC 3
19	Juha KANKKUNEN - Juha REPO	Hyundai Accent WRC 3
20	Thomas RADSTRÖM - D. GIRAUDET	Citroën Xsara WRC
21	Sébastien LOEB - Daniel ELENA	Citroën Xsara WRC
23	Gilles PANIZZI - Hervè PANIZZI	Peugeot 206 WRC
24	Francois DUVAL - Jean-Marc FORTIN	Ford Focus RS WRC 02
25	Sebastian LINDHOLM - T. HANTUNEN	Peugeot 206 WRC
26	Armin KREMER - D. SCHNEPPENHEIM	Ford Focus RS WRC 02
27	Juuso PYKALISTO - Esko MERTSALMI	Peugeot 206 WRC
28	Janne TUOHINO - Petri VIHAVAINEN	Ford Focus RS WRC 02
33	Timo SALONEN - Launo HEINONEN	Peugeot 206 WRC
34	Tomasz KUCHAR - Maciej SZCEPANIAK	Toyota Corolla WRC
53	Alessandro FIORIO - V. BRAMBILLA	Mitsubishi Lancer Evo 6
54	Ramon FERREYROS - Diego VALLEJO	Mitsubishi Lancer Evo 6
55	Saulius GIRDAUSKAS - Z. SAKALAUSKAS	Mitsubishi Lancer Evo 6
58	Luca BALDINI - Marco MUZZARELLI	Mitsubishi Lancer Evo 6
66	Dimitar ILIEV - Petar SIVOV	Mitsubishi Lancer Evo 7
73	Martin ROWE - Chris WOOD	Mitsubishi Lancer Evo 7
74	Karamjit SINGH - Allen OH	Proton Pert
75	Kristian SOHLBERG - Jakke HONKANEN	Mitsubishi Lancer Evo 7

Special Stage Times

SS1 SSS Killeri I (2,05 km)
1.Burns 1'16"7; 2.Sainz & Solberg +0"8;
4.C. McRae +1"1; 5.Grönholm +1"3;
6.Rovanperä +1"4; FIA Prod. (33) Ligato +6"5

SS2 Valkola (8,42 km)
1.Grönholm 4'27"9; 2.Rovanperä +1"7;
3.C. McRae +2"5; 4.Pykalisto +3"3;
5.Burns +4"0; 6.Solberg +5"7;
FIA Prod. (33) Ligato +27"7

SS3 Lankamaa I (23,44 km)
1.Burns 11'28"7; 2.Grönholm +1"7;
3.Pykalisto +1"8; 4.Rovanperä +3"1;
5.Lindholm +12"6; 6.C. McRae +13"6;
FIA Prod. (31) Ligato +1'02"3

SS4 Laukaa I (11,80 km)
1.Rovanperä 5'47"0; 2.Burns +0"3;
3.Pykalisto +2"9; 4.Grönholm +4"1;
5.Lindholm +5"0; 6.Märtin +5"7;
FIA Prod. (31) Sohlberg +32"1

SS5 Mokkipera (13,38 km)
1.Burns 6'22"6; 2.Grönholm +0"6;
3.Rovanperä +1"4; 4.Pykalisto +5"5;
5.Solberg +6"5; 6.Märtin +6"6;
FIA Prod. (31) Ligato +43"1

SS6 Palsankyla (25,47 km)
1.Burns 13'33"0; 2.Rovanperä +2"9;
3.Grönholm +5"0; 4.C. McRae +14"1;
5.Sainz +14"8; 6.Solberg +18"3;
FIA Prod. (27) Ligato +1'26"8

SS7 Ruuhimaki (8,78 km)
1.Burns 4'44"6; 2.Grönholm +0"2;
3.Rovanperä +1"0; 4.Sainz +4"8; 5.Märtin &
Radström +6"4; FIA Prod. (27) Ligato +30"2

SS8 Laukaa II (11,80 km)
1.Grönholm 5'42"9; 2.Burns +1"0;
3.Rovanperä +1"8; 4.3.Solberg +3"9;
5.Sainz, C. McRae & Märtin +7"4;
FIA Prod. (31) Manfrinato +46"8

SS9 Lankamaa II (23,44 km)
1.Burns 11'21"5; 2.Rovanperä +4"3;
3.Solberg +9"4; 4.Sainz +12"8;
5.Grönholm +14"8; 6.Kankkunen 16"0;
FIA Prod. (26) Fiorio +1'46"4

SS10 SSS Killeri II (2,05 km)
1.Sainz 1'17"2; 2.Grönholm +0"2;
3.Rovanperä +0"4;
4.C. McRae & Solberg +0"6; 6.Burns +0"7;
FIA Prod. (25) Fiorio +6"2

SS11 Talviainen (25,73 km)
1.Burns 12'47"3; 2.Grönholm +7"3;
3.Rovanperä +8"3; 4.Märtin +24"7;
5.Lindholm +25"4; 6.Solberg +28"7;
FIA Prod. (26) Sohlberg +1'27"5;

SS12 Ouuninpohja I (34,13 km)
1.Rovanperä 15'58"6; 2.Grönholm +6"3;
3.C. McRae +30"4; 4.Sainz +30"5;
5.Märtin +36"4; 6.Lindholm +36"7;
FIA Prod. (20) Sohlberg +1'44"

SS13 Moksi-Leustu (40,84 km)
1.Grönholm 20'31"9; 2.Burns +13"4;
3.C. McRae +22"4; 4.Sainz +33"0;
5.Solberg +34"6; 6.Märtin +37"4;
FIA Prod. (25) Fiorio +1'10"8

SS14 Ehikki (14,89 km)
1.Grönholm 6'57"8; 2.Burns +1"4;
3.C. McRae +2"2; 4.Sainz +3"6;
5.Solberg +4"4; 6.Märtin +6"8;
FIA Prod. (18) Sohlberg +36"5

SS15 Ouuninpohja II (34,13 km)
1.Grönholm 11'26"; 2.Solberg +5"6;
3.Burns +8"6; 4.Märtin +10"3;
5.McRae +10"8; 6.Sainz +16"1;
FIA Prod. (19) Sohlberg +1'09"8

SS16 Vaheri-Himos (35,83 km)
1.Burns 17'58"0; 2.Grönholm +3"9;
3.C. McRae +8"4; 4.Sainz +10"5;
5.Märtin +18"4; 6.Solberg +23"8;
FIA Prod. (16) Fiorio +1'37"5

SS17 Keuruu I (11,80 km)
1.Burns 5'28"2; 2.Märtin +0"3;
3.Grönholm +0"5; 4.Paasonen +1"1;
5.Sainz +1"3; 6.Solberg +2"5;
FIA Prod. (19) Sohlberg +28"1

SS18 Jukojarvi I (22,70 km)
1.C. McRae 11'11"2; 2.Burns & Sainz +0"4;
4.Solberg +2"7; 5.Märtin +3"7;
6.Grönholm +4"1;

FIA Prod. (18) Sohlberg +59"1

SS19 Kuunpera I (12,67 km)
1. Solberg 6'06"4; 2.Märtin +0"7;
3.C. McRae +2"0; 4.Grönholm +2"4;
5.Burns +2"9; 6.Radström +3"1;
FIA Prod. (18) Sohlberg +39"1

SS20 Keuruu II (11,80 km)
1.Märtin 5'20"9; 2.Burns +1"0;
3.Solberg +1"1; 4.Sainz +2"4;
5.Grönholm +2"5; 6.C. McRae +5"5;
FIA Prod. (18) Sohlberg +33"4

SS21 Jukojarvi II (22,70 km)
1.Märtin 11'02"4; 2.Burns & Solberg +2"8;
4.Grönholm +4"6; 5.Sainz +5"6; 6.Mäkinen
+8"3; FIA Prod. (17) Fiorio +1'12"9

SS22 Kuunpera II (12,67 km)
1.Burns & Grönholm 6'02"2; 3.Märtin +0"5;
4.Sainz +1"7; 5.Solberg +3"1;
6.Gardemeister +5"4;
FIA Prod. (20) Sohlberg +41"1

Results   WRC

	Driver/Navigator	Car	Gr.	Time
1	Grönholm – Rautiainen	Peugeot 206 WRC	A	3h17'52"5
2	Bruns – Reid	Peugeot 206 WRC		+ 1'27"3
3	Solberg – Mills	Subaru Impreza WRC 2002		+ 2'49"6
4	Sainz – Moya	Ford Focus RS WRC 02		+ 2'53"8
5	Märtin – Park	Ford Focus RS WRC 02		+ 3'10"0
6	Mäkinen – Lindström	Subaru Impreza WRC 2002		+ 4'34"1
7	Lindholm – Hantunen	Peugeot 206 WRC		+ 5'36"4
8	Paasonen – Kapanen	Mitsubishi Lancer Evo WRC 2		+ 5'55"3
9	Loix – Smeet	Hyundai Accent WRC 3		+ 6'07"8
10	Loeb – Elena	Citroën Xsara WRC		+ 6'13"6
18	Fiorio – Brambilla	Mitsubishi Lancer Evo 7	Prod.	+ 24'49"3

Leading Retirements (47)

SS 21	Radström – Giraudet	Citroën Xsara WRC	Off
SS.20	C. McRae – Grist	Ford Focus RS WRC 02	Fire
SS.18	A. McRae – Senior	Mitsubishi Lancer Evo WRC 2	Suspension
SS.13	Rovanperä – Silander	Peugeot 206 WRC	Puncture
SS.11	Kankkunen – Repo	Hyundai Accent WRC 3	Off
SS.9	Duval – Fortin	Ford Focus RS WRC 02	Suspension
SS.9	Delecour – Grataloup	Mitsubishi Lancer Evo WRC 2	Suspension
SS.6	Eriksson – Thorner	Skoda Octavia WRC Evo 2	Out of fuel
SS.6	Pykälistö – Mertsalmi	Peugeot 206 WRC	Gearbox

Championship Classifications

FIA Drivers (9/14)
1. Grönholm 47; 2. C. McRae 30; 3. Sainz 26; 4. Burns 25;
5. Panizzi 21; 6. Solberg 19; 7. Rovanperä 18; 8. Mäkinen 15;
9. Märtin 9; 10. Loeb 8; 11. Bugalski 7; 12. Radström 4;
13. A. McRae, Gardemeister 2; 15. Eriksson 1

FIA Constructors (9/14)
1. Peugeot 99; 2. Ford 74; 3. Subaru 40; 4. Skoda 8; 5. Mitsubishi 7;
6. Hyundai 6

FIA Production Car WRC (6/8)
1. Singh 28; 2. Ferreyros 20; 3. Sohlberg 16; 4. Fiorio 13; 5. Arai,
Trelles 12; 7. Iliev 9; 8. Girdauskas 7; 9. Rowe 5; 10. Ipatti, Baldini 4;
12. Ligato, Harrach, Marrini, Kollevold & De Dominics 2

FIA Junior WRC (3/6)
1. Sola 13; 2. Tuohino, Dallavilla 12; 4. Duval 11; 5. Caldani 10;
6. Feghali, Basso 4; 8. Carlsson, Galli 3; 10. Doppelreiter, Rowe 2;
12. Schelle, Foss 1

Performers

	1	2	3	4	5	6
Burns	10	7	1	–	2	1
Grönholm	6	7	2	3	3	1
Rovanperä	2	3	5	1	–	1
Märtin	2	2	1	2	5	4
Solberg	1	3	2	3	4	5
Sainz	1	2	–	8	4	1
C. McRae	1	–	6	3	2	2
Pykalisto	–	–	2	2	–	–
Paasonen	–	–	–	1	–	–
Lindholm	–	–	–	–	2	1
Radström	–	–	–	–	1	1
Kankkunen	–	–	–	–	–	1
Gardemeister	–	–	–	–	–	1
Mäkinen	–	–	–	–	–	1

Event Leaders

SS.1	Burns
SS.2 > SS.3	Grönholm
SS.4 > SS.10	Burns
SS.11 > SS.12	Rovanperä
SS.13 > SS.22	Grönholm

Previous winners

1973	Mäkinen – Liddon Ford Escort RS 1600	1988	Alen – Kivimaki Lancia Delta Integrale
1974	Mikkola – Davenport Ford Escort RS 1600	1989	Ericsson – Billstam Mitsubishi Galant VR4
1975	Mikkola – Aho Toyota Corolla	1990	Sainz – Moya Toyota Celica GT-Four
1976	Alen – Kivimaki Fiat 131 Abarth	1991	Kankkunen – Piironen Lancia Delta Integrale 16v
1977	Hamalaiinen – Tiukkanen Ford Escort RS	1992	Auriol – Occelli Lancia Delta Integrale
1978	Alen – Kivimaki Fiat 131 Abarth	1993	Kankkunen – Giraudet Toyota Celica Turbo 4WD
1979	Alen – Kivimaki Fiat 131 Abarth	1994	Mäkinen – Harjanne Ford Escort RS Cosworth
1980	Alen – Kivimaki Fiat 131 Abarth	1995	Mäkinen – Harjanne Mitsubishi Lancer Ev.3
1981	Vatanen – Richards Ford Escort RS	1996	Mäkinen – Harjanne Mitsubishi Lancer Ev.3
1982	Mikkola – Hertz Audi Quattro	1997	Mäkinen – Harjanne Mitsubishi Lancer Ev.4
1983	Mikkola – Hertz Audi Quattro	1998	Mäkinen – Mannisenmäki Mitsubishi Lancer Ev.5
1984	Vatanen – Harryman Peugeot 205 T16	1999	Kankkunen – Repo Subaru Impreza WRC
1985	Salonen – Harjanne Peugeot 205 T16	2000	Grönholm – Rautiainen Peugeot 206 WRC
1986	Salonen – Harjanne Peugeot 205 T16	2001	Grönholm – Rautiainen Peugeot 206 WRC
1987	Alen – Kivimaki Lancia Delta HF Turbo		

Deutschland

Sébastien Loeb secured his maiden World Championship win ahead of a gaggle of World Champions, foremost among them Marcus Grönholm and Richard Burns. "My first second win," joked the Frenchman as he got his own back for Monte Carlo.

10

As lively as ever on tarmac, Bruno Thiry put in a great drive for fifth in his privateer 206 WRC.

A pumped-up Armin Schwarz completed a fine opening leg in front of his home fans, but then had a big off shortly before the end of the second.

THE RACE
A FIRST FOR LOEB!

No-one can rewrite the record books, but Gilles Panizzi's absence weighed heavily on the Rally of Germany. The top tarmac driver played no part in the event after an accident at home in which he fell from a ladder and broke his shoulder. That left Peugeot with a decision to make: who could they give the car to and expect him to score some points for them? The French management could have thrown top national driver and Jean-Pierre Nicolas protégé Cédric Robert in at the deep end, or they could have called up Bruno Thiry,

who had been driving a Belgian privateer 206 and was about to have a superb rally, though of course they weren't to know that. They might just as easily have brought back a great ex-driver of theirs who knew the car, such as Didier Auriol: the veteran was the only man to have beaten Panizzi in equal 206 equipment (Catalonia 2001), but the dispute between team and driver goes too deep for reason and common sense to prevail. So in the face of all those logical solutions, the one they came up with was Harri Rovanperä.

The Scandinavian Lucky Luke look-alike is a nice guy, one who can be quick on gravel or ice, but on tarmac

Matching Delecour's times in equal machinery on tarmac is no simple task, but Alister McRae really shone early in the event.

he is less than great. The alleged aim of this choice was to maintain the harmony in the team.

Nevertheless, by handing Rovanperä that poisoned chalice – he again proved very uncomfortable on the bitumen – Peugeot was letting him know that his pretensions to an all-round, full-time drive were perhaps a wee bit ill-founded. No-one in the Lion camp will confirm that interpretation, but in the end it all seemed to fit.

The things we do in the name of politics! Thank goodness the French team management are also passionate supporters of this wonderful sport: otherwise you might be inclined to think they have been spending too much time with their Anglo-Saxon arch-rivals.

What it all added up to was that the French outfit arrived ill-equipped for battle. Mind you, Grönholm had done the event in non-Championship guise the year before, an advantage the bold Marcus exploited to the full. And he wasn't the only one: Philippe Bugalski won it in a Xsara in 2001, and Francois Delecour had also graced the event in a Ford Focus.

Gronholm wasn't having anybody else opening the scoring on the first special, he and his 206 flung themselves into the fight straight away. He shared the fastest time with Richard Burns – Panizzi may not have been there, but the Peugeots certainly were. So was Loeb. The Alsace man – the local hero (though some Belgian onlookers did point out that Bruno Thiry lives closer to the heart of the

Marcus Grönholm just keeps getting better on tarmac, as his drive in Germany showed. No-one was more surprised than the man himself – at times he was really flirting with disaster.

No luck for Carlos Sainz at all. Gearbox problems, a poor tyre choice and engine trouble saw the Ford driver plummet down the leaderboard.

German event than the Citroën driver) – drew on the massive crowd support to grab all the other scratch times for the remainder of the opening leg. Hats off! He managed to avoid the woes that afflicted Jesus Puras (a timely stand-in for Thomas Radstrom, injured in Finland and on rather frosty terms with his team), who was forced out by a problem with a circuit-breaker contact, and Philippe Bugalski, slowed by major brake trouble.

Grönholm was also having his share of problems, a hydraulic pump failure bringing with it a 30-second penalty on exit from the service park where his team had been fixing the 206. Before that misadventure, which came about on the third stage, the Finn had been leading the rally. Would he have stayed there?

Lacking confidence in the car, Tommi Mäkinen tinkered with its settings throughout the rally.

We shall never know, but Loeb was certainly making some impression, and logically enough it was he who won the first leg.

The next morning a fired-up Grönholm was determined to catch the Frenchman, setting the fastest times on the first three stages. On the slick and damp surfaces of the morning he really threw himself into it. It helped him up the order but not back to first place, where Loeb was putting up superb resistance. Helped by re-cut TA's – the Citroën was on the same TA's but uncut – Peugeot's Finn shot back through the field. A spin caused by a collision with a large rock left Loeb's steering slightly skewed. That, and Grönholm's challenge, were enough to really get Loeb going: despite a less-than-perfect Xsara he set the next fastest time. 'I just went for it,' he

Colin McRae's sole aim was to finish as the first driver in a non-PSA, Pirelli-shod car, and he did it with an encouraging fourth place.

confessed. 'I wanted to stay in the lead, I gave it everything and I surprised even myself. I was focussed like never before: I just had to do it, and I did it.' Not everyone did: Grönholm had his own spin on that same 13th stage, but the day spent on the very different roads of a mlitary training-ground was all about that twosome. Burns, with a scratch time of his own, was the only one to rein them in a bit, managing to keep his teammate in check and even taking a bit off the gap to the leader.

But Marcus Grönholm wasn't finished yet. As the last day loomed he felt he could still win it, despite starting with a 25.4s handicap. His tarmac driving had improved, he was more determined than ever, and so back on the attack he went. He promptly overshot – twice – on the first test. Loeb felt the breeze from the bullet, though, and kept his own

foot right in it, splitting the scratches for the rest of the leg with Burns, determined that Grönholm wasn't going to get past. That was probably all about being top dog at Peugeot, Burns having so often had to play second fiddle to Grönholm. The only unhappy Lion driver was the lacklustre Rovanperä, 11th on the first and second legs. He then lost his rear wing, an unbalanced 206 ending up in a ditch and out. Despite Grönholm's charge and Burns not backing off one bit, Loeb took his first World Championship win and erased the memory of his Monte Carlo disappointment. Not even a attempt by Subaru, who complained that Loeb had travelled the wrong way for a few metres after a spin on the St Wendel super-special, could take the gloss off. 'My first second win!' he joked, and rightly so. It was all very heartening for Citroën Sport, for whom Germany was their

For once Richard Burns was ahead of teammate Grönholm, but as he kept reminding us he had to keep attacking all the way.

seventh and final official outing. At the season's start Guy Fréquelin set them one specific target: at least one victory. Thanks to Seb, they got it just in time.

While the result put Peugeot's noses out of joint, the world champion team were still the big winners from this rally. With the chevroned cars not scoring any constructors' points, that gave the Lion another 16, the equivalent of a one-two finish thanks to Burns and Grönholm, the former in front for once. But we shall never know if Panizzi could have caught Loeb! Colin McRae, fourth in front of a hard-charging Bruno Thiry and a very consistent Markko Märtin, pulled something out of the bag for Ford and for himself, but he was still left with an 18-point gap to Grönholm – virtually two victories' worth. In the constructors' championship Peugeot widened the gap still further (115 to second-placed Ford's 81), chalking up maximum points for the

sixth time in as many events, all this without the help of Panizzi. But there was only one winner, and his name was Sébastien Loeb, the 17th Frenchman to get his name on a World Championship trophy. He was the first of the new generation of drivers to win. He didn't crack under pressure, he didn't make the mistake that might have eliminated him, he kept it all together to the finish. Little Seb is going to make a big name for himself.

Loeb is probably the benchmark after his achievements in the Junior World Championship. Spaniard Daniel Sola's Citroën Saxo was a fairly easy winner of the fourth round on their calendar from Italian Andrea Dallavilla (Saxo) and Germany's Schelle, giving the Suzuki Ignis a podium finish, which confirmed Sola's lead in the category, ahead of same Dallavilla and Finland's Tuohino, victim of an off in Germany. ∎

Spain's Daniel Sola maintained his assault on the Junior Championship, triumphing on German tarmac for his second win of the season.

Champagne time for Sébastien Loeb and Daniel Eléna as they celebrate their first World Championship win.

The Step 2 Lancer WRC (this is Delecour) had its first tarmac rally in Germany. It was an inconclusive run for a cumbersome car that still doesn't seem to hold the road as it should.

be a big step forward.

The event was certainly a hit with the fans. Rallying doesn't come naturally to a country where circuit racing is king, thanks to the Schumi effect and the efforts of Mercedes and BMW in F1, and those of Audi and Porsche, then and now, in the DTM and at Le Mans. The discipline did give us two German legends in Walter Röhrl and the Audi Quattro. The crowd was remarkable, with the organisers claiming 225,000, half of them jammed in as the cars went through the second leg. Another reason to be happy was the breakdown of that crowd, as Denis Giraudet, there purely as a

tourist, put it. Germans first and foremost, of course, but others flocked to central Europe from Belgium, Italy, France (Alsace!), Switzerland, Great Britain and even Estonia – the Märtin effect – and made it not only a cosmopolitan crowd but a very young one. That is reassuring for the constructors: the customers had come along. Germany, after all, is one of the continent's major markets. And before encouraging the German marques to come into rallying, as David Richards so fondly hopes they will, success depends on keeping the ones who are already there happy. ∎

THE ORGANISATION
COULD DO BETTER!

No new event had been accepted on the calendar since Cyprus found its way into the World Championship back in 2000.

That followed the defection of the Chinese, whose event took place once and only once (Didier Auriol won it in a Toyota Corolla WRC in 1999). Ratified a year earlier when a non-Championship event was given a pass mark by the FIA, the latest version of the German Rally, a combination of two former local events of which the ADAC Rally was one, made its debut from August 22 to 25. Based at Trier, it gave us three very strikingly different legs, from the Moselle vineyards to the roads – bitumen-covered, of course, since it was a tarmac event – of the Baumholder army camp where tanks had been

the most recent to try out their caterpillar tracks. Among the vines the biggest trap was the kerbstones; on tank territory there were mud and earth slides, loose stones, blind corners and some very unnatural roads. More than one driver got caught out. It all presented a bit of a challenge in road-holding terms, which prompted Michelin to come up with a new tyre which they aptly called Baumholder. Unanimity didn't reign among the drivers when asked for comments on that rather bizarre terrain: some found it too quick, others thought it held no interest from a driving point of view, others liked it.

But that's how it is at every event. There will always be different opinions. Organising a new event is never easy, and although the organisers realise that there is still plenty of room for improvement, they have made a solid start. Next year's Rallye Deutschland should

As the season drew to a close Markko Märtin proved he is the coming man at Ford. Sixth place showed he is not so unhappy on tarmac as some would have us believe.

10th leg of the 2002 World Rally Championship for constructors and drivers. 4th leg of WRC Junior Championship.

Date 22nd to 25th August 2002

Route
1449,19 km divided in 3 legs. 23 tarmac stages scheduled (415,89 km) and 22 contested (393,61 km)

1st leg
Friday 23rd August (06h45-19h30): Trier > Trier, 498 km; 8 special stages scheduled (148,62 km), 7 contested (126,34 km)

2nd leg
Saturday 24th August (07h30-21h44): Trier > Bostalsee > Trier, 585 km; 8 special stages (164,41 km)

3rd leg
Sunday 25th August (06h30-16h00): Trier > Bostalsee > Trier, 363 km; 7 special stages (102,86 km)

Entry List - Starters - Finishers:
90 - 86 - 40

Conditions: cloudy, followed by rain.

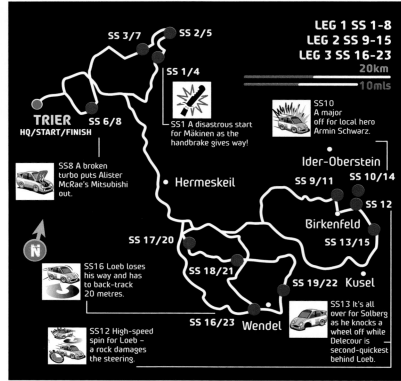

LEG 1 SS 1-8
LEG 2 SS 9-15
LEG 3 SS 16-23
20km
10mls

SS 3/7   SS 2/5

SS 1/4

TRIER   SS 6/8
HQ/START/FINISH

SS1 A disastrous start for Mäkinen as the handbrake gives way!

SS10 A major off for local hero Armin Schwarz.

SS8 A broken turbo puts Alister McRae's Mitsubishi out.

Hermeskeil

Ider-Oberstein

SS 9/11   SS 10/14

SS 12

Birkenfeld

SS 17/20   SS 13/15

SS16 Loeb loses his way and has to back-track 20 metres.

SS 18/21   Kusel

SS 19/22

SS13 It's all over for Solberg as he knocks a wheel off while Delecour is second-quickest behind Loeb.

SS 16/23   Wendel

SS12 High-speed spin for Loeb – a rock damages the steering.

Es gibt nur einen Walter Röhrl.

Special Stage Times

SS1 Dhrontal I (12,42 km)
1.Grönholm & Burns 8'27"9; 3.Loeb +4"6;
4.Sainz +5"1; 5.C. McRae +6"2; 6.Solberg
+7"4; Jr. (24) Dallavilla +0'52"3

SS2 Schönes Moselland I (23,81 km)
1.Loeb 14'10"8; 2.Grönholm +0"2;
3.Burns +1"3; 4.Bugalski +7"5;
5 Schwarz +8"7; 6.Loix +12"3;
Jr. (27) Dallavilla +1'20"5

SS3 Moselwein I (22,28 km)
1.Loeb 13'24"2; 2.Bugalski +14"0;
3.Burns +14"3; 4.Solberg +14"7;
5.C. McRae +15"5; 6.Thiry +18"3;
Jr. (23) Mcshea +1'37"6

SS4 Dhrontal II (12,42 km)
1.Loeb 8'23"8; 2.Grönholm +4"6;
3.C. McRae +5"1; 4.Burns +5"2;
5.Solberg +6"4; 6.Bugalski +6"7;
Jr. (23) Dallavilla +49"7

SS5 Schönes Moselland II (23,81km)
1.Loeb 13'53"8; Bugalski +2"0;
3.Loix +5"9; 4.Grönholm +5"9;
5.Burns +9"5; 6.C. McRae +12"2;
Jr. (21) Sola +1'20"0

SS6 Stein und Wein /Fel (15,80 km)
1.Loeb 8'33"5; 2.Burns +0"9;
3.Grönholm +2"7; 4.Bugalski +8"9;
5.Schwarz +7"7; 6.C. McRae +8"3;
Jr. (24) Haaf +54"8

SS7 Moselwein II (22,28 km)
Cancelled for safety reasons - too many
spectators.

SS8 Stein und Wein / Fel (15,80 km)
1.Loeb 8'31"5; 2.Burns +0"4;
3.Grönholm +1"9; 4.Bugalski +4"7;
5.Schwarz +6"6; 6.C. McRae & Thiry
+8"9; Jr. (22) Duval +49"2

SS9 Maiwald I (18,72 km)
1.Grönholm 10'58"6; 2.Burns +13"1;
3.Solberg +18"3; 4.C. McRae +18"8;
5.Rovanperä +18"9; 6.Loeb +20"0;
Jr. (17) Duval +55"8

SS10 Panzerplatte I (35,56 km)
1.Grönholm 21'27"0; 2.Loeb +7"6;
3.Burns +17"7; 4.Solberg +18"9;
5.C. McRae +27"1; 6.Gardemeister
+30"1; Jr. (15=) Dallavilla +2'00"1

SS11 Maiwald II (18,72 km)
1.Grönholm 10'52"0; 2.Burns +3"1;
3.Mäkinen +4"0; 4.C. McRae +6"4;
5.Märtin +8"3; 6.Sainz +9"2;
Jr. (17) Duval +52"5

SS12 Halkreuz (8,31 km)
1.Burns 4'53"3; 2.Mäkinen +1"2;
3.Grönholm +1"9; 4.Sainz +2"3;
5.Delecour +3"8; 6.Märtin +6"4;
Jr. (19) Dallavilla +19"8

SS13 Erzweiler I (20,87 km)
1.Loeb 12'56"6; 2.Delecour +1"3;
3.Sainz +6"2; 4.Märtin +7"4;
5.C. McRae +7"8; 6.Grönholm +9"2;
Jr. (12) Dallavilla +43"8

SS14 Panzerplatte II (35,56 km)
1.Grönholm 20'39"7; 2.Burns +4"8;
3.Loeb +8"1; 4.Mäkinen +25"7;
5.C. McRae +26"9; 6.Sainz +30"5;
Jr. (14) Dallavilla +1'47"5

SS15 Erzweiler II (20,87 km)
1.Loeb 12'21"1; 2.Grönholm +0"2;
3.Burns +3"1; 4.Rovanperä +18"0;
5.Mäkinen +19"4; 6.Sainz +19"6;
Jr. (17) Dallavilla +1'05"2

SS16 St Wendel I (5,80 km)
1.Grönholm 3'36"5; 2.Burns +1"4;
3.Mäkinen +3"6; 4.Märtin +3"9;
5.Thiry +4"4; 6.Rovanperä +4"6;
Jr. (15) Schelle +23"6

SS17 Peterberg I (15,02 km)
1.Loeb 8'07"6; 2.Burns +1"9;
3.Mäkinen +6"4; 4.Märtin +9"4;
5.C. McRae +10"6; 6.Rovanperä +11"3;
Jr. (14) Duval +53"5

SS18 St Wendeler Land I (17,70 km)
1.Burns 8'46"4; 2.Loeb +3"9;
3.Grönholm +14"6; 4.Rovanperä +15"5;

SS19 Bosenberg I (15,81 km)
1.Loeb 7'39"4; 2.Burns +5"2;
3.Grönholm +15"9; 4.C. McRae +18"1;
5.Sainz +18"4; 6.Mäkinen +22"3;
Jr. (16) Basso +1'00"2

SS20 Peterberg II (15,02 km)
1.Burns 8'09"1; 2.Loeb +1"1; 3.Mäkinen
& Grönholm +6"7; 5.Märtin +8"1;
6.Sainz +10"5; Jr. (16) Duval +56"0

SS21 St Wendeler Land II (17,70 km)
1.Burns 8'46"3; 2.Loeb +0"1;
3.Grönholm +4"3; 4.Mäkinen +8"8;
5.Sainz +11"2; 6.Märtin +15"5;
Jr. (15) Basso +1'00"7

SS22 Bosenberg II (15,81 km)
1.Loeb 7'38"9; 2.Burns +2"6;
3.Grönholm +5"4; 4.Mäkinen +6"0;
5.C. McRae +12"7; 6.Sainz +12"8;
Jr. (13) Basso +0'51"7

SS23 St Wendel II (5,80 km)
1.Burns 3'39"6; 2.Loeb +0"4;
3.Grönholm +0"8; 4.Märtin +3"8;
5.Mäkinen +5"0; 6.Thiry +5"5;
Jr. (14) Schelle +0'24"5

Others:
5.C. McRae +19"1; 6.Märtin +21"2;
Jr. (16) Sola +1'00"9

Results ᵔᴝᴿᴄ

	Driver/Navigator	Car	Gr.	Time
1	Loeb - Elena	Citroën Xsara WRC	A	3h47'17"3
2	Burns - Reid	Peugeot 206 WRC		+14"3
3	Grönholm - Rautiainen	Peugeot 206 WRC		+1'19"1
4	C. McRae - Grist	Ford Focus RS WRC 02		+3'45"3
5	Thiry - Prevot	Peugeot 206 WRC		+5'18"8
6	Märtin - Park	Ford Focus RS WRC 02		+5'33"0
7	Mäkinen - Lindström	Subaru Impreza 2002		+5'39"2
8	Sainz - Moya	Ford Focus RS WRC 02		+6'17"0
9	Delecour - Grataloup	Mitsubishi Lancer Evo WRC 2		+6'35"9
10	Eriksson - Thörner	Skoda Octavia WRC Evo 3		+13'34"2
12	**Sola - Romani**	**Citroën Saxo**	**Jr.**	**+23'22"3**

Leading Retirements (44)

SS.19	Rovanperä - Silander	Peugeot 206 WRC	Off
SS.15	Gardemeister - Lükander	Skoda Octavia WRC Evo 3	Off
SS.11	Solberg - Mills	Subaru Impreza WRC 2002	Wheel torn off
SS.10	Schwarz - Hiemer	Hyundai Accent WRC 3	Off
SS.9	Mörtl - Wicha	Subaru Impreza WRC 2002	Off
SS.9	Bugalski - Chiaroni	Citroën Xsara WRC	Oil pump
SS.9	Loix - Smeets	Hyundai Accent WRC 3	Oil pressure
SS.7	A. McRae - Senior	Mitsubishi Lancer Evo WRC 2	Turbo
SS.5	Arai - Sircombe	Subaru Impreza WRC 2002	Gearbox
SS.3	Kahle - Goebel	Skoda Octavia WRC Evo 3	Engine
SS.3	Puras - Marti	Citroën Xsara WRC	Electrics

Performers

	1	2	3	4	5	6
Loeb	1	5	2	-	-	1
Burns	6	9	4	1	1	-
Grönholm	6	3	9	1	1	1
Bugalski	-	2	-	3	-	1
Mäkinen	-	1	2	4	3	-
Delecour	-	1	-	-	1	-
C. McRae	-	-	2	2	7	3
Sainz	-	1	3	1	5	
Solberg	-	-	1	2	1	1
Loix	-	-	1	-	-	1
Märtin	-	-	3	2	3	
Rovanperä	-	-	-	-	-	2
Schwarz	-	-	-	-	3	-
Thiry	-	-	-	-	1	4
Gardemeister	-	-	-	-	-	-
Eriksson	-	-	-	-	-	1

Event Leaders

SS.1	Burns & Grönholm
SS.2	Grönholm
SS.3 > SS.23	Loeb

Championship Classifications

FIA Drivers (10/14)
1. Grönholm 51; 2. C. McRae 33; 3. Burns 31; 4. Sainz 26;
5. Panizzi 21; 6.Solberg 19; 7. Rovanperä, Loeb 18; 9. Mäkinen 15;
10. Märtin 10; 11. Bugalski 7; 12. Radström 4; 13. A. McRae,
Gardemeister & Thiry 2; 16. Eriksson 1

FIA Constructors (10/14)
1. Peugeot 115; 2. Ford 81; 3. Subaru 42; 4. Skoda 8; 5. Mitsubishi 8;
6. Hyundai 6

FIA Production Car WRC (6/8)
1. Singh 28; 2. Ferreyros 20; 3. Sohlberg 16; 4. Fiorio 13; 5. Arai,
Trelles 12; 7. Iliev 9; 8. Girdauskas 7; 9. Rowe 5; 10. Ipatti, Baldini 4;
12. Ligato, Harrach, Marrini, Kollevold & De Dominics 2

FIA Junior WRC (4/6)
1. Sola 23; 2. Dallavilla 18; 3. Tuohino 12; 4. Duval 11; 5. Caldani 10;
6. Schelle 5; 7. Feghali, Basso & Rowe 4; 10. Carlsson, Galli &
Baldacci 3; 13. Doppelreiter 2; 14. Foss, Katajamäki 1

Italy

Sanremo

Despite being hampered by the broken shoulder he suffered a month and a half earlier, Gilles Panizzi won the Italian round in magnificent style. Marcus Grönholm came second for another Peugeot 1-2, and there was more good news in the shap of their latest newcomer, Cédric Robert

Good news for Tommi Mäkinen, at last getting his hands on a Subaru that allowed him to set some splendid times. The show was over by the end of the first leg when a driveshaft broke.

One day Marcus Grönholm will be a winner on tarmac. He is slowly creeping closer to Panizzi, even if the Tarmac Master is still just a notch above him.

Entered by the Piedrafita team, the only way Philippe Bugalski could match Panizzi's pace was by taking some huge risks, and he paid the price with a big accident.

saw one major retirement. That was Armin Schwarz, just getting over the effects of his German accident and now out with a wheel ripped off. But Panizzi piled it on in the second stage, Hervé surprised and delighted to see his brother back to his best, on the attack and spot-on with his braking. The only tricky thing now was the hairpins, where he couldn't quite get the hand-braking right and opted instead to just roll round. In fact he admitted that he had been having a hard time in all of the twisty stuff where precision and on-the-edge driving are called for.

Nevertheless, a newly confident Panizzi is worth any number of frustrated souls. Before the start several people had been saying that with Gilles at less than peak fitness, as his body langauge seemed to suggest, maybe there was a chance of a tarmac win. Not least of all the other members of the 206 WRC club,

THE RACE
PANIZZI DRIVES
THROUGH THE PAIN

Ten days before the rally got under way a test session had been arranged in Corsica. The man they call Zebulon, it seemed, had turned into a Zombie: his driving was all over the place, he couldn't last the distance and brother Hervé admitted he didn't like what he was seeing from the front right seat. Instead of running for two full days, the eldest son went home 24 hours ahead of schedule to try and recover completely. The Sanremo rally had seemed so far away, now here it was

looming up. There was an air of real uncertainty at Peugeot: would the 'Tarmac Master' be able to compete in Italy's World Championship round? The point was not so much to try for the win as to contain the Fords and stop the blue oval coming away with too many constructors' points.

The reason for all this anxiety was simple. On July 31, Gilles was trying to change a lighting tube in the games room in his home at Sospel – and fell off the ladder. With a broken right collarbone and new damage to ligaments chewed up in a road accident some time before, there was nothing for it but to have an operation

and endure the slow process of rehabilitation. The Finnish and German rallies went by, and now Sanremo was coming up at full tilt. In the pre-rally testing, the shakedown on the eve of the start, doubt still reigned in the French crew.

Gilles wasn't on top form, Hervé was even more unsure how things would pan out. But whether it was those racing demons, his own intensity or sheer will power – probably all of the above – the driver was right back in the groove as soon as they were off and running. Keeping something in reserve, he left Marcus Grönholm to take the first scratch on a test that

Toni Gardemeister just fades away on tarmac, and the Sanremo proved no exception to that rule.

all, no doubt, were the Subaru drivers, especially their four-time World Champion. Putting on a fine show, he was enjoying himself more than at any time this season, so it was sad that he had to retire before the last timed section with a broken driveshaft. The second leg proved a much sterner test for the man in front. Marcus Grönholm had got the measure of Richard Burns yet again and he was on a charge. Right from the word go he strung scratch times together, contemptuous of his hapless stablemate.

The day before a laughing Finn had told us he'd found the key to winning on tarmac. 'As soon as I get back home to Finalnd,' he said, 'I'm going to climb a ladder and throw myself off!' Meantime, it was all going wrong for Panizzi, even if he was credited with a fastest time for a stage he took very easy indeed. First time through Colle Langan, Philippe Bugalski had a big off, thankfully without too much damage, though Jean-Paul Chiaroni had to spend the next two days in hospital with a haemorrhaging eye. The Xsara's crew were the only ones to match the 206's pace, but had they overdone it? Maybe – the driver himself had been knocked out in the accident and remembered nothing about it. First to arrive on the scene were the Panizzi brothers, who started the stage just after the Xsara, and they stopped to give first aid to their colleagues before quietly heading for the exit. So as not to throw the event out of kilter, the stewards rightly decided to give them the same time as Grönholm's scratch.

Bugalski wasn't the only one caught out at Colle Langan. Burns broke a shock absorber and damaged his

Armin Schwarz, not fully recovered from his Deutschland Rally accident, was below his best, abandoning after a mistake on the first stage.

Messrs Grönholm and Burns. The time had come for the Englishman to put a solid result on the board and break the stranglehold the Finn had had on him since the season got under way. And he had good grounds for optimism, the championship leader having decided that he would base his rally on what Burns was doing.

leg, though the driver did look more and more drawn as the miles went by and fatigue took its toll. We knew how talented he was, but Panizzi also has a big heart. Things were getting lively behind him as Bugalski, Burns, Grönholm, Mäkinen and McRae all took it in turns to shine. Happiest of

Loix was badly held up by a broken suspension after a bump, but he got in some real-life testing by finishing the event.

Bugalski had already got the better of 'Zebulon' before when the latter was at his best, so little 'Bug' was hoping to thumb his nose not only at Panizzi but at the whole World Championship mob in his Xsara. Once again it was in semi-works or semi-privateer form and, like the Jesus Puras car, a Piedrafita entry. It was harder to hold out much hope for the Fords, since neither the Focus, its Pirellis nor McRae are currently up to it on tarmac. The blue boys at Subaru, on the other hand, felt sure they could do something with the excellent Impreza WRC chassis and its Italian rubber, now much better suited to the bitumen.

In the end, as the French crew's confidence flooded back, the event soon settled back into its logical course, and that course took it their way. They missed out on just one of the eight special stages on the first

Märtin was impressive on the Italian tarmac, completely overshadowing his teammates and hounding the cars that sport the tricolour.

11

Three scratch times and a podium finish: Petter Solberg took full advantage of the progress made by both the Subaru and the Pirellis on tarmac.

steering after a little tap, Puras was running minus brakes and Colin McRae with a broken centre diff. But our wounded soldier felt he was under threat and gave himself a bit of a shake in the 12th stage.

That was all about being number one and showing his Finnish teammate that, even at less than 100 per cent, he was still the boss. It wasn't pain that was his problem so much as sheer fatigue. But there was no way he was going to let people see he was weary or down – the predatory Grönholm would have pounced on his hapless prey all the harder. And it worked beautifully: the 2000 World Champion, having shaken off Burns as the latter slipped to fourth with that mid-leg mistake, resigned himself to being second-best to his stablemate. A wiser, more sensible man these days, he felt those six points were a

better bet than taking silly risks chasing after a possible ten for the win.

As the leg came to a close Solberg, dragging his Subaru in among the Peugeots for a brilliant third place, took the last two fastest times. The Norwegian had his work cut out in the final stage to keep Burns in check but he did so in fine style to deprive the French outfit of another 1-2-3. As well as that splendid, unexpected win for Panizzi and Marcus Grönholm's second place, another fine double meaning yet another 16 points were in the bag, there were plenty of other reasons for celebrations in the lion's den. That superb result meant the tricolors were in great shape to secure a third constructors' title in New Zealand on the next round. Ford could still see the faintest glimmer of hope thanks to Märtin, in the points again in fifth

Though he tried his heart out, the World Champion couldn't match his Peugeot teammates' pace.

and much more on it than his famous teammates Sainz and McRae. Like his employers, Marcus Grönholm could also look forward to being crowned champion again in the Antipodes.

And seventh place was a fine reward for a superb drive by Cédric Robert, making his World Championship debut in a customer 206 WRC with the same Peugeot shock absorbers as the works cars. The Jean-Pierre Nicolas protégé confirmed his talent by setting some fine times as he came home just behind Puras. So the Lion not only knows how to win, it also knows how to plan for the future – and don't let anyone forget it. ∎

THE JUNIORS
DALLAVILLA BACK ON TOP

The Junior Championship, led for so long by Daniel Sola, took a different turn after the Sanremo, the fifth of the scheduled six events. A fiercely contested event went to Andrea Dallavilla in his Saxo.

The Italian had won the category here on home ground in 2001, a race which saw his main rival of the day, Sébastien Loeb, in a Xsara WRC, but he had the devil of a job to shake off the Fiat Puntos of Nicola Caldani and

Marcus Grönholm had his fair share of trouble (turbo, brakes, gearbox), otherwise he might have been a threat to Panizzi.

On tarmac the Focus WRC cars (this is McRae) were outperformed by the Subarus, even though they were on the same Pirellis, so what could they expect against the Peugeots? It was enough to demotivate McRae completely.

Citroën drivers on 28 and 27 respectively. Caldani, third on 13, Tuohino and Duval, both on 12, were out of the running to be successor to 2001 champion Sébastien Loeb.

The title would be fought out in Britain between the two leading lights of the season, adding spice to that event as neither of them is what you'd call a gravel specialist.

Once again, though, it was not a Junior Championship car that won the Super 1600 class. Victory went to Roberto Travaglia, driving

an Espace Competition-prepared French 206. He was in Sanremo as part of the build-up to the 2003 Championship, which he will contest in the same car. The Italian had a stroke of luck when his main rival, Simon Jean-Joseph, had to retire his Clio early on.

Soon after the start of the second leg the car from the diamond marque lost its engine with a broken gudgeon pin. But the man from Martinique had had time to impress once again, having shaken off the after-effects of broken ribs suffered in a fall on a boat.

The Clio and the 206 had clearly shown their potential again, to the detriment of the Saxos, Puntos and the rest. Still, as they are not in the Junior Championship, Jean-Joseph and Travaglia aren't governed by the same regulations.

'No significant advantage,' Renault claimed all season long; 'they're on a different planet,' retorted the Junior Championship contestants.

Roll on 2003, when the doubts and suspicions will be dispelled as the two cars compete on an equal footing with the rest. ∎

Sixth on this running of the Sanremo, Jesus Puras was a pale shadow of the man who led for so long last year.

Giandomenico Basso. The transalpine trio were also threatened by Spaniard Sola, intent on damage limitation.

It started disastrously for Sola after a poor choice of tyres for the first special and a puncture that cost him time. A magnificent fightback saw him grab fourth place at the expense of Caldani by just four-tenths of a second.

That's what it took to get those three points rather than just two. It meant Dallavilla took over the title lead, but by the narrowest of margins (a single point), the

11th leg of the 2002 World Rally Championship for constructors and drivers. 5th leg of WRC Junior Championship.

Date 19th to 22nd September 2002

Route
1407,04 km divided in 3 legs.
18 special stages on tarmac roads (385,72 km)

Start
Thursday 19th September (20h30): Sanremo
1st leg
Friday 20th September (06h00-20h01): Sanremo > Imperia > Sanremo, 538,88 km; 8 special stages (147,18 km)
2nd leg
Saturday 21st September (06h00-20h01): Sanremo > Imperia > Sanremo, 540,88 km; 6 special stages (150,54 km)
3rd leg
Sunday 22nd September (06h00-15h00): Sanremo > Imperia > Sanremo, 327,28 km; 4 special stages (88 km)

Entry List - Starters - Finishers:
57 - 53 - 35

Conditions: fine, roads dry.

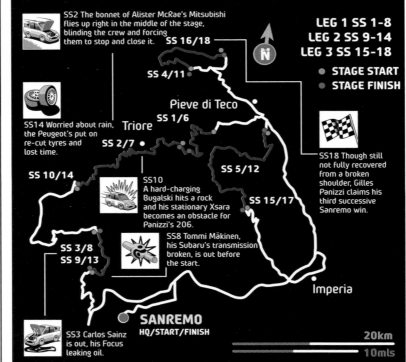

SS2 The bonnet of Alister McRae's Mitsubishi flies up right in the middle of the stage, blinding the crew and forcing them to stop and close it.

SS14 Worried about rain, the Peugeot's put on re-cut tyres and lost time.

SS10 A hard-charging Bugalski hits a rock and his stationary Xsara becomes an obstacle for Panizzi's 206.

SS8 Tommi Mäkinen, his Subaru's transmission broken, is out before the start.

SS3 Carlos Sainz is out, his Focus leaking oil.

SS18 Though still not fully recovered from a broken shoulder, Gilles Panizzi claims his third successive Sanremo win.

LEG 1 SS 1-8
LEG 2 SS 9-14
LEG 3 SS 15-18
● STAGE START
● STAGE FINISH

SS 16/18
SS 4/11
Pieve di Teco
SS 1/6
Triore
SS 2/7
SS 5/12
SS 10/14
SS 15/17
SS 3/8
SS 9/13
Imperia
SANREMO HQ/START/FINISH
20km
10mls

TOP ENTRIES

TOP ENTRIES

1 Richard BURNS - Robert REID
   Peugeot 206 WRC
2 Marcus GRÖNHOLM - Timo RAUTIAINEN Peugeot 206 WRC
3 Gilles PANIZZI - Hervè PANIZZI
   Peugeot 206 WRC
4 Carlos SAINZ - Luis MOYA
   Ford Focus RS WRC 02
5 Colin McRAE - Nicky GRIST
   Ford Focus RS WRC 02
6 Markko MÄRTIN - Michael PARK
   Ford Focus RS WRC 02
7 Francois DELECOUR - Daniel GRATALOUP Mitsubishi Lancer Evo WRC
8 Alister McRAE - David SENIOR
   Mitsubishi Lancer Evo WRC
10 Tommi MÄKINEN - Kaj LINDSTROM
   Subaru Impreza WRC 2002
11 Petter SOLBERG - Philip MILLS
   Subaru Impreza WRC 2002
12 Achim MÖRTL - Klaus WICHA
   Subaru Impreza WRC 2002
14 Kenneth ERIKSSON - Tina THORNER
   Skoda Octavia WRC Evo 3
15 Toni GARDEMEISTER - Paavo LUKANDER Skoda Octavia WRC Evo 3
16 Roman KRESTA - Jan TOMANEK
   Skoda Octavia WRC Evo 3
17 Armin SCHWARZ - Manfred HIEMER
   Hyundai Accent WRC 3
18 Freddy LOIX - Sven SMEETS
   Hyundai Accent WRC 3
24 Philippe BUGALSKI - Jean-Paul CHIARONI Citroën Xsara WRC
25 Harri ROVANPERÄ - Voitto SILANDER
   Peugeot 206 WRC
26 Bruno THIRY - Stèphane PREVOT
   Peugeot 206 WRC
27 Jésus PURAS - Carlos DEL BARRIO
   Citroën Xsara WRC
28 Cedric ROBERT - Gerald BEDON
   Peugeot 206 WRC
51 Andréa DALLAVILLA - Giovanni BERNACCHINI Citroën Saxo Super 1600
52 Niall McSHEA -Michael ORR
   Opel Corsa 1.6
53 Giandomenico BASSO - Luigi PIROLLO
   Fiat Punto Super 1600
55 François DUVAL - Jean-Marc FORTIN
   Ford Puma Super 1600
60 Nicola CALDANI - Dario D'ESPOSITO
   Fiat Punto Super 1600
62 Janne TUOHINO - Petri VIHAVAINEN
   Citroën Saxo Super 1600
63 Martin ROWE - Chris WOOD
   Ford Puma Super 1600
64 Gianluigi GALLI - Guido D'AMORE
   Fiat Punto Super 1600
65 Daniel SOLA - David MORENO
   Citroën Saxo Super 1600
66 Mirco BALDACCI - Maurizio BARONE
   Citroën Saxo Super 1600
67 Daniel CARLSSON - Mattias ANDERSSON
   Ford Puma Super 1600
68 Nikolaus SCHELLE - Tanja GEILHAUSEN
   Suzuki Ignis Super 1600
78 Roger FEGHALI - Nicola ARENA
   Ford Puma Super 1600
100 Simon JEAN-JOSEPH - Jack BOYERE
   Renault Clio Super 1600

Special Stage Times

SS1 Passo Teglia I (14,43 km)
1.Grönholm 10'23"5; 2.Bugalski +0"8;
3.Burns +2"8; 4.Mäkinen/Panizzi +3"1;
6.Märtin +5"4; Jr. (22) Duval +57"7

SS2 Passo Drego I (26,45 km)
1.Panizzi 17'41"9; 2.Grönholm +3"7;
3.Burns +4"7; 4.Solberg +4"8;
5.Martin +5"5; 6.Puras +5"6;
Jr. (22) Dallavilla +1'23"9

SS3 Ghimbegna I (10,43 km)
1.Panizzi 6'38"9; 2.Burns +2"5;
3.Solberg +2"2; 4.Martin +2"3;
5.Puras +3"3; 6.Bugalski +3"6;
Jr. (23) Galli +33"3

SS4 Cosio I (19,19 km)
1.Panizzi 12'13"0; 2.Grönholm +1"4;
3.Burns +3"; 4.Bugalski +4"3;
5.Mäkinen/Märtin +6"0;
Jr. (22) Basso +1'05"3

SS5 San Bartolomeo I (25,37 km)
1.Panizzi 15'03"7; 2.Bugalski +1"3;
3.Burns +6"1; 4.Grönholm +13"6;
5.Puras +16"9; 6.Märtin +17"6;
Jr. (21) Galli +1'16"7

SS6 Passo Teglia II (14,43 km)
1.Panizzi 10'19"4; 2.Bugalski +0"3;
3.Grönholm +3"1; 4.Puras +5"7;
5.Solberg +6"7; 6.Robert +8"2;
Jr. (22) Dallavilla +58"9

SS7 Passo Drego II (26,45 km)
1.Panizzi 17'30"0; 2.Bugalski +3"6;
3.Grönholm +5"1; 4.Puras +8"1;
5.Burns +12"6; 6.Solberg +14";
Jr. (21) Sola +1'23"2

SS8 Ghimbegna II (10,43 km)
1.Panizzi 6'40"4; 2.Grönholm +1"2;
3.Märtin +2"4; 4.Solberg +3"6;
5.Robert +4"1; 6.Thiry/Loix +4"5;
Jr. (20) Sola +30"7

SS9 San Romolo I (10,68 km)
1.Grönholm 6'45"6; 2.Burnis +3"8;
3.Bugalski +4"5; 4.Panizzi +4"6;
5.Solberg +6"2; 6.Puras +7"2;
Jr. (18) Basso +32"9

SS10 Colle Lagan I (42,31 km)
1.Grönholm/Panazzi 28'52"8;
3.Solberg +18"0; 4.Märtin +23"2;
5.Rovanperä +32"2; 6.Robert +32"3;
Jr. (12) Dallavilla +52"0

SS11 Cosio II (19,19 km)
1.Grönholm 12'11"4; 2.Panizzi +1"0;
3.Solberg +4"9; 4.Märtin +5"6;
5.Puras +6"9; 6.Burns +7"5;
Jr. (16) Dallavilla +1'01"2

SS12 San Bartolomeo II (25,37 km)
1.Panizzi 15'03"3; 2.Burns +5"6;
3.Solberg +6"0; 4.Grönholm +7"0;
5.Puras +9"5; 6.Robert +11"3;
Jr. (16) Basso +1'13"6

SS13 San Romolo II (10,68 km)
1.Solberg 7'03"1; 2.Grönholm +1"8;
3.Märtin +3"8; 4.C. McRae +4"2;
5.Panizzi +5"4; 6.Burns +7"4;
Jr. (16) Basso +30"2

SS14 Colle Langan II (42,31 km)
1.Solberg 28'59"9; 2.Märtin +13"8;
3.Puras +19"1; 4.Grönholm +22"1;
5.Burns +22"5; 6.Rovanperä +23"4;
Jr. (13) Sola +2'10"

SS15 Pantasina I (25,03 km)
1.Solberg 14'55"2; 2.Panizzi +0"3;
3.Burns +0"9; 4.Grönholm +1"8;
5.Märtin +6"1; 6.Puras +7"5;
Jr. (16) Basso +59"

SS16 Mendatica I (18,97 km)
1.Grönholm 12'03"0;
3.Burns/Panizzi +3"1; 4.Märtin 8"2;
5.Solberg/Thiry +9"2;
Jr. (15) Dallavilla +54"6

SS17 Pantasina II (25,03 km)
1.Burns 14'51"4; 2.Panizzi +1"2;
3.Solberg +2"0; 4.Grönholm +4"2;
5.Robert +10"5; 6.Märtin +12"2;
Jr. (15) Basso +58"7

SS18 Mendatica II (18,97 km)
1.Grönholm 12'01"0; 2.Burns +1"3;
3.Panizzi +2"6; 4.Solberg +2"7;
5.Robert +8"6; 6.Märtin +8"8;
Jr. (15) Sola +51"5

Results WRC

	Driver/Navigator	Car	Gr.	Time
1	**Panizzi - Panizzi**	**Peugeot 206 WRC**	**A**	**4h10'15"6**
2	Grönholm - Rautiainen	Peugeot 206 WRC		+ 20"9
3	Solberg - Mills	Subaru Impreza WRC 2002		+ 1'06"4
4	Burns - Reid	Peugeot 206 WRC		+ 1'18"9
5	Märtin - Park	Ford Focus RS WRC 02		+ 1'54"9
6	Puras - Del Barrio	Citroën Xsara WRC		+ 2'39"3
7	Robert - Bedon	Peugeot 206 WRC		+ 3'01"3
8	C. McRae - Grist	Ford Focus RS WRC 02		+ 5'17"5
9	Rovanperä - Silander	Peugeot 206 WRC		+ 6'18"9
10	Delecour - Grataloup	Mitsubishi Lancer Evo WRC 2		+ 7'24"4
15	Dallavilla - Bernacchini	Citroën Saxo Super 1600 Jr.		+ 18'10"8

Leading Retirements (18)

SS.14	Gardemeister - Lukander	Skoda Octavia WRC Evo 3	Off
SS.10	Mörtl - Wicha	Subaru Impreza WRC 2002	Withdraw
SS.10	Bugalski - Chiaroni	Citroën Xsara WRC	Off
SS.9	A. McRae - Senior	Mitsubishi Lancer Evo WRC 2	Withdraw
SS.8	Mäkinen - Lindström	Subaru Impreza WRC 2002	Transmission
SS.4	Sainz - Moya	Ford Focus RS WRC 02	Oil leak
SS.1	Schwarz - Hiemer	Hyundai Accent WRC 3	Off

Performers

	1	2	3	4	5	6
Panizzi	8	4	1	2	1	-
Grönholm	6	4	2	5	-	-
Solberg	3	1	4	3	3	1
Burns	1	5	5	-	2	2
Bugalski	-	4	1	1	-	1
Märtin	-	1	3	3	3	4
Puras	-	-	1	2	4	4
Mäkinen	-	-	-	1	1	-
Rovanperä	-	-	-	1	-	1
C. McRae	-	-	-	1	-	-
Robert	-	-	-	-	4	2
Thiry	-	-	-	-	1	1
Loix	-	-	-	-	-	1

Event Leaders

SS.1	Gronhölm
SS.2 > SS.18	Panizzi

Previous winners

1973	Thérier - Jaubert Alpine Renault A110	1988	Biasion - Siviero Lancia Delta Integrale
1975	Waldegaard - Thorszelius Lancia Stratos	1989	Biasion - Siviero Lancia Delta Integrale
1976	Waldegaard - Thorszelius Lancia Stratos	1990	Auriol - Occelli Lancia Delta Integrale
1977	Andruet - Delferrier Fiat 131 Abarth	1991	Auriol - Occelli Lancia Delta Integrale
1978	Alen - Kivimaki Lancia Stratos	1992	Aghini - Farnocchia Lancia Delta HF Integrale
1979	Fassina - Mannini Lancia Stratos	1993	Cunico - Evangelisti Ford Escort RS Cosworth
1980	Rohrl - Geistdorfer Fiat 131 Abarth	1994	Auriol - Occelli Toyota Celica Turbo 4WD
1981	Mouton - Pons Audi Quattro	1995	Liatti - Alessandrini Subaru Impreza
1982	Blomqvist - Cederberg Audi Quattro	1996	McRae - Ringer Subaru Impreza
1983	Alen - Kivimaki Lancia Rally 037	1997	McRae - Grist Subaru Impreza WRC
1984	Vatanen - Harryman Peugeot 205 T16	1998	Mäkinen - Mannisenmäki Mitsubishi Lancer Ev.5
1985	Rohrl - Geistdorfer Audi Sport Quattro S1	1999	Mäkinen - Mannisenmäki Mitsubishi Lancer Ev.6
1986	Alen - Kivimaki Lancia Delta S4	2000	Panizzi - Panizzi Peugeot 206 WRC
1987	Biasion - Siviero Lancia Delta HF 4WD	2001	Panizzi - Panizzi Peugeot 206 WRC

Championship Classifications

FIA Drivers (11/14)
1. Grönholm 57; 2. Burns 34; 3. C. McRae 33; 4. Panizzi 31; 5. Sainz 26;
6. Solberg 23; 7. Rovanperä, Loeb 18; 9. Mäkinen 15; 10. Märtin 12;
11. Bugalski 7; 12. Radström 4; 13. A. McRae, Gardemeister & Thiry 2;
16. Puras, Eriksson 1

FIA Constructors (11/14)
1. Peugeot 131; 2. Ford 86; 3. Subaru 46; 4. Mitsubishi 9; 5. Skoda 8;
6. Hyundai 6

FIA Production Car WRC (6/8)
1. Singh 28; 2. Ferreyros 20; 3. Sohlberg 16; 4. Fiorio 13; 5. Arai,
Trelles 12; 7. Iliev 9; 8. Girdauskas 7; 9. Rowe 5; 10. Ipatti, Baldini 4;
12. Ligato, Harrach, Marrini, Kollevold & De Dominics 2

FIA Junior WRC (5/6)
1. Dallavilla 28; 2. Sola 27; 3. Caldani 13; 4. Tuohino, Duval 12;
6. Basso 10; 7. Schelle, Galli 5; 9. Feghali, Rowe 4; 11. Carlsson,
Baldacci 3; 13. Doppelreiter 2; 14. Foss, Katajamäki 1

New Zealand

On an event that became one-way traffic for the omnipotent 206's, Grönholm and Peugeot took the drivers' and constructors' titles in the Antipodes. The weak links in the Kiwi chain of events were British ones as offs for McRae and Burns handed them both crowns.

WRC
WORLD RALLY
CHAMPIONSHIP

12

McRae threw away what slim chances he had of taking the drivers' title with an off after misunderstanding his navigator.

THE RACE
PEUGEOT'S HAT-TRICK

In 2000 they were crowned in the mists of Wales, last year it happened under the Australian sun, and this season Peugeot claimed the constructors' title even earlier in the season, before the end of the 11th round, the New Zealand Rally. But for a few unfortunate slip-ups, like that double disqualification in Argentina, the Velizy steam-roller's record would have been even better. Underlining that outstanding achievement, Marcus Grönholm took his own second world crown to add to the one he won in 2000, this time after a much smoother, more impressive campaign than two years before. And since hat-tricks were the order of the day, the New Zealand event resulted in yet another one-two finish, the new champion coming home ahead of Harri Rovanperä. Seven one-two finishes in 11 rounds: that's some performance.

But before we got round to all those coronations there was a rally to be fought out. It took place just as the America's Cup qualifying races, better known as the Louis Vuitton Cup, were getting under way off the harbour city of Auckland, the base for all the challengers trying to wrest away the world's oldest sporting

trophy. Compared to the Auld Mug, the World Rally Championship is a babe in arms: the elite sailing competition first took place in 1871 – 102 years before the first world series on the roads! Given the Kiwi passion for all things maritime, motor sport had to take a bit of a back seat, so it was lucky there wasn't an All Blacks rugby match scheduled for New Zealand's major city as well.

Despite the relative lack of interest, the North Island still has the loveliest and most popular stages the World Championship has to offer, backed up by flawless organisation. Right at the start the 206 WRC's were literally flying on the first leg. As usual, though, the starting order skewed things more than somewhat. Once again Marcus Grönholm paid a heavy price for leading the title race, sweeping the road for his pals. Even second position was a definite bonus for Richard Burns, and that state of affairs was more obvious still when it came to Rovanperä, who ran seventh on the road. But as we know, the amiable Finn is a notch below the World Champions he has to live with at Peugeot. He managed just one scratch time all day, and even then he shared it with Burns. For the day belonged to the Englishman. Determined to lay the Grönholm bogey that has seen Marcus dominate him all season

long, Burns attacked confidently from the start, still seeing a faint glimmer of hope for the title. Setting four fastest times out of eight, including the first, he was the undisputed leader after that leg, finishing with an 18s advantage over Rovanperä and 37s on Grönholm. The handicap of his road position apart, the latter was also the only one of the Peugeot trio to complain of any

And one makes two! Marcus Grönholm chased down his second title in New Zealand. Any other result would have been a travesty after such a dominant season.

Consistent rather than brilliant, Juha Kankkunen dragged his Hyundai up to fifth place ahead of the Korean firm's usual drivers.

Only Mäkinen's third podium in 12 events: things went better in New Zealand, but 2002 just wasn't his year.

technical trouble, his car's hydraulics and clutch playing up. But those were minor details as he threw himself into the fray with his usual gusto.

Around midday the Finn also learned that his assault on the title had become a little easier. At Whaanga Coast, probably the most popular stage on the whole calendar, Colin McRae got carried away, missing the braking-point for a right-hander he tried to take in third when it fact it was a second-gear corner. The Focus wound up off the road, nosed up against a fir tree, and a few minutes later it was hit by a local Group N Mitsubishi whose driver

adjustments had been made to his Impreza's brakes and diff. Backed up by Petter Solberg, he was showing that the Subarus were getting back to something like their form.

But that didn't mean they could hope to match the 206's pace. And when they at last get the chance to start from more favourable positions, their superiority becomes even more stark. That's exactly what happened on the second leg. Winner the day before, Burns set off from 15th and Grönholm 13th, which meant they could also fight each other on a level playing-field. The two of them went at it hammer and tongs, and Rovanperä was the one to suffer quickly knocked off second spot by the bold Marcus. The latter soon realised, however, that if nothing untoward happened there was

no way he could make up his earlier handicap to Burns, so he signalled he was going to cease hostilities. For all that, the man just doesn't know the meaning of 'go easy' and he kept the pace up throughout the leg, just so Burns shouldn't think the pressure was off altogether.

Incidentally, we ought to congratulate Peugeot for the commitment they have shown: not once did the French constructor issue team orders to their two thoroughbreds, they just let them go at each other as hard as they liked. That broadmindedness might have been revised if there had been any threat to the constructors' title – the only one that matters to the Lion – but the French team never found themselves in that situation all season long. Not only that, but the title was handed to them on a plate in the course of that second

You had to go back to New Zealand 2001 for Richard Burns' last win – and 12 months is a long time for a driver of his class.

made the same mistake. His chances of another crown –– something the record-holder for rally wins hasn't enjoyed since 1995 – had really gone before the start, but now the Scot had left both his Ford and any hopes well and truly in the ditch. Of the three title contenders before the event began just Grönholm and Burns remained.

With McRae out and the Peugeots out of sight, there was still an interesting battle going on for the minor placings. First of all there was the brilliant Finnish prospect Jani Paasonen, standing in for Alister McRae. The Scot suffered abdominal injuries in a mountain-

bike fall before Sanremo, where he took the start but had to withdraw after the first leg, and there was no question of his being here. Paasonen set the first scratch by a Lancer WRC on the fifth stage, Te Hutewai, a feat that temporarily earned him third place in the rally – this after he had gone through two stages with a bent steering arm! The youngster was in seventh heaven, and he must have been making François Delecour and the absent Alister feel very old indeed. Unfortunately Paasonen had to give best to Grönholm and Mäkinen by the end of that leg, the latter recovering his get up and go once

Paasonen With Alister McRae not back to full fitness after his mountain-bike fall, Mitsubishi put the second Lancer WRC in the hands of Paasonen. The stand-in gave his employers a promising scratch time.

leg. To prolong what little suspense was left, Ford had to have two Focuses finish high up among the points. They got off on the wrong foot when McRae retired and Märtin and Sainz found themselves seventh and 10th after the first leg, but that unrealistic target was finally blown away on SS13, Waipu Gorge, when a mistake sent the Estonian off the road. So the blue oval brigade must wait at least another year to get their hands on a crown they haven't held since way back in 1979.

The rest of the rally, of course, was fairly meaningless. Though both leader and champion, Grönholm stayed on his toes, thinking it wise to maintain a good pace rather than let himself be lulled into easing off. He promptly set every fastest time till the finish, reaching the superb total of 15 out of a possible 26. The only one of them who caused the team a flutter was Rovanperä with hydraulic and gearbox woes, but his mechanics moved heaven and earth and got the car fixed before the crew incurred a penalty. He made it a Peugeot 1-2 after fighting off the threat from Solberg, though Petter still couldn't make it to the podium – he retired with a dead engine on the penultimate stage – and that rather flattering place went to Mäkinen. But both he and the Norwegian had the look of men who had been playing in the second division, a long way below the level of the Peugeots, not just here but all season long. ■

Running minus brakes on the first stage, Eriksson couldn't avoid going off – and out – in the second.

THOSE TITLES
ON A DIFFERENT PLANET...

It was clean, clear-cut and it was virtually flawless. The papers handed in by Peugeot and Grönholm were too good for their rivals, even before the end of season report cards were issued. Driver first: the Finn was wound up both by the disappointment of a wasted 2001 season and by Richard Burns's arrival in 'his' team, and he was simply majestic throughout. He came out on top when playing to his strengths (Sweden, Finland, New Zealand), broke the jinx of the car-breaking rallies (Cyprus), bounced back when things went wrong (Argentine disqualification, Monte Carlo disappointment), nearly won his first tarmac event (Germany) and utterly overwhelmed his English teammate. They may publicly and dutifully deny it, but Grönholm and Burns do not get on: they work together, but friends is something they will never be. Apart from the fact that they are completely opposite

None too happy with his Ford in the early stages, Sainz finished strongly to be fourth.

Grönholm – Rautiäinen – 206: THE threesome of the year!

Yes, it's another ditch: this is the one in which Colin McRae buried any hopes he held out for 2002.

A relaxed Rovanperä made sure of another Peugeot 1-2 behind Grönholm, thereby making his own contribution to the French team's third world crown.

characters, they have always had a thing about who was number one. It started in 2000 when they were fighting it out for the title. Ever since that time they have consistently outshone the oldies, not only Sainz and Auriol but also McRae and Mäkinen, both not much older than them maybe, but a bit more battle-scarred. As Jean-Pierre Nicolas so rightly says, 'It's no secret that there are always four or five drivers ahead of the rest, and only one of them comes out on top each season. This year it was Marcus's turn.' And how. Not for nearly a decade had a driver been crowned so early in the season, and with two titles he is now up there with Röhrl, Biaision and Sainz. Meanwhile, for the 2003 Monte Carlo, the no. 1 will migrate from Burns's doors to his, and that in itself must be mighty pleasing to him.

As for the 206, it now has a third title, the third on the trot, and that's a feat that only Lancia (twice) and Subaru have ever achieved before. The car gets quicker and quicker, but it is also so much more reliable than it used to be. Its Cyprus success proved it could be a winner everywhere. Seven 1-2 finishes, one of them a treble, so far this year; 19 wins from 45 events since 1999; five world titles, three constructors', two drivers' in just three full seasons: this is the absolute benchmark among

the WRC's. Peugeot Sport is the absolute trendsetter, a young, dynamic, ultra-competent team making maximum use of the considerable resources the parent company provides to destroy the competition. Their level of excellence and, with it, their success have become the yardstick by which all others must be measured. The others will need to go into overdrive to get anywhere near them, all the more so because this 206 is far from being a spent force. 'Even if we can do no more than a few minor adjustments,' says Marcus Grönholm, 'it will still be the top car in 2003, or at least good enough for us to go for the titles again.' So Peugeot are under no pressure to bring the 307 WRC out ahead of its scheduled 2004 debut. That means the technical people have all the time they need to perfect that car – and the competition has been duly warned. ■

Grönholm is the main man at Peugeot – and that's well worth a good cigar, given him by the real boss man, Corrado Provera

Richard Burns was hoping for a first win in a 206, but he was trying so hard he overcooked it – terminally, as his car shows.

Propecia Rally New Zealand 2002

12th leg of the 2002 World Rally Championship for constructors and drivers. 7th leg of FIA Production Car WRC Championship.

Date 3rd to 6th October 2002

Route
1792,48 km divided in 3 legs.
24 special stages on dirt roads (411,26 km)

Start
Thursday 3rd October: Auckland City
1st leg
Friday 4th October (05h30-20h30): Auckland > Raglan > Auckland, 611 km; 8 special stages (117,03 km)
2nd leg
Saturday 5th October (06h00-23h00): Auckland > Ruawai > Auckland, 760,46 km; 10 special stages (204,07 km)
3rd leg
Sunday 6th October (06h00-15h45): Auckland > Te Kauwhata > Auckland, 421,02 km; 8 special stages (90,16 km)

Entry List - Starters - Finishers:
81 - 81 - 42

Conditions: dirt roads with a layer of gravel and pebbles.

SS14 Markko Märtin crashes and his Ford Focus catches fire briefly.

SS14 A camera crew is injured after a car crashes into them.

SS24 Carlos Sainz crashes into a tree but loses little time.

SS15 Richard Burns crashes out, handing the 2002 World Champion title to Marcus Grönholm.

SS5 Jani Paasonen sets his and the Mitsubishi Lancer WRC's first ever fastest stage time.

SS3 Skoda driver Kenneth Eriksson retires with brake problems

LEG 1 SS 1-8
LEG 2 SS 9-18
LEG 3 SS 19-26

● STAGE START
● STAGE FINISH

AUCKLAND HQ/START
MANUKAU FINISH
Te Kauwhata
Raglan
Ruawai

SS 16 SS 14
SS 17 SS 13
SS 9
SS 11 SS 12
SS 15
SS 10/18
SS 7/8
SS 22/24
SS 21/23
SS 19
SS 1
SS 20
SS 2
SS 4/5 SS 3/6

140km
80mls

TOP ENTRIES

1　Richard BURNS - Robert REID
　　Peugeot 206 WRC
2　Marcus GRÖNHOLM - Timo RAUTIAINEN Peugeot 206 WRC
3　Harri ROVANPERÄ - Voitto SILANDER Peugeot 206 WRC
4　Carlos SAINZ - Luis MOYA
　　Ford Focus RS WRC 02
5　Colin McRAE - Nicky GRIST
　　Ford Focus RS WRC 02
6　Markko MÄRTIN - Michael PARK
　　Ford Focus RS WRC 02
7　Francois DELECOUR - Daniel GRATALOUP Mitsubishi Lancer Evo WRC 2
9　Jani PAASONEN - Arto KAPANEN
　　Mitsubishi Lancer Evo WRC 2
10　Tommi MÄKINEN - Kaj LINDSTROM
　　Subaru Impreza WRC 2002
11　Petter SOLBERG - Philip MILLS
　　Subaru Impreza WRC 2002
14　Kenneth ERIKSSON - Tina THORNER
　　Skoda Octavia WRC Evo 3
15　Toni GARDEMEISTER - Paavo LUKANDER Skoda Octavia WRC Evo 3
17　Armin SCHWARZ - Manfred HIEMER
　　Hyundai Accent WRC 3
18　Freddy LOIX - Sven SMEETS
　　Hyundai Accent WRC 3
19　Juha KANKKUNEN - Juha REPO
　　Hyundai Accent WRC 3
23　Gilles PANIZZI - Hervè PANIZZI
　　Peugeot 206 WRC
32　Tomasz KUCHAR - Maciej SZCEPANIAK
　　Toyota Corolla WRC
52　Marcos LIGATO - Ruben GARCIA
　　Mitsubishi Lancer EVO 7
53　Alessandro FIORIO - V. BRAMBILLA
　　Mitsubishi Carisma GT Evo 7
54　Ramon FERREYROS - Jorge DEL BUONO
　　Mitsubishi Lancer Evo 7
57　Toshihiro ARAI - Tony SIRCOMBE
　　Subaru Impreza WRX
58　Luca BALDINI - Marco MUZZARELLI
　　Mitsubishi Lancer Evo 6
65　Beppo HARRACH - Peter MÜLLER
　　Mitsubishi Lancer Evo 6
66　Dimitar ILIEV - Petar SIVOV
　　Mitsubishi Lancer Evo 7
69　Bernt KOLLEVOLD - Ola FLOENE
　　Mitsubishi Lancer Evo 7
70　Giovanni MANFRINATO - Claudio CONDOTTA Mitsubishi Lancer Evo 6
71　Stefano MARRINI - Tiziana SANDRONI
　　Mitsubishi Lancer Evo 7
73　Martin ROWE - Chris WOOD
　　Mitsubishi Lancer Evo 7
74　Karamjit SINGH - Allen OH
　　Proton Pert
75　Kristian SOHLBERG - Jakke HONKANEN
　　Mitsubishi Lancer Evo 7
77　Alfredo DE DOMINICIS - Rudy POLLET
　　Mitsubishi Lancer Evo 7
100　Juuso PYKALISTO - Esko MERTSALMI
　　Mitsubishi Lancer Evo 6
101　Manfred STOHL - Ilka PETRASKO
　　Mitsubishi Lancer Evo 6
110　Stig BLOMQVIST - Ana GONI
　　Mitsubishi Lancer Evo 7

Special Stage Times

SS1 Te Akau North (32,36 km)
1.Burns 17'50"4; 2.Rovanperä +6"5;
3.Grönholm +9"4; 4.Mäkinen +13"6;
5.Paasonen +15"5; 6.C. McRae +15"1;
FIA Prod. (20) Ligato +1'02"8

SS2 Maungatawhiri (6,51 km)
1.Burns/Rovanperä 3'41"3; 3.Sainz +0"2;
4.Solberg +0"3; 5.Mäkinen +1"3;
6.Gardemeister +2"0; FIA Prod. (20) Arai +10"6

SS3 Te Papatapu I (16,62 km)
1.Burns 11'05"2; 2.Rovanperä +0"3;
3.Solberg +4"7; 4.C. McRae +5"9;
5.Sainz +6"2; 6.Grönholm/Märtin +7"0;
FIA Prod. (22) Sohlberg +30"8

SS4 Whaanga Coast (29,60 km)
1.Burns 21'27"0; 2.Rovanperä +7"4;
3.Grönholm +9"8; 4.Paasonen +10"2;
5.Kankkunen +14"4; 6.Märtin +15"0;
FIA Prod. (20) Manfrinato +54"2

SS5 Te Hutewai (11,14 km)
1.Paasonen 7'59"8; 2.Solberg +1"2; 3.Märtin
+2"3; 4.Mäkinen +4"1; 5.Burns +4"5; 4.Schwarz
+5"2; FIA Prod. (22) Manfrinato +20"4

SS6 Te Papatapu II (16,62 km)
1.Grönholm 10'37"7; 2.Burns +2"4;
3.Rovanperä +4"0; 4.Solberg +4"9;
5.Märtin +5"3; 6.Mäkinen +8"2;
FIA Prod. (15) Sohlberg +39"9

SS7 Manukau Super I (2,09 km)
1.Solberg 1'21"3; 2.Sainz +0"3;
3.Grönholm +0"5; 4.Burns +0"6;
5.Rovanperä +0"7; 6.Loix +1"8;
FIA Prod. (22) Ligato +7"4

SS8 Manukau Super II (2,09 km)
1.Solberg 1'20"8;
2.Burns/Grönholm +0"6; 4.Mäkinen +0"9;
5.Rovanperä +1"1; 6.Märtin +1"4;
FIA Prod. (17) Sohlberg +6"4

SS9 Mititai Finish (20,14 km)
1.Burns 10'05"2; 2.Grönholm +1"7;
3.Rovanperä +11"4; 4.Solberg +19"7;
5.Mäkinen +25"8; 6.Paasonen +26"4;
FIA Prod. (17) Ligato +58"

SS10 Tokatoka I (10,14 km)
1.Grönholm 5'09"9; 2.Burns +0"5;
3.Rovanperä +3"6; 4.Paasonen +10"0;
5.Mäkinen +12"8; 6.Solberg +13"0;
FIA Prod. (19) Ligato +22"

SS11 Parahi-Ararua (59 km)
1.Burns 33'37"7; 2.Grönholm +6"9;
3.Rovanperä +17"6; 4.Solberg +35"3;
5.Mäkinen +39"8; 6.Sainz +58"6;
FIA Prod. (17) Ligato +2'38"4

SS12 Batley (17,45 km)
1.Grönholm 9'36"4; 2.Burns +3"8;
3.Rovanperä +13"7; 4.Solberg +16"6; 5.Sainz
+19"7; 6.Märtin +24"2;
FIA Prod. (15) Ligato +51"1

SS13 Waipu Gorge (11,23 km)
1.Burns 6'25"5; 2.Grönholm +1"3;
3.Rovanperä +2"9; 4.Solberg +4"9; 5.Mäkinen
+12"6; 6.Sainz +13"1;
FIA Prod. (20) Ligato +33"1

SS14 Brooks (16,03 km)
1.Burns 9'37"1; 2.Grönholm +0"9;
3.Rovanperä +6"8; 4.Solberg +12"7;

5.Mäkinen +15"5; 6.Sainz +18"2;
FIA Prod. (16) Ligato +48"9

SS15 Paparoa Station (11,64 km)
1.Grönholm 6'11"9; 2.Rovanperä +6"0;
3.Solberg +6"9; 4.Sainz +11"2;
5.Kankkunen +13"7; 6.Panizzi +14"6;
FIA Prod. (15) Sohlberg +32"8

SS16 Cassidy (21,63 km)
1.Grönholm 12'16"0; 2.Rovanperä +10"8;
3.Solberg +12"8; 4.Mäkinen +17"2;
5.Sainz +24"5; 6.Loix +30"5;
FIA Prod. (13) Rowe +1'10"8

SS17 Mititai (26,67 km)
1.Grönholm 13'32"8; 2.Rovanperä/
Solberg +8"9; 4.Sainz +15"7;
5.Mäkinen +19"4; 6.Kankkunen +25"9;
FIA Prod. (13) Sohlberg +1'23"9

SS18 Tokatoka II (10,14 km)
1.Grönholm 5'18"4; 2.Solberg +3"2;
3.Rovanperä +3"9; 4.Mäkinen +6"1;
5.Gardemeister +6"6; 6.Sainz +8"6;
FIA Prod. (12) Sohlberg +35"3

SS19 Otorohea Trig (4,61 km)
1.Grönholm 3'05"6; 2.Rovanperä +2"1;
3.Solberg 2"6; 4.Mäkinen +4"1;
5.Sainz +4"3; 6.Panizzi +6"5;
FIA Prod. (14) Ligato +17"8

SS20 Te Akau South (32,43 km)
1.Grönholm +18'43"3; 2.Rovanperä +28"7;
3.Solberg +35"1; 4.Sainz +41"0;
5.Mäkinen +41"8; 6.Kankkunen +49"9;
FIA Prod. (14) Ligato +1'23"7

SS21 Ridge I (8,52 km)
1.Grönholm 4'45"8; 2.Mäkinen +5"4;
3.Solberg +7"1; 4.Sainz +7"9;
5.Rovanperä +9"0; 6.Loix +11"4;
FIA Prod. (11) Ligato +21"9

SS22 Campbell (7,44 km)
1.Grönholm 3'55"8; 2.Solberg +0"4;
3.Mäkinen +2"7; 4.Rovanperä +3"5;
5.Sainz +5"0; 6.Kankkunen +7"6;
FIA Prod. (12) Rowe +18"2

SS23 Ridge II (8,52 km)
1.Grönholm 4'43"4; 2.Mäkinen +4"2;
3.Solberg +4"4; 4.Sainz +5"9;
5.Rovanperä/Gardemeister +6"8;
FIA Prod. (13) Rowe +22"9

SS24 Campbell II (7,44 km)
1.Grönholm 3'52"9; 2.Solberg +3"0;
3.Mäkinen +3"2; 4.Panizzi +5"9;
5.Kankkunen +6"1; 6.Gardemeister +7"0;
FIA Prod. (10) Rowe +17"2

SS25 Fyfe I (10,60 km)
1.Grönholm 5'47"4; 2.Mäkinen +1"8;
3.Sainz +6"9; 4.Panizzi/Kankkunen +7"0;
6.Gardemeister +7"7;
FIA Prod. (16) Ligato +24"3

SS26 Fyfe II (10,60 km)
1.Grönholm 5'40"1; 2.Mäkinen +3"3;
3.Panizzi +6"6; 4.Gardemeister +8"3;
5.Sainz +9"7; 6.Kankkunen +12"1;
FIA Prod. (12) Fiorio +23"1

Results — WRC

	Driver/Navigator	Car	Gr.	Time
1	Grönholm - Rautiainen	Peugeot 206 WRC	A	+ 3h58'45"4
2	Rovanperä - Silander	Peugeot 206 WRC		+ 3'47"6
3	Mäkinen - Lindström	Subaru Impreza WRC 2002		+ 4'26"3
4	Sainz - Moya	Ford Focus RS WRC 02		+ 5'48"9
5	Kankkunen - Repo	Hyundai Accent WRC 3		+ 7'10"2
6	Loix - Smeets	Hyundai Accent WRC 3		+ 7'52"5
7	Panizzi - Panizzi	Peugeot 206 WRC		+ 8'24"4
8	Gardemeister - Lukander	Skoda Octavia WRC Evo 3		+ 8'56"1
9	Delecour - Grataloup	Mitsubishi Lancer Evo WRC 2		+ 10'43"6
10	Schwarz - Hiemer	Hyundai Accent WRC 3		+ 11'34"8
14	Sohlberg - Honkanen	Mitsubishi Lancer Evo 7	Prod.	+ 19'35"1

Leading Retirements (39)

SS.25	Solberg - Mills	Subaru Impreza WRC 2002	Engine
SS.15	Burns - Reid	Peugeot 206 WRC	Accident
SS.14	Märtin - Park	Ford Focus RS WRC 02	Accident
SS.11	Paasonen - Kapanen	Mitsubishi Lancer Evo WRC 2	Accident
SS.4	C. McRae - Grist	Ford Focus RS WRC 02	Accident
SS.2	Eriksson - Thörner	Skoda Octavia WRC Evo 3	Accident

Championship Classifications

FIA Drivers (12/14)
1. Grönholm 67; 2. Burns 34; 3. C. McRae 33; 4. Panizzi 31; 5. Sainz 29;
6. Rovanperä 24; 7. Solberg 23; 8. Mäkinen 19; 9. Loeb 18; 10. Märtin 12;
11. Bugalski 7; 12. Radström 4; 13. A. McRae, Gardemeister, Thiry &
Kankkunen 2; 17. Puras, Eriksson & Loix 1

FIA Constructors (12/14)
1. Peugeot 147; 2. Ford 89; 3. Subaru 50; 4. Mitsubishi, Hyundai 9;
6. Skoda 8

FIA Production Car WRC (7/8)
1. Singh 28; 2. Sohlberg 26; 3. Ferreyros 20; 4. Fiorio 16; 5. Arai, Trelles 12;
7. Rowe 11; 8. Iliev 9; 9. Girdauskas 7; 10. Ipatti, Baldini, Manfrinato &
Ligato 4; 14. Kollevold 3; 15. Harrach, De Dominicis & Marini 2

FIA Junior WRC (5/6)
1. Dallavilla 28; 2. Sola 27; 3. Caldani 13; 4. Tuohino, Duval 12; 6. Basso 10;
7. Schelle, Galli 5; 9. Feghali, Rowe 4; 11. Carlsson, Baldacci 3;
13. Doppelreiter 2; 14. Foss, Katajamäki 1

Performers

	1	2	3	4	5	6
Grönholm	15	5	3	–	–	1
Burns	8	4	–	1	1	–
Solberg	2	5	7	7	–	–
Rovanperä	1	8	8	1	4	–
Paasonen	1	–	–	2	1	1
Mäkinen	–	4	2	6	8	2
Sainz	–	1	2	5	6	4
Panizzi	–	–	1	2	–	2
Märtin	–	–	1	–	1	4
Kankkunen	–	–	–	1	3	4
Gardemeister	–	–	–	1	2	3
C. McRae	–	–	–	1	–	1
Loix	–	–	–	–	–	2
Schwarz	–	–	–	–	–	1

Event Leaders

SS.1 > SS.14	Burns
SS.15 > SS.26	Grönholm

Previous winners

1977	Bacchelli - Rosetti Fiat 131 Abarth	1992	Sainz - Moya Toyota Celica Turbo 4WD
1978	Brookes - Porter Ford Escort RS	1993	McRae - Ringer Subaru Legacy RS
1979	Mikkola - Hertz Ford Escort RS	1994	McRae - Ringer Subaru Impreza
1980	Salonen - Harjanne Datsun 160J	1995	McRae - Ringer Subaru Impreza
1982	Waldegaard - Thorzelius Toyota Celica GT	1996	Burns - Reid Mitsubishi Lancer Ev.3
1983	Rohrl - Geistdorfer Opel Ascona 400	1997	Eriksson - Parmander Subaru Impreza WRC
1984	Blomqvist - Cederberg Audi Quattro A2	1998	Sainz - Moya Toyota Corolla WRC
1985	Salonen - Harjanne Peugeot 205 T16	1999	Mäkinen - Mannisenmäki Mitsubishi Lancer Evo 6
1986	Kankkunen - Piironen Peugeot 205 T16	2000	Grönholm - Rautiainen Peugeot 206 WRC
1987	Wittmann - Patermann Lancia Delta HF 4WD	2001	Grönholm - Rautiainen Peugeot 206 WRC
1988	Haider - Hinterleitner Opel Kadett GSI		
1989	Carlsson - Carlsson Mazda 323 Turbo		
1990	Sainz - Moya Toyota Celica GT-Four		
1991	Sainz - Moya Toyota Celica GT-Four		

141

Australia

Marcus Grönholm didn't
need to push for his fifth
win of the season. With
the world title in his
pocket since New Zealand
Peugeot's Finnish driver
only had to keep
teammate Harri Rovanperä
in check once mechancal
failure had sidelined
Richard Burns. The two
Scandinavians completed
the French cars' eighth 1-
2 finish in 13 rallies

Good things come in threes: Marcus Grönholm had no need to push hard for a third win in the Antipodes this year to go with his 2000 and 2001 Australian successes.

THE RACE
GRÖNHOLM AT HIS LEISURE

Some say this is the most dangerous rally on the calendar, others believe that unwanted honour goes to Corsica. It's all a question of background.

For a Latin brought up on tarmac, taking on the rally of a thousand turns may not be child's play, but it is second nature; for the rest, mainly Scandinavians and Brits, coping with those slippery roads on the island continent is somehow in their genes. To each his own. But the Australian event certainly has some characteristics that make it a one-off. The roads that fan out

When the car doesn't break, the Hyundai drivers often do. Loix was brilliant early on but went off near the end of the first leg.

from Perth, on the west coast, and back are covered in small gravel balls, in colour and size exactly like the ones you put in the bottom of your flower pots to keep the moisture in. Just think about it: walking on a footing like that without a slip calls for a tightrope walker's skills, so driving at high speed must be for the true artist. Especially on narrow roads where, as Petter Solberg put it, it always looks as if the trees are about to cross – in which case a rally driver comes close to a slalom skier shouldering aside the posts that mark his gates.

That, then, was the playing-field – and it's one that François Delecour can't seem to get the hang of. In 1995, his last full season before being unfairly overlooked, the great late braker damaged his Ford Escort RS here; last year he used his Focus WRC to attack a eucalypt; and this time he lost control of his Mitsubishi Lancer WRC on the first leg. Our colleagues at the British specialist magazine Autosport said the resultant, terrifying 100mph crash was the

biggest ever to happen to a World Rally Car. And the sight of the smoking wreck, its engine block quietly dying ten metres away from the chassis, was not a pretty one. Worse still, Daniel Grataloup was in a bad way when they removed him from the cockpit. It came about on the seventh special, Murray Pines South, where the driver hit a stump at the apex of a left-hander with his front left wheel. Thrown off balance, the car went straight on into the forest like a chain saw. The driver was knocked out on impact, with no serious damage, which was more than could be said for his navigator. Daniel Grataloup had let out a shriek of fear just before the machine slammed into an unyielding tree. He was airlifted immediately to hospital in Perth with fractures to his pelvis, his right leg, two ribs and his collarbone. All heart and determination, he was flown home to France and family many days later. Grataloup had been

This was Ford's Estonian driver's first real crack at this event (he retired on the first special stage in 2000), and it was a good one, with an encouraging fifth-place finish.

thinking about giving up competitive rallying, but since then he has decided against it.

Needless to say, the rest of the rally was run under a considerable cloud. But there was a race on, and a damn fine one it was too. A scratch time on the first special stage had put Petter Solberg in the lead as Marcus Grönholm scratched his head for a way round the handicap of opening the road,

probably worse in Australia than anywhere else. Thankfully for the new champion, the rain before the start had helped settle the gravel layer, which meant that after the Norwegian and Freddy Loix, who set scratch in the second stage, had their little bit of fun, Marcus and his 206 rolled up their sleeves and went into the lead on the third. Just for the record, he never relinquished it, setting every scratch time for the rest of the first leg bar the

Langley Park show won by Harri Rovanperä.
And yet there were those – Richard Burns in particular – who were determined to give him a hard time of it. On this course the Englishman felt he had a real chance of winning for the first time in a 206 and bringing the super-confident Grönholm to heel. The 2001 World Champion tried everything, but fell short of ever becoming a real danger. On the abovementioned Murray Pines South stage, before Delecour's accident, he had to retire with a broken clutch. He

would have been hard pressed to beat his teammate in any case. And of course Gronholm didn't loosen his grip on the rest of Rally Australia. Solberg, 29.5s down after the first leg, tried hard to breathe life into proceedings after that, but an untroubled Grönholm was in control and extending his advantage bit by bit. So it was left to the rest of the field to provide the interest in this 13th round. Thank goodness Colin McRae knows how to put on a show! He started the event with Derek Ringer in place of Nicky Grist: the tension that had been

Not sure of a drive for 2003, Sainz put himself in the shop window, sneaking another points finish – his ninth from a possible 13.

Once Burns was out Rovanperä drove one of his best events of the season, getting right up into Grönholm's slipstream.

simmering between the two for months had boiled over and brought their partnership, begun on the 1997 Monte, to an end.

They took one leg to get run in, by which the two old mates – McRae was 1995 World Champion with Ringer – had got the hang of each other again, not only in their way of going about the event but in their mutual denial of the laws of physics. Let's not forget that it was with this same chap by his side that the Scot got saddled with the glorious tag of "Colin McCrash". On Muresk 1, landing over one of the most famous jumps in the Championship, now making a timely reappearance, the Ford dug its nose in, burst its radiator and was unable to go on. In an identical car François Duval had also flirted with disaster on landing but luckily for the young Belgian he got away with it. But not with the mistake he made on the last leg: on the last but one stage he got it wrong and a tree

thumped into the passenger door of his Focus. The incident forced his navigator Jean-Marc Fortin to hospital for a check-up.

Grönholm was going along nicely at the front ahead of Harri Rovanperä, who took advantage of the leader's serene progress to set a string of scratch times and snatch the runner-up spot from Solberg. We needed a third man to make up the podium, and it lay between Subaru's Norwegian, a wound-up Carlos Sainz and Tommi Mäkinen. In the end, the coveted position as first of the non-Peugeots went to the young Scandinavian, his teammate finding himself disqualified towards the end of the rally. On exit from the 23rd special stage, his Subaru weighed in at 1222 kilos, some eight below the minimum. Poor Mäkinen: he had already been outshone by his teammate, and here he was suffering the same agony as two years before when his Mitsubishi was excluded over

an illegal turbo. With one major difference: that time he was the winner on the road, now he was fighting for the minor placings.

A word about Sébastian Loeb to finish. The Frenchman contested the event in a semi-privateer, semi-works Xsara WRC. The entry came hard on the heels of a five-day test fitted in before the reonnaissance runs. The point was to gain some experience for the 2003 running of the event, because next season testing will be banned in countries outside Europe where a World Championship rally is being staged. Smart thinking, Citroën. The driver duly came home seventh after a measured, sensible drive.

But that, of course, fell a long way short of Peugeot's performance. The Lion claimed

another double, with Grönholm leading Rovanperä home, their eighth from 13 opportunities through the season. How could you ask for more? ∎

GROUP N
SINGH TAKES CHARGE

One round after the major drivers' and constructors' titles had been settled, Rally Australia saw the identity of the FIA Production category revealed. The name of course refers to Group N, for production cars. Coming to Australia, three drivers were in contention to succeed the Argentine Gabriel Pozzo:

Malaysian Karamjit Singh, Finland's Kristian Sohlberg and Ramon Ferreyros of Peru. The last-named's chances were slimmest as he had to count on

The consistent, valiant Toni Gardemeister helped Skoda to another constructors' championship point.

Loeb and Citroën went out to Australia on a learning mission for 2003. As usual, the driver coped very well with the challenge those tricky conditions presented.

Trying hard, no doubt, to revive past glories together, Colin McRae and Derek Ringer, who replaced Nicky Grist, made too spectacular – and too hard – a landing for the Focus to withstand.

For the time being, Marcus Grönholm at the wheel is still a level above Petter Solberg. But the Norwegian tried his hardest to knock him off that pedestal...

Once again Mäkinen was disqualified in Australia, but it was his team's fault – the Subaru was eight kilos underweight!

his rivals' retiring. The other two got straight down to a ferocious struggle, but on the Muresk stage the Nordic driver's Mitsubishi gave up the ghost on landing over one of the course's murderous bumps. With a rear crossmember broken, retirement was the only option, so Singh inherited the lead. He just had to keep it going while looking out for the South American in his mirrors. 'You really have to keep your eyes peeled,' Singh said. 'After the WRC cars have gone through, the going is pretty tough for our Group N cars, and you need a bit of luck to be in at the finish.' With his rival off his back, the Malaysian made no mistake and finished the event at the head of that group. While Toshi Araï took the category overall, both of them left Manfred Stohl to fight

it out with local drivers Ed Ordynski, Bourke, Crocker, Evans and the rest for the production honours. When Bourne fell victim to his Subaru's broken suspension, the Austrian took the lead and though Crocker threatened he too eventually retired with electrical failure. Stohl finished a fine tenth, Group N entry winner Araï 14th and new champion Singh 18th. His win is not only the first for a Malaysian in an FIA World Championship, but also for a car of the Proton brand. A copy of the Mitsubishi Lancer it may be, but it was also a first for a car from that same country. Karamjit Singh, World Champion in a Proton Pert: a big taste of the exotic for the World. Championship, and so much the better for that. ∎

Telstra Rally Australia 2002

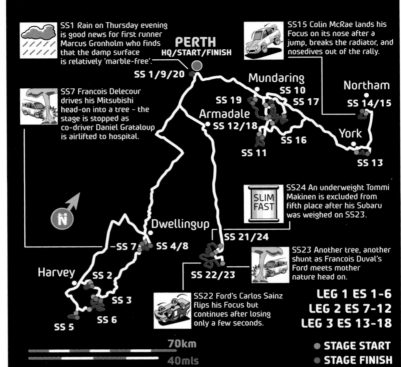

SS1 Rain on Thursday evening is good news for first runner Marcus Gronholm who finds that the damp surface is relatively 'marble-free'.

SS15 Colin McRae lands his Focus on its nose after a jump, breaks the radiator, and nosedives out of the rally.

SS7 Francois Delecour drives his Mitsubishi head-on into a tree - the stage is stopped as co-driver Daniel Grataloup is airlifted to hospital.

SS24 An underweight Tommi Makinen is excluded from fifth place after his Subaru was weighed on SS23.

SS23 Another tree, another shunt as Francois Duval's Ford meets mother nature head on.

SS22 Ford's Carlos Sainz flips his Focus but continues after losing only a few seconds.

PERTH HQ/START/FINISH

Mundaring SS 10 SS 17

Northam SS 14/15

SS 19

Armadale SS 12/18

SS 16

York

SS 11

SS 13

Dwellingup

SS 21/24

SS 7 — SS 4/8

Harvey SS 2

SS 22/23

SS 3

SS 5 SS 6

SS 1/9/20

LEG 1 ES 1-6
LEG 2 ES 7-12
LEG 3 ES 13-18

70km
40mls

● STAGE START
● STAGE FINISH

13rd leg of the 2002 World Rally Championship for constructors and drivers. 8th leg of FIA Production Car WRC Championship.

Date 31st October to 3rd November 2002

Route
1571,98 km divided in 3 legs
24 special stages on dirt roads
(388,55 km)

Superspecial
Thursday 31 October (18h50-21h00):
Langley Park (2,20 km)
1st leg
Friday 1st November (07h00-20h21):
Perth > Dwellinup > Perth, 679,04 km;
8 special stages (133,45 km)
2nd leg
Saturday 2nd November (07h00-20h41):
Perth > Chidlow > Perth, 539,15 km;
11 special stages (147,23 km)
3rd leg
Sunday 3rd November (06h00-15h46):
Perth > Bunnings (Sotico) > Perth,
353,79 km; 4 special stages (105,67 km)

Entry List - Starters - Finishers:
73 - 69 - 37

Conditions: Fine and warm.

TOP ENTRIES

1. Richard BURNS - Robert REID
   Peugeot 206 WRC
2. Marcus GRÖNHOLM - Timo RAUTIAINEN Peugeot 206 WRC
3. Harri ROVANPERÄ - Voitto SILANDER Peugeot 206 WRC
4. Carlos SAINZ - Luis MOYA
   Ford Focus RS WRC 02
5. Colin McRAE - Derek RINGER
   Ford Focus RS WRC 02
6. Markko MÄRTIN - Michael PARK
   Ford Focus RS WRC 02
7. Francois DELECOUR - Daniel GRATALOUP Mitsubishi Lancer Evo WRC
9. Jani PAASONEN - Arto KAPANEN
   Mitsubishi Lancer Evolution WRC
10. Tommi MÄKINEN - Kaj LINDSTRÖM
    Subaru Impreza WRC 2002
11. Petter SOLBERG - Philip MILLS
    Subaru Impreza WRC 2002
14. Kenneth ERIKSSON - Tina THORNER
    Skoda Octavia WRC Evo 3
15. Toni GARDEMEISTER - Paavo LUKANDER Skoda Octavia WRC Evo 3
17. Armin SCHWARZ - Manfred HIEMER
    Hyundai Accent WRC 3
18. Freddy LOIX - Sven SMEETS
    Hyundai Accent WRC 3
19. Juha KANKKUNEN - Juha REPO
    Hyundai Accent WRC 3
24. Francois DUVAL - Jean-Marc FORTIN
    Ford Focus RS WRC 02
25. Sébastien LOEB - Daniel ELENA
    Citroen Xsara WRC
32. Tomasz KUCHAR - Maciej SZCEPANIAK
    Toyota Corolla WRC
52. Marcos LIGATO - Ruben GARCIA
    Mitsubishi Lancer Evo 7
53. Alessandro FIORIO - Vittorio BRAMBILLA
    Mitsubishi Lancer Evo 7
54. Ramon FERREYROS - Jorge DEL BUONO
    Mitsubishi Lancer Evo 7
57. Toshihiro ARAI - Tony SIRCOMBE
    Subaru Impreza WRX
65. Beppo HARRACH - Peter MÜLLER
    Mitsubishi Lancer Evo 6
69. Bernt KOLLEVOLD - Ola FLOENE
    Mitsubishi Lancer Evo 7
70. Giovanni MANFRINATO - Claudio CONDOTTA Mitsubishi Lancer Evo 6
71. Stefano MARRINI - Tiziana SANDRONI
    Mitsubishi Lancer Evo 7
73. Martin ROWE - Chris WOOD
    Mitsubishi Lancer Evo 7
74. Karamjit SINGH - Allen OH
    Proton Pert
75. Kristian SOHLBERG - Jakke HONKANEN
    Mitsubishi Lancer Evo 7
77. Alfredo DE DOMINICIS - Nicola ARENA
    Mitsubishi Lancer Evo 7
101. Manfred STOHL - Ilka PETRASKO
     Mitsubishi Lancer Evo 6
106. Stig BLOMQVIST - Ana GONI
     Mitsubishi Lancer Evo 7
108. Juuso PYKALISTO - Esko MERTSALMI
     Mitsubishi Lancer Evo 6
117. Saulius GIRDAUSKAS - Audrius SHOSHAS
     Mitsubishi Lancer Evo 6

Special Stage Times

SS1 Langley Park I (2,20 km)
1.Solberg 1'28"7; 2.Grönholm + 0"3;
3.Sainz/Burns +0"9; 5.Rovanperä +1"1;
6.Mäkinen +1"3; FIA Prod. (21) Arai +7"7

SS2 Harvey Weir (6,96 km)
1.Loix 4'00"7; 2.Solberg +0"8;
3.Grönholm +1"2; 4.Rovanperä +1"3;
5.Sainz +1"6; 6.C. McRae +1"9;
FIA Prod. (17) Ligato +12"3

SS3 Stirling West (15,89 km)
1.Grönholm 9'19"9; 2.Solberg +2"3;
3.Burns +2"4; 4.Rovanperä +3"6;
5.Sainz +8"6; 6.Loix +9"5;
FIA Prod. (19) Sohlberg +50"3

SS4 Murray River I (20,44 km)
1.Grönholm 12'15"0; 2.Sainz +1"7; 3.Burns
+4"9; 4.Solberg +7"7; 5.C. McRae +8"8;
6.Mäkinen +9"4; FIA Prod. (20) Ligato +55"6

SS5 Brunswick (16,62 km)
1.Grönholm 9'08"7; 2.Burns +1"4;
3.Solberg +3"8; 4.Sainz +7"7;
5.Mäkinen +8"3; 6.Rovanperä +9"3;
FIA Prod. (21) Arai +59"0

SS6 Stirling East Revers (38,93 km)
1.Grönholm 22'44"9; 2.Sainz +4"2;
3.Mäkinen +7"6; 4.Burns +10"0;
5.Solberg +10"1; 6.Rovanperä/Märtin +15"7;
FIA Prod. (20) Rowe +1'51"9

SS7 Murray Pines South (11,97 km)
1.Grönholm 6'29"5; 2.Solberg +1"7;
3.C. McRae/Rovanperä +4"2; 5.Sainz +4"8;
6.Märtin +6"6; FIA Prod. (=) Arai +19"5

SS8 Murray River II (20,44 km)
1.Grönholm 11'47"8; 2.Solberg +5"0;
3.Sainz +5"4; 4.Mäkinen/Rovanperä +9"3;
6.Märtin/Loeb +18"6;
FIA Prod. (17) Singh +1'08"2

SS9 Langley Park II (2,20 km)
1.Rovanperä 1'28"3; 2.C. McRae +0"1;
3.Sainz/Grönholm +0"5; 5.Solberg +1"0;
6.Mäkinen +2"4; FIA Prod. (21) Rowe +9"2

SS10 Kev's (9,56 km)
1.Solberg 5'51"8; 2.Rovanperä 0"5;
3.Grönholm 1"; 4.Sainz 3"5; 5.Mäkinen 4"4;
6.C. McRae 7"8; FIA Prod. (17) Rowe +32"8

SS11 Beraking (26,45 km)
1.Rovanperä 14'23"3; 2.Grönholm +1"7;
3.Solberg 4"3; 4.C. McRae +8"9;
5.Mäkinen +11"8; 6.Sainz 18"0;
FIA Prod. (17) Arai +1'27"2

SS12 Helena South I (18,43 km)
1.Rovanperä 9'28"9; 2.Solberg +0"4;
3.Grönholm +1"5; 4.C. McRae +2"1;
5.Mäkinen +7"0; 6.Sainz +9"4;
FIA Prod. (17 =) Arai +49"3

SS13 York Railwail (5,30 km)
1.Rovanperä 3'45"9; 2.Solberg +1"7;
3.Grönholm +1"2; 4.Sainz +2"6;
5.Solberg +2"6; 6.Mäkinen +3"2;
FIA Prod. (19) Sohlberg +17"1

SS14 Muresk I (6,80 km)
1.Mäkinen 3'24"9; 2.Solberg +0"4;
3.C. McRae +0"7; 4.Sainz +1"9;
5.Rovanperä +2"9; 6.Grönholm +3"8;
FIA Prod. (20) Arai +28"4

SS15 Muresk II (6,80 km)
1.Rovanperä/Sainz 3'24"0; 3.Grönholm +0"1;
4.Mäkinen +0"3; 5.Kankkunen +3"5;
6.Solberg +4"3; FIA Prod. (20) Arai +25"8

SS16 Flynns Short (19,97 km)
1.Grönholm 11'33"8; 2.Solberg +6"0;
3.Rovanperä +6"2; 4.Sainz +9"7;
5.Mäkinen +13"5; 6.Duval +19"7;
FIA Prod. (13) Arai +57"4

SS17 Helena North Extended (28,87 km)
1.Grönholm 16'20"7; 2.Solberg +9"4;
3.Rovanperä +13"2; 4.Sainz +14"4;
5.Mäkinen +21"3; 6.Gardemeister +35"3;
FIA Prod. (20) Arai +1'33"8

SS18 Helena South II (18,43 km)
1.Grönholm 9'20"7; 2.Solberg +0"8;
3.Rovanperä +2"5; 4.Sainz +5"2;
5.Mäkinen +5"3; 6.Märtin +15"5;
FIA Prod. (16) Arai +51"1

SS19 Atkins (4,42 km)
1.Grönholm 2'58"2; 2.Mäkinen/Solberg +1"1;
4.Rovanperä +1"4; 5.Sainz +2"0;
6.Duval +4"9; FIA Prod. (14) Arai +12"5

SS20 Langley Park III (2,20 km)
1.Solberg 1'27"6; 2.Grönholm +1"2;
3.Duval +1"2; 4.Märtin +1"3;
5.Eriksson +1"7; 6.Gardemeister +1"9;
FIA Prod. (16) Fiorio +7"1

SS21 Bannister Central (5,63 km)
1.Rovanperä 3'22"4; 2.Sainz +3"0;
3.Grönholm +3"8; 4.Mäkinen +4"3;
5.Solberg +5"1; 6.Märtin +7"1;
FIA Prod. (19) Arai +21"8

SS22 Bannister South (28,64 km)
1.Rovanperä 16'07"3; 2.Grönholm +11"3;
3.Mäkinen +21"2; 4.Solberg +25"0;
5.Duval +29"6; 6.Märtin +37"0;
FIA Prod. (20) Arai +1'57"4

SS23 Bannister West (34,56 km)
1.Rovanperä 17'09"2; 2.Grönholm +4"6;
3.Solberg +16"3; 4.Mäkinen +18"0;
5.Sainz +23"1; 6.Märtin +42"6;
FIA Prod. (18) Rowe +2'03"3

SS24 Bannister North (36,84 km)
1.Grönholm 19'15"7; 2.Rovanperä +4"3;
3.Mäkinen +9"0; 4.Solberg +13"7;
5.Sainz +18"5; 6.Gardemeister +41"0;
FIA Prod. (14) Arai +2'15"2

Results WRC

	Driver/Navigator	Car	Gr.	Time
1	**Grönholm - Rautiainen**	**Peugeot 206 WRC**	A	3h35'56"5
2	Rovanperä - Pietilainen	Peugeot 206 WRC		+ 57"3
3	Solberg - Mills	Subaru Impreza WRC 2002		+ 1'28"7
4	Sainz - Moya	Ford Focus RS WRC 02		+ 3'09"0
5	Märtin - Park	Ford Focus RS WRC 02		+ 6'21"5
6	Gardemeister - Lukander	Skoda Octavia WRC Evo 3		+ 7'11"6
7	Loeb - Elena	Citroën Xsara WRC		+ 9'06"1
8	Eriksson - Thorner	Skoda Octavia WRC Evo 3		+ 12'46"4
9	Paasonen - Kapanen	Mitsubishi Lancer Evo WRC		+ 13'25"5
10	Stohl - Petrasko	Mitsubishi Lancer Evo 6		+ 19'20"7
14	**Arai - Sircombe**	**Subaru Impreza WRX**	Prod.	+ 22'13"0

Leading Retirements (32)

SS.24	Kankkunen - Repo	Hyundai Accent WRC 3	Engine
SS.23	Duval - Fortin	Ford Focus RS WRC 02	Accident
SS.14	C. McRae - Ringer	Ford Focus RS WRC 02	Accident
SS.7	Schwarz - Hiemer	Hyundai Accent WRC 3	Engine
SS.7	Delecour - Grataloup	Mitsubishi Lancer Evo WRC	Accident
SS.7	Burns - Reid	Peugeot 206 WRC	Clutch
SS.6	Loix - Smeets	Hyundai Accent WRC 3	Accident
CH24E	Mäkinen - Lindstöm	Subaru Impreza WRC 2002	Disqualified (underweight)

Performers

	1	2	3	4	5	6
Grönholm	11	5	7	-	-	1
Rovanperä	8	2	4	4	2	2
Solberg	3	10	4	3	4	1
Sainz	1	3	3	7	6	2
Mäkinen	1	1	3	4	7	4
C. McRae	1	1	2	2	1	2
Loix	1	-	-	-	-	1
Burns	-	1	3	1	-	-
Duval	-	1	-	-	1	2
Märtin	-	-	-	1	-	7
Kankkunen	-	-	-	1	-	1
Eriksson	-	-	-	1	-	1
Gardemeister	-	-	-	-	3	3

Event Leaders

SS.1 > SS.2	Solberg
SS.3 > SS.24	Grönholm

Championship Classifications

FIA Drivers (13/14)
1. Grönholm 77; 2. Burns 34; 3. C. McRae 33; 4. Sainz 32; 5. Panizzi 31;
6. Rovanperä 30; 7. Solberg 27; 8. Mäkinen, Loeb 18; 10. Märtin 14;
11.Bugalski 7; 12. Radström 4; 13. Gardemeister 3; 14. A. McRae, Thiry & Kankkunen 2; 17.Eriksson, Puras & Loix 1

FIA Constructors (13/14)
1. Peugeot 163; 2. Ford 94; 3. Subaru 54; 4. Mitsubishi, Skoda & Hyundai 9

FIA Production Car WRC (8/8)
1. Singh 32; 2. Sohlberg 26; 3. Ferreyros 23; 4. Arai, Fiorio 22; 6. Rowe 13;
7. Trelles 12; 8. Iliev 9; 9. Girdauskas 7; 10. Baldini, Ipatti, Kollevold, Ligato & Manfrinato 4; 15. De Dominicis, Harrach & Marini 2

FIA Junior WRC (5/6)
1. Dallavilla 28; 2. Sola 27; 3. Caldani 13; 4. Tuohino, Duval 12;
6. Basso 10; 7. Schelle, Galli 5; 9. Feghali, Rowe 4; 11. Carlsson, Baldacci 3;
13. Doppelreiter 2; 14. Foss, Katajamäki 1

Previous winners

1989	Kankkunen - Piironen Toyota Celica GT-Four		1996	Mäkinen - Harjanne Mitsubishi Lancer Ev.3
1990	Kankkunen - Piironen Lancia Delta Integrale		1997	McRae - Grist Subaru Impreza WRC
1991	Kankkunen - Piironen Lancia Delta Integrale		1998	Mäkinen - Mannisenmäki Mitsubishi Lancer Ev.5
1992	Auriol - Occelli Lancia Delta HF Integrale		1999	Burns - Reid Subaru Impreza WRC
1993	Kankkunen - Grist Toyota Celica Turbo 4WD		2000	Grönholm - Rautiainen Peugeot 206 WRC
1994	McRae - Ringer Subaru Impreza		2001	Grönholm - Rautiainen Peugeot 206 WRC
1995	Eriksson - Parmander Mitsubishi Lancer Ev.2			

Great Britain

When Marcus Grönholm
made a rare error, running
off the road while well in
front, the battle for victory
boiled down to a two-man
fight between Markko Märtin
and Petter Solberg. Subaru's
Norwegian finally won the
day in style, breaking into
the rally winners' circle and
just snatching the 2002
runner-up spot overall.

Inheriting the lead, Markko Märtin had a chance to win his first World Championship rally – until Hurricane Solberg blew it out of his hands near the end.

It's not often you see Delecour go off, but in Britain he visited the scenery again – the second time in a row, after doing the same in Australia.

Ford put their faith in Mark Higgins by giving him one of the official Focuses to drive, and he made the most of it by finishing eighth.

Mark you, it's no easy thing to make your debut on a rally like that, but the MotoGP calendar left Rossi little room for manoeuvre. And he stumbled on a nice, cosy old RAC, not visited by the rain maybe, but still full of pitfalls after the soakings of the past few days, partly dried – but only partly! – by an invigorating breeze. Brechfa had claimed the motorcycle ace, but there were others who also went off: Briton Justin Dale, brought in to bolster the Mitsubishi effort, remodelled his Lancer as a pick-up truck, Sebastien Loeb had a nasty bump and Colin McRae missed his braking at a

THE RACE
SOLBERG GETS IN AMONG THE BIG BOYS

The whole operation had been carefully put together. On the technical side, the redoubtable, highly efficient Scuderia Grifone provided their services; Michelin did the same with finance and the media certainly weren't about to be left out. This was the proper rally debut for Valentino Rossi, 2002 MotoGP World Champion (formerly 500cc), just the latest of his titles. A keen road racer, the livewire Italian had expressed the wish many times to try his hand at something other than the twists and turns of the Champions' Trophy or other Mickey Mouse transalpine events. Entered with his usual employer Honda's blessing in a 206 WRC, the man they laughingly call "The Doctor" was a touch feverish but raring to go. Once they got through the superspecial curtain-raiser, like his opponents he had to get to grips with the hard going in the Welsh

forests. On the first real special stage, Rossi was determined to observe the old saying – 'gently does it' – that he never pays any heed to on two wheels. Just 10 miles after the Brechfa start, his 206 ended its run – in reverse, and off the track. He had made a mess of a long left-hander, getting the apex all wrong. The car was stuck on too steep a slope to get back on to the road. Not only that, but there was not a single spectator around, and thus no-one to lend a hand. A desperately disappointed Rossi immediately headed for London, leaving navigator Carlo Cassina to bring the car – a bit dirty, granted, but otherwise intact – back to the service park. It had taken a truck just a few seconds to drag it out of its unhappy resting-place, albeit too late. It was a shame: the eminently likeable young fellow had won over the rally world, and his attraction to the discipline had in turn attracted attention from people other than the usual aficionados. Let's hope it was a case of 'Au revoir' and not 'Goodbye'!

This was Colin McRae's final Ford fling after three seasons at the wheel of a Focus. Highlander will be a Citroën driver in 2003.

had had big moments, happily with no serious consequences, and they were both making their famous teammates, Mäkinen in Solberg's case, Sainz and McRae in Märtin's, feel their age.

As the second leg got under way Marcus Grönholm was well aware that there was only one man who could come between him and victory – and that was himself! In fact Solberg was 48.3 seconds behind, Märtin 51, big enough gaps for him to be relatively relaxed. All big Marcus had to do to take his sixth win of the season, equalling Didier Auriol's record, was turn up. But this was not to be the Finn's year to match the Frenchman. In Halfway he had a violent off, flinging the 206 into a series of rolls that were great for the show, not too good for the machine but happily did no harm at all to its crew. Not ducking out at all, Grönholm was quick to admit his mistake. "I went in too quick," he said afterwards. "I went through a series of bumps too hard before the back end hit, and that sent us into the

junction and had to be helped back on track by spectators. On the next section Richard Burns went off hard in his 206, flattening his machine's exhaust and depriving the engine of all its power. McRae and Burns delayed – the former Princes of Wales cut down to size. And that wasn't the end of it: an uninspired Rovanperä stalled twice on the same stage before picking up a penalty in the next for a jump start then having a spin on SS6. As for Tommi Mäkinen, though he was blameless for once this season, his Subaru was at it again with an anaemic turbo.

So it was a question of who could survive long enough to finish this one-day holiday on mud in front. And the answer, of course, was Marcus Grönholm! Yet again he skipped through the leg, taking all the scratch times that really mattered and leaving the one for the last superspecial to Solberg. The Norwegian matched Markko Märtin's performance there the previous day, a time that had earned the Estonian a short-lived rally lead before the Grönholm machine got going. Those were the three men in the three podium places on that Friday evening. The young, headstrong members of the Subaru and Ford camps had made a remarkable start, though they made a point of saying how slippery and dangerous the roads had been. Both

Fifth place in Britain was small consolation: this was a season Tommi Mäkinen will want to forget in a hurry.

Ten miles and then he was out of here: Valentino Rossi made a mess of his first real rally start.

Freddy Loix's eighth place brought Hyundai another constructors' point and fourth place overall.

Toni Gardemeister outshone his teammate this season to guarantee himself his 2003 drive with Skoda.

rolls." To be precise it happened at Dixies, a particularly tricky spot because there was a short tarred section on which, of course, the gravel tyres on the cars weren't up to the job. Not only that but Grönholm, without hydraulic pressure since the previous stage and forced into making manual changes, had lost concentration and simply not been careful enough. He wasn't the only one either, for Paasonen performed the same figure a few minutes later at exactly the same place, his Mitsubishi expiring just a few yards from the stricken Peugeot. Of course the French constructors couldn't really hold it against their star driver, especially as they and Grönholm had both secured their titles some time before.

Naturally the retirement injected some fresh interest in the rally. A surprised and happy Markko Märtin inherited the lead ahead of Solberg and Sainz, the three men then covered by 16.7 seconds. For all his verve, and the fact that his 206 was

working particularly well in those conditions, Burns was giving the leader 52.8 seconds, far too big a gap for him to entertain any hopes of getting back. With a first World Championship win just a bonnet's length away, the two young Turks up front made a thunderous finish to that leg, though the Norwegian didn't do it as well as the Estonian. But with that wolfish grin of his and his iron will, Märtin was clinging on to the lead, and just kept it as they got back to Cardiff on the Saturday night. It was down to just 1.6 seconds. Sainz, on the other hand, hadn't been able to keep pace and was now 30 seconds adrift. And just to show how much spirit these youngsters have, Sébastien Loeb had also put in a high-class effort on the second leg, even though he was having his first drive in a WRC. A second-fastest time, a third and a fourth showed how quickly he was adapting and took him from ninth to sixth. He had benefited from Grönholm's retirement and Rovanperä's woes with suspension and brakes, and again when McRae

stalled at the start of the superspecial, but it was no more than he deserved. It was some consolation for Citroën too following the nasty bump that had sidelined Radstrom.

So the last day was to see the coming of a new rally winner! The forecasts were flying: Solberg from Märtin, Märtin from Solberg... As short of common sense as you would expect any top-class driver to be, the Norwegian flung himself into the attack on a final day that comprised four special stages. A super-quick time on the first took him into the lead; his Ford rival hit back on the next, though it wasn't good enough to win it back; stung into action, the Subaru man made a whirlwind finish to both the rally and the season with the last two scratch times, and that was enough to seal the victory. Märtin was 24.4 seconds behind. Disappointed but gracious in defeat, he congratulated the winner. "Petter drove very well," he said. "And in any case it was a fantastic weekend for both of us." Solberg could really give

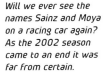

Will we ever see the names Sainz and Moya on a racing car again? As the 2002 season came to an end it was far from certain.

Caught out at the same spot, Grönholm and Paasonen both barrel-rolled their cars, the two wrecks ending up almost side-by-side.

No wonder a joyful Solberg was spraying the champagne: he was a World Championship rally winner at last. Bravo!

Once again Jean-Joseph and his Clio dominated the Super 1600 class. Pity they didn't contest the Junior Championship!

vent to his feelings, in the nicest way and with his usual infectious exuberance. On the eve of his 28th birthday, here he was joining the elite club of World Championship Rally winners! And he had done it in style, never shirking danger until the very end although his advantage was getting bigger all the time. "It was a bit on the limit at times," he said joyfully. "I could have thrown it all away with a spin, but I kept my nerve and that's what counts. And what a reward!" All the more so because those 10 points for winning meant he leap-frogged a star quintet – Sainz, McRae, Burns, Panizzi and Rovanperä – in the drivers' championship and, right at the death, finished as Marcus Grönholm's runner-up.

That left the unfortunate Märtin still knocking at the door to the winners' circle, where Solberg was warmly welcomed by Sainz, but it shouldn't be long before he pushes his way in too. Behind those two the Spaniard made sure of a double podium finish, on the event and overall, though not

of his future: as the rally ended the two-time World Champion didn't have a definite drive for 2003. A frustrated Tommi Mäkinen was fourth. True, he had been held up by a host of technical troubles, but what was worse was that he had never been able to match his young Subaru teammate's pace. Colin McRae and, surprisingly, Mark Higgins, both driving works Focuses, snaffled the last two points on offer. Richard Burns and Sébastien Loeb had both fallen off the leaderboard since the penultimate special, the Englishman going off, the Frenchman with suspension broken by repeated pounding over embedded rocks. That meant the 2001 World Champion, chasing his first win in a 206, hadn't had a victory for 14 months! Finishing fifth overall, his worst result since 1998, he will have to put the season behind him as quickly as he can. Peugeot, for their part, had a rather anonymous rally. It was a most unusual thing for none of the Lionesses to be in the top six finishers, a 'feat' that no-one will hold against the remarkable French team after a season so dominated by their 206 and their talented people. ∎

THE JUNIORS
SOLA IS LOEB'S SUCCESSOR

The last rally of the 2002 season was a decisive one in the outcome of the FIA Junior Championship. As the race started, the only drivers with a chance of succeeding 2001 champion Sébastien Loeb – it was then called the Super 1600 – were Citroën drivers Andrea Dallavilla and Daniel Sola. There was just one point between the two men, the experienced Italian having the edge. The Catalan didn't mess about: he won it after a fine, fiercely-fought race, finishing ahead of the redoubtable British specialist McShea

in his Opel Corsa and the Fiat Punto of Italy's Basso. Dallavilla could do no better than sixth after losing eight minutes halfway through with a puncture. As in 2001 he had to be content with second place.

Seen in Spain as a worthy successor to Carlos Sainz, 'Dani' Sola, clearly an all-rounder unlike other Iberian tarmac specialists such as Jesus Puras, has a real future. Winner of three of the six events on the calendar, he was driving a privateer Citroën Saxo entered by the efficient French PH Sport outfit. They are obviously the ones who guarantee

success: it was the same team that helped Loeb to the title in 2001. The marque with the double chevron must have been happy with the way the 2002 series turned out, having three cars in the first three places, with Finland's Tuohino rounding out the podium behind Sola and Dallavilla. Despite the bigger and better competition, the Saxo showed no signs of weakness or age all year. It remains to be seen how it will cope with some sharper cars in 2003, starting with the brand-new Clio driven with so much panache by Simon Jean-Joseph from time to time this year. ∎

Spain's 'Dani' Sola fought splendidly to clinch the junior world title. He is a worthy successor to Sébastien Loeb.

Network 0 Rally of Great Britain 2002

14th and final leg of the 2002 World Rally Championship for constructors and drivers. 6th and final leg of WRC Junior Championship.

Date 14th to 17th November 2002

Route
1637,86 km divided in 3 legs.
17 special stages on dirt roads scheduled (390,53 km) and 16 contested (367,41 km)

1st leg
Friday 15th November (05h15-20h30):
Cardiff > Felindre > Cardiff, 638,66 km;
6 special stages scheduled (135,01 km) and 5 contested (111,89 km)

2nd leg
Saturday 16th November (06h00-20h30):
Cardiff > Felindre > Cardiff, 508,39 km;
6 special stages (117,03 km)

3rd leg
Sunday 17th November (05h30-16h40):
Cardiff > Felindre > Cardiff, 490,81 km;
4 special stages (138,49 km)

Entry List - Starters - Finishers:
93 - 89 - 39

Conditions: cloudy then sunny, slippery dirt roads.

SS2 Italian bike ace Valentino Rossi rolls out of the rally early to the dissappointment of his fans.

SS3 Drivers are unprepared for the sunshine and the glare makes driving conditions difficult.

LEG 1 SS 1-7
LEG 2 SS 8-13
LEG 3 SS 14-17

● STAGE START
● STAGE FINISH

SS10 Ice cool Marcus Gronholm makes an atypical mistake and rolls out of the rally, as does Mitsubishi's Jani Paasonen and Francois Delecour.

SS8 Armin Schwarz's Hyundai catches fire and he is left gasping for breath in the smoke.

SS17 An ecstatic Petter Solberg takes his first WRC victory for Subaru.

SS16 Richard Burns blows his chances after sliding off the road near the infamous Margam tree.

CARDIFF
HQ/START/FINISH

70km
40mls

Llandovery
Brecon
Carmarthen
Swansea
Port Talbot

SS 9/11
SS 2/4
SS 3/5
SS 10/12
SS 6/15
SS 8/14
SS 16/17
SS 1/7/13

TOP ENTRIES

1 Richard BURNS - Robert REID
Peugeot 206 WRC

2 Marcus GRÖNHOLM - Timo RAUTIAINEN Peugeot 206 WRC

3 Harri ROVANPERÄ - Risto PIETILÄINEN Peugeot 206 WRC

4 Carlos SAINZ - Luis MOYA
Ford Focus RS WRC 02

5 Colin McRAE - Derek RINGER
Ford Focus RS WRC 02

6 Markko MÄRTIN - Michael PARK
Ford Focus RS WRC 02

7 François DELECOUR - D. SAVIGNONI
Mitsubishi Lancer Evo WRC 2

8 Justin DALE - Andrew BARGERY
Mitsubishi Lancer Evo WRC 2

9 Jani PAASONEN - Arto KAPANEN
Mitsubishi Lancer Evo WRC 2

10 Tommi MÄKINEN - Kaj LINDSTROM
Subaru Impreza WRC 2002

11 Petter SOLBERG - Philip MILLS
Subaru Impreza WRC 2002

14 Kenneth ERIKSSON - Tina THORNER
Skoda Octavia WRC Evo 3

15 Toni GARDEMEISTER - Paavo LUKANDER Skoda Octavia WRC Evo 3

16 Roman KRESTA - Jan TOMANEK
Skoda Octavia WRC Evo 3

17 Armin SCHWARZ - Manfred HIEMER
Hyundai Accent WRC 3

18 Freddy LOIX - Sven SMEETS
Hyundai Accent WRC 3

19 Juha KANKKUNEN - Juha REPO
Hyundai Accent WRC 3

20 Thomas RADSTRÖM - D. GIRAUDET
Citroën Xsara WRC

21 Sébastien LOEB - Daniel ELENA
Citroën Xsara WRC

23 Gilles PANIZZI - Hervè PANIZZI
Peugeot 206 WRC

24 Mark HIGGINS - Bryan THOMAS
Ford Focus RS WRC 02

25 Juuso PYKALISTO - Esko MERTSALMI
Peugeot 206 WRC

26 Armin KREMER - D. SCHNEPPENHEIM
Ford Focus

27 I. PAPADIMITRIOU - Allan HARRYMAN
Ford Focus WRC

28 Mikko HIRVONEN - Jarmo LEHTINEN
Subaru Impreza WRC

29 Manfred STOHL - Ilka PETRASKO
Ford Focus WRC

31 Txus JAIO - Lucas CRUZ
Ford Focus WRC

46 Valentino ROSSI - Carlo CASSINA
Peugeot 206 WRC

51 Andréa DALLAVILLA - Giovanni BERNACCHINI Citroën Saxo VTS

52 Niall McSHEA - Michael ORR
Opel Corsa

53 Giandomenico BASSO - Luigi PIROLLO
Fiat Punto HGT

55 François DUVAL - Jean-Marc FORTIN
Ford Puma

62 Janne TUOHINO - Petri VIHAVAINEN
Citroën Saxo VTS

64 Gianluigi GALLI - Guido D'AMORE
Fiat Punto HGT

65 Daniel SOLA - Alex ROMANI
Citroën Saxo VTS

Special Stage Times

SS1 Cardiff Super Special (2,45 km)
1.Märtin 2'07"7; 2.Solberg +6"0;
3.C. McRae +1"1; 4.Sainz +1"3;
5.Rovanperä +1"5; 6.Grönholm +2"6;
Jr. (44) Evans +14"1

SS2 Brechfa I (23,12 km)
1.Grönholm 13'24"2; 2.Burns +0"5;
3.Sainz +12"0; 4.Märtin +12"8;
5.Solberg +17"5; 6.Rovanperä +17"9;
Jr. (38) Tuohino +2'16"6

SS3 Trawscoed I (27,96 km)
1.Grönholm 16'36"5; 2.Solberg +13"8;
3.Märtin +18"3; 4.Sainz +24"3;
5.C. McRae +26"6; 6.Mäkinen 27"3;
Jr. (38) Sola +2'44"2

SS4 Brechfa II (23,12 km)
Cancelled - too many spectators.

SS5 Trawscoed II (27,96 km)
1.Grönholm 16'52"6; 2.Solberg +8"2;
3.C. McRae +9"8; 4.Märtin +11"0;
5.Burns +13"8; 6.Mäkinen +15"2;
Jr. (35) Dallavilla +2"33

SS6 Rheola I (27,95 km)
1.Grönholm 15'55"5; 2.Burns +5"8;
3.Solberg +11"1; 4.Märtin +11"3;
5.C. McRae +12"6; 6.Sainz +13"7;
Jr. (28) Sola +2'34"7

SS7 Cardiff Super Spéciale (2,45 km)
1.Solberg 2'07"2; 2.Märtin +0"5;
3.Sainz +1"2; 4.Grönholm 1"3;
5.C. McRae 2"1; 6.Burns 2"4;
Jr. (41) Dallavilla +14"4

SS8 Resolfen I (54,68 km)
1.Grönholm 28'56"5; 2.Burns +5"2;
3.Rovanperä 16'55"8;
4.Sainz 17'24"8; 5.Märtin 16"7;
6.Solberg 27"7; Jr. (33) Sola +4'31"3

SS9 Crychan I (12,67 km)
1.Solberg 7'03"6; 2.Burns +1"1;
3.Grönholm +3"1; 4.Märtin +3"4;
5.Sainz +4"0; 6.Rovanperä +6"1;
Jr. (34) Sola +1'06"7

SS10 Halfway I (17,28 km)
1.Burns 9'50"8; 2.Loeb +1"9;
3.Solberg +3"1; 4.C.McRae +3"9;
5.Märtin +4"5; 6.Sainz +8"1;
Jr. (19) Dallavilla +59"2

SS11 Crychan II (12,67 km)
1.Solberg 7'07"1; 2.Märtin +0"6;
3.Burns +2"0; 4.Mäkinen +4"5;
5.Sainz +4"9; 6.Loeb +4"9;
Jr. (41) Dallavilla +14"4

SS12 Halfway II (17,28 km)
1.Solberg 9'59"9; 2.Märtin +1"1;
3.Loeb +1"6; 4.Mäkinen +2"4;
5.C. McRae +3"7; 6.Burns +4"1;
Jr. (22) McShea +1'15"6

SS13 Cardiff Super Special (2,45 km)
1.Solberg 2'07"9; 2.Märtin +0"2;
3.Sainz +0"9; 4.Burns +1"4;
5.Loeb +1"4; 6.Higgins +1"4;
Jr. (33) Baldacci +4'25"3

SS14 Resolfen II (54,68 km)
1.Solberg 28'49"4; 2.Burns +2"8;
3.Rovanperä +19"3; 4.Märtin +21"9;
5.Sainz +25"5; 6.C. McRae +26"0;
Jr. (21) Baldacci +4'25"3

SS15 Rheola II (27,95 km)
1.Märtin 15'49"6; 2.Burns +4"5;
3.Solberg +7"5; 4.Mäkinen +9"4;
5.C. McRae +9"5; 6.Rovanperä +10"9;
Jr. (24) Välimäki +2'24"4

SS16 Margam I (27,93 km)
1.Solberg 16'12"3; 2.Märtin +8"5;
3.Mäkinen +8"9; 4.Sainz +16"9;
5.Higgins +18"8; 6.C. McRae +20"1;
Jr. (20) McShea +2'20"9

SS17 Margam II (27,93 km)
1.Solberg 16'06"1; 2.Märtin +3"1;
3.Mäkinen +5"5; 4.Rovanperä +9"7;
5.C. McRae +11"5; 6.Sainz 16"1;
Jr. (18) McShea +2'30"0

Results — WRC

	Driver/Navigator	Car	Gr.	Time
1	Solberg - Mills	Subaru Impreza WRC 2002	A	3h30'36"4
2	Märtin - Park	Ford Focus RS WRC 02		+ 24"4
3	Sainz - Moya	Ford Focus RS WRC 02		+ 1'35"7
4	Mäkinen - Lindström	Subaru Impreza WRC 2002		+ 2'37"5
5	C. McRae - Grist	Ford Focus RS WRC 02		+ 3'01"5
6	Higgins - Thorley	Ford Focus RS WRC 02		+ 5'01"9
7	Rovanperä - Rautiainen	Peugeot 206 WRC		+ 5'15"8
8	Loix - Smeets	Hyundai Accent WRC 3		+ 5'15"9
9	Kankkunen - Repo	Hyundai Accent WRC 3		+ 5'29"1
10	Gardemeister - Lukander	Skoda Octavia WRC Evo 3		+6'02"9
21	**Sola - Romani**	**Citroën Saxo VTS**		**+ 32'30"2**

Leading Retirements (47)

SS.16	Burns - Reid	Peugeot 206 WRC	Off
SS.16	Loeb - Elena	Citroën Xsara WRC	Suspension
SS.10	Grönholm - Rautiainen	Peugeot 206 WRC	Off
SS.10	Delecour - Savignoni	Mitsubishi Lancer Evo WRC	Off
SS.10	Paasonen - Kapanen	Mitsubishi Lancer Evo WRC	Off
SS.8	Radström - Giraudet	Citroën Xsara WRC	Engine
SS.8	Schwarz - Hiemer	Mitsubishi Lancer Evo WRC 2	Withdraw
SS.3	Dale - Bargery	Mitsubishi Lancer Evo WRC 2	Off
SS.2	Rossi - Cassina	Peugeot 206 WRC	Off

Championship Classifications

FIA Drivers (14/14)
1. Grönholm 77; 2. Solberg 37; 3. Sainz 36; 4. C. McRae 35; 5. Burns 34;
6. Panizzi 31; 7. Rovanperä 30; 8. Mäkinen 22; 9. Märtin 20; 10. Loeb 18;
11.Bugalski 7; 12. Radström 4; 13. Gardemeister 3; 14. A. McRae, Thiry &
Kankkunen 2; 17. Eriksson, Puras, Loix & Higgins 1

FIA Constructors (14/14)
1. Peugeot 165; 2. Ford 104; 3. Subaru 67; 4. Hyundai 10; 5. Skoda, Mitsubishi 9

FIA Production Car WRC (8/8)
1. Singh 32; 2. Sohlberg 26; 3. Ferreyros 23; 4. Arai, Fiorio 22; 6. Rowe 13;
7. Trelles 12; 8. Iliev 9; 9. Girdauskas 7; 10. Baldini, Ipatti, Kollevold, Ligato
& Manfrinato 4; 15. De Dominicis, Harrach & Marini 2

FIA Junior WRC (6/6)
1. Sola 37; 2. Dallavilla 29; 3. Tuohino 15; 4. Basso 14; 5. Caldani 13;
6. Duval 12; 7. McShea 6; 8. Galli, Schelle 5; 10. Feghali, Rowe 4;
12. Carlsson, Baldacci 3; 14. Doppelreiter, Välimäki 2; 16. Foss, Katajamäki 1

Performers

	1	2	3	4	5	6
Solberg	8	3	3	-	1	1
Grönholm	5	-	1	1	-	1
Märtin	2	6	1	5	2	-
Burns	1	6	1	1	1	2
Loeb	-	1	1	1	1	-
Sainz	-	-	3	4	3	3
Mäkinen	-	-	2	3	-	2
C. McRae	-	-	2	1	6	2
Rovanperä	-	-	2	1	1	3
Higgins	-	-	-	1	1	-

Event Leaders

SS.1	Märtin
SS.2 > SS.9	Grönholm
SS.10 > SS.13	Märtin
SS.14 > SS.17	Solberg

Previous winners

1974	Makinen - Liddon Ford Escort RS 1600		1988	Alen - Kivimaki Lancia Delta Integrale
1975	Makinen - Liddon Ford Escort RS		1989	Airikkala - McNamee Mitsubishi Galant VR4
1976	Clark - Pegg Ford Escort RS		1990	Sainz - Moya Toyota Celica GT-Four
1977	Waldegaard - Thorszelius Ford Escort RS		1991	Kankkunen - Piironen Lanica Delta Integrale
1978	Mikkola - Hertz Ford Escort RS		1992	Sainz - Moya Toyota Celica Turbo 4WD
1979	Mikkola - Hertz Ford Escort RS		1993	Kankkunen - Piironen Toyota Celica Turbo 4WD
1980	Toivonen - White Talbot Sunbeam Lotus		1994	McRae - Ringer Subaru Impreza
1981	Mikkola - Hertz Audi Quattro		1995	McRae - Ringer Subaru Impreza
1982	Mikkola - Hertz Audi Quattro		1996	Schwarz - Giraudet Toyota Celica GT-Four
1983	Blomqvist - Cederberg Audi Quattro		1997	McRae - Grist Subaru Impreza WRC
1984	Vatanen - Harryman Peugeot 205 T16		1998	Burns - Reid Mitsubishi Carisma GT
1985	Toivonen - Wilson Lancia Delta S4		1999	Burns - Reid Subaru Impreza WRC
1986	Salonen - Harjanne Peugeot 205 T16		2000	Burns - Reid Subaru Impreza WRC 2000
1987	Kankkunen - Piironen Lancia Delta HF		2001	Gronhölm - Rautiainen Peugeot 206 WRC

2002 FIA World Rally Championship / Drivers

DRIVERS	Nationalities	Monte Carlo	Sweden	France	Spain	Cyprus	Argentina	Greece	Kenya	Finland	Germany	Italy	New Zealand	Australia	Great Britain	POINTS
1. Marcus Grönholm	(SF)	2	10	6	3	10	0	6	0	10	4	6	10	10	0	77
2. Petter Solberg	(N)	1	0	2	2	2	6	2	0	4	0	4	0	4	10	37
3. Carlos Sainz	(E)	4	4	1	0	0	10	4	0	3	0	0	3	3	4	36
4. Colin McRae	(GB)	3	1	0	1	1	4	10	10	0	3	0	0	0	2	35
5. Richard Burns	(GB)	0	3	4	6	6	0	0	0	6	6	3	0	0	0	34
6. Gilles Panizzi	(F)	0	0	10	10	0	0	0	1	-	-	10	0	-	0	31
7. Harri Rovanperä	(SF)	0	6	0	0	3	0	3	6	0	0	0	6	6	0	30
8. Tommi Mäkinen	(SF)	10	0	0	0	4	0	0	0	1	0	0	4	0	3	22
9. Markko Märtin	(EST)	0	0	0	0	0	3	1	3	2	1	2	0	2	6	20
10. Sébastien Loeb	(F)	6	0	-	0	-	-	0	2	0	10	-	-	0	0	18
11. Philippe Bugalski	(F)	0	-	3	4	-	-	-	-	-	0	0	-	-	-	7
12. Thomas Radström	(S)	0	0	0	0	-	-	0	4	0	-	-	-	-	0	4
13. Toni Gardemeister	(SF)	0	0	0	0	0	2	0	0	0	0	0	0	1	0	3
14. Alister McRae	(GB)	0	2	0	0	0	0	0	0	0	0	0	0	-	-	-	2
15. Juha Kankkunen	(SF)	-	0	-	-	0	0	0	0	0	-	-	2	0	0	2
16. Bruno Thiry	(B)	-	-	-	-	-	-	-	-	-	2	0	-	-	-	2
17. Kenneth Eriksson	(S)	0	0	0	0	0	1	0	0	0	0	0	0	0	0	1
18. Freddy Loix	(B)	0	0	0	0	0	0	0	0	0	0	0	1	0	0	1
19. Jésus Puras	(E)	-	-	-	-	-	-	-	-	-	-	-	1	-	-	1
20. Mark Higgins	(GB)	-	-	-	-	-	-	-	-	-	-	-	-	-	1	1
21. Stig Blomqvist	(S)	-	0	-	0	-	-	0	-	-	-	-	-	-	-	0
22. François Delecour	(F)	0	0	0	0	0	0	0	0	0	0	0	0	0	0	0
23. Roman Kresta	(CZ)	0	-	0	0	0	-	-	0	-	-	0	-	-	0	0
24. Armin Schwarz	(D)	0	0	0	0	0	0	0	0	0	0	0	0	0	0	0

2002 FIA World Rally Championship / Manufacturers

MANUFACTURERS	Nationalities	Monte Carlo	Sweden	France	Spain	Cyprus	Argentina	Greece	Kenya	Finland	Germany	Italy	New Zealand	Australia	Great Britain	POINTS
1. Peugeot	(F)	4	16	16	16	16	0	9	6	16	16	16	16	16	2	165
2. Ford	(GB)	10	6	4	5	2	14	14	14	5	7	5	3	5	10	104
3. Subaru	(GB)	12	0	4	4	7	6	2	0	5	2	4	4	4	13	67
4. Hyundai	(ROK)	0	1	0	0	1	1	1	2	0	0	0	3	0	1	10
5. Skoda	(CZ)	0	0	0	0	0	5	0	3	0	0	0	0	1	0	9
5. Mitsubishi	(GB)	0	3	2	1	0	0	0	1	0	1	1	0	0	0	9

REGULATIONS: DRIVERS'CHAMPIONSHIP: All result count. 1st - 10 points, 2nd - 6 points, 3rd - 4 points, 4th - 3 points, 5th - 2 points, 6th - 1 point.
CONSTRUTORS'CHAMPIONSHIP: To be eligible, the constructors who have registered with FIA, must take part in all the events with a minimum of two cars.
The first two cars score the points according to their finishing position. All results are taken into consideration. Points scale is the same as for the drivers

World Championship for Manufacturers

World Championship for Drivers

2002 FIA Production Car World Rally Championship (for Drivers)

	DRIVERS	Nationalities	Sweden	France	Cyprus	Argentina	Kenya	Finland	New Zealand	Australia	POINTS
1.	Karamjit Singh	(MAL)	-	-	10	4	10	4	-	4	32
2.	Kristian Sohlberg	(SF)	10	-	0	-	-	6	10	-	26
3.	Ramon Ferreyros	(PE)	-	10	0	10	-	-	-	3	23
4.	Toshihiro Arai	(J)	6	-	0	6	-	-	-	10	22
4.	Alessandro Fiorio	(I)	3	-	0	-	-	10	3	6	22
6.	Martin Rowe	(GB)	1	4	0	-	-	-	6	2	13
7.	Gustavo Trelles	(ROU)	-	3	6	3	-	-	-	-	12
8.	Dimitar Iliev	(BG)	0	6	3	-	-	-	-	-	9
9.	Saulius Girdauskas	(LT)	2	-	2	-	-	3	-	-	7
10.	Luca Baldini	(I)	-	0	4	-	-	-	-	-	4
11.	Marco Ipatti	(SF)	4	-	0	-	-	-	-	-	4
12.	Bernt Kollevold	(N)	0	0	1	-	-	1	1	1	4
13.	Marcos Ligato	(RA)	-	-	-	2	-	-	2	-	4
14.	Giovanni Manfrinato	(I)	-	-	-	-	-	-	4	-	4
15.	Alfredo De Dominics	(I)	-	-	-	-	-	2	-	-	2
16.	Beppo Harrach	(A)	-	2	0	-	-	-	-	-	2
17.	Stefano Marrini	(I)	-	1	0	1	-	-	-	-	2
18.	Natalie Barratt	(GB)	0	-	0	-	-	-	-	-	0
19.	Ben Briant	(GB)	0	-	0	-	-	-	-	-	0
20.	Joakim Roman	(S)	0	0	0	-	-	-	-	-	0
21.	Federico Villagra	(RA)	-	-	0	-	-	-	-	-	0

Production Car Championship (Gr. N)

1987 Alex Fiorio (I)
1995 Rui Madeira (PT)
1988 Pascal Gaban (B)
1996 Gustavo Trelles (ROU)
1989 Alain Oreille (F)
1997 Gustavo Trelles (ROU)
1990 Alain Oreille (F)
1998 Gustavo Trelles (ROU)
1991 Grégoire de Mevius (B)
1999 Gustavo Trelles (ROU)
1992 Grégoire de Mevius (B)
2000 Manfred Stohl (D)
1993 Alex Fassina (I)
2001 Gabriel Pozzo (RA)
1994 Jesus Puras (E)
2002 Karamjit Singh (MAL)

2002 FIA Junior World Rally Championship (for Drivers)

	DRIVERS	Nationalities	Monte-Carlo	Spain	Greece	Germany	Italy	Great Britain	POINTS
1.	Daniel Sola	(E)	0	10	3	10	4	10	37
2.	Andréa Dallavila	(I)	0	6	6	6	10	1	29
3.	Janne Tuohino	(SF)	0	2	10	-	-	3	15
4.	Giandomenico Basso	(I)	0	4	0	-	6	4	14
5.	Nicola Caldani	(I)	6	0	4	-	3	-	13
6.	François Duval	(B)	10	1	0	-	1	-	12
7.	Niall McShea	(GB)	-	-	-	-	-	6	6
8.	Gianluigi Galli	(I)	0	3	0	-	2	-	5
9.	Nikolaus Schelle	(D)	1	0	0	4	-	-	5
10.	Roger Feghali	(RL)	4	0	0	-	-	-	4
11.	Martin Rowe	(GB)	0	0	2	2	-	-	4
12.	Mirco Baldacci	(RSM)	-	-	-	3	-	-	3
13.	Daniel Carlsson	(S)	3	0	0	-	-	-	3
14.	Jussi Välimäki	(SF)	-	-	-	-	2	-	2
14.	David Doppelreiter	(A)	2	0	0	-	-	-	2
16.	Alexander Foss	(N)	-	-	-1	-	-	-	1
17.	Kosti Katajamäki	(SF)	-	-	-	1	-	-	1
18.	Christian Chemin	(I)	0	0	0	-	-	-	0
19.	Alejandro Galanti	(PY)	0	0	0	-	-	-	0
20.	Juha Kangas	(SF)	0	0	0	-	-	-	0

World Junior Championship

2001 Sébastien Loeb (F)
2002 Daniel Sola (E)

DRIVERS WHO HAVE WON WORLD CHAMPIONSHIP RALLIES FROM 1973 TO 2002

DRIVERS	NATIONALITIES	Nbr. of WINS	RALLIES
Andrea Aghini	(I)	1	1992 I
Pentti Airikkala	(SF)	1	1989 GB
Markku Alen	(SF)	20	1975 PT • 1976 SF • 1977 PT • 1978 PT-SF-I • 1979 SF • 1980 SF • 1981 PT • 1983 F-I • 1984 F • 1986 I-USA • 1987 PT-GR-SF • 1988 S-SF-GB
Alain Ambrosino	(F)	1	1988 CI
Ove Andersson	(S)	1	1975 EAK
Jean-Claude Andruet	(F)	3	1973 MC • 1974 F • 1977 I
Didier Auriol	(F)	20	1988 F • 1989 F • 1990 MC-F-I • 1991 I • 1992 MC-F-GR-RA-SF-AUS • 1993 MC • 1994 F-RA-I • 1995 F • 1998 E • 1999 C • 2001 E
Fulvio Bacchelli	(I)	1	1977 NZ
Bernard Beguin	(F)	1	1987 F
Miki Biasion	(I)	17	1986 RA • 1987 MC-RA-I • 1988 PT-EAK-GR-USA-I • 1989 MC-PT-EAK-GR-I • 1990 PT-RA • 1993 GR
Stig Blomqvist	(S)	11	1973 S • 1977 S • 1979 S • 1982 S-I • 1983 GB • 1984 S-GR-NZ-RA-CI
Walter Boyce	(CDN)	1	1973 USA
Philippe Bugalski	(F)	2	1999 E-F
Richard Burns	(GB)	9	1998 EAK • 1999 GR-AUS-GB • 2000 EAK-PT-RA-GB • 2001 NZ
Ingvar Carlsson	(S)	2	1989 S-NZ
Roger Clark	(GB)	1	1976 GB
Gianfranco Cunico	(I)	1	1993 I
Bernard Darniche	(F)	7	1973 MA • 1975 F • 1977 F • 1978 F • 1979 MC-F • 1981 F
François Delecour	(F)	4	1993 PT-F-E • 1994 MC
Ian Duncan	(EAK)	1	1994 EAK
Per Eklund	(S)	1	1976 S
Mikael Ericsson	(S)	2	1989 RA-SF
Kenneth Eriksson	(S)	6	1987 CI • 1991 S • 1995 S-AUS • 1997 S-NZ
Tony Fassina	(I)	1	1979 I
Guy Frequelin	(F)	1	1981 RA
Marcus Grönholm	(SF)	12	2000 S-NZ-F-AUS • 2001 FIN-AUS-GB • 2002 S-CY-SF-NZ-AUS
Sepp Haider	(A)	1	1988 NZ
Kyosti Hamalainen	(SF)	1	1977 SF
Mats Jonsson	(S)	2	1992 S • 1993 S
Harry Kallstom	(S)	1	1976 GR
Juha Kankkunen	(SF)	23	1985 EAK-CI • 1986 S-GR-NZ • 1987 USA-GB • 1989 AUS • 1990 AUS • 1991 EAK-GR-SF-AUS-GB • 1992 PT • 1993 EAK-RA-SF-AUS-GB • 1994 PT • 1999 RA-SF
Anders Kullang	(S)	1	1980 S
Piero Liatti	(I)	1	1997 MC
Sébastien Loeb	(F)	1	2002 D
Colin McRae	(GB)	25	1993 NZ • 1994 NZ-GB • 1995 NZ-GB • 1996 GR-I-E • 1997 EAK-F-I-AUS-GB • 1998 PT-F-GR • 1999 EAK-PT • 2000 E-GR • 2001 ARG-CY-GR • 2002 GR-EAK
Timo Makinen	(SF)	4	1973 SF-GB • 1974 GB • 1975 GB
Tommi Mäkinen	(SF)	24	1994 SF • 1996 S-EAK-RA-SF-AUS • 1997 PT-E-RA-SF • 1998 S-RA-NZ-SF-I-AUS • 1999 Mc-S-NZ-I • 2000 MC • 2001 MC-POR-EAK • 2002 MC
Shekhar Mehta	(EAK)	5	1973 EAK • 1979 EAK • 1980 EAK • 1981 EAK • 1982 EAK
Hannu Mikkola	(SF)	18	1974 SF • 1975 MA-SF • 1978 GB • 1979 PT-NZ-GB-CI • 1981 S-GB • 1982 SF-GB • 1983 S-PT-RA-SF • 1984 PT • 1987 EAK
Joaquim Moutinho	(PT)	1	1986 PT
Michèle Mouton	(F)	4	1981 I • 1982 PT-GR-BR
Sandro Munari	(I)	7	1974 I-CDN • 1975 MC • 1976 MC-PT-F • 1977 MC
Jean-Pierre Nicolas	(F)	5	1973 F • 1976 MA • 1978 MC-EAK-CI
Alain Oreille	(F)	1	1989 CI
Jesus Puras	(E)	1	2001 FR
Gilles Panizzi	(F)	5	2000 F-I • 2001 IT • 2002 F-E-I
Rafaelle Pinto	(PT)	1	1974 PT
Jean Ragnotti	(F)	3	1981 MC • 1982 F • 1985 F
Jorge Recalde	(RA)	1	1988 RA
Walter Röhrl	(D)	14	1975 GR • 1978 GR-CDN • 1980 MC-PT-RA-I • 1982 MC-CI • 1983 MC-GR-NZ 1984 MC • 1985 I
Harri Rovanperä	(SF)	1	2001 S
Bruno Saby	(F)	2	1986 F • 1988 MC
Carlos Sainz	(E)	24	1990 GR-NZ-SF-GB • 1991 MC-PT-F-NZ-RA • 1992 EAK-NZ-E-GB • 1994 GR 1995 MC-PT-E • 1996 RI • 1997 GR-RI • 1998 MC-NZ 2000 CY • 2002 RA
Timo Salonen	(SF)	11	1977 CDN • 1980 NZ • 1981 CI • 1985 PT-GR-NZ-RA-SF • 1986 SF-GB • 1987 S
Armin Schwarz	(D)	1	1991 E
Kenjiro Shinozuka	(J)	2	1991 CI • 1992 CI
Joginder Singh	(EAK)	2	1974 EAK • 1976 EAK
Petter Solberg	(N)	1	2002 GB
Patrick Tauziac	(F)	1	1990 CI
Jean-Luc Thèrier	(F)	5	1973 PT-GR-I • 1974 USA • 1980 F
Henri Toivonen	(SF)	3	1980 GB • 1985 GB • 1986 MC
Ari Vatanen	(SF)	10	1980 GR • 1981 GR-BR-SF • 1983 EAK • 1984 SF-I-GB • 1985 MC-S
Bjorn Waldegaard	(S)	16	1975 S-I • 1976 I • 1977 EAK-GR-GB • 1978 S • 1979 GR-CDN • 1980 CI • 1982 NZ • 1983 CI • 1984 EAK • 1986 EAK-CI • 1990 EAK
Achim Warmbold	(D)	2	1973 PL-A
Franz Wittmann	(A)	1	1987 NZ

A: Austria – AUS: Australia – B: Belgium – BG: Bulgaria – BR: Brazil – C: China – CDN: Canada – CI: Ivory Coast – CY: Cyprus – CZ: Czech Republic – D: Germany – E: Spain – EAK: Kenya – EST: Estonia – F: France – GB: Great Britain – GR: Greece – I: Italy – J: Japan – LT: Lithuania – MA: Marocco – MAL: Malaysia – MC: Monaco – N: Norway – NZ: New Zealand – PE: Peru – PL: Poland – PT: Portugal – PY: Paraguay – RA: Argentina – RI: Indonesia – RL: Lebanon – ROK; Republic of Korea – ROU: Uruguay – RSM: San Marino – S: Sweden SF: Finland – USA : United States of America